THE PICTORIAL
ENCYCLOPEDIA OF
RAILWAYS

THE PICTORIAL ENCYCLOPEDIA OF
RAILWAYS

HAMILTON ELLIS
A I Loco E, FRSA

PAUL HAMLYN

Published by
The Hamlyn Publishing Group Ltd
Hamlyn House ● The Centre ● Feltham ● Middlesex
© Copyright 1968 Hamilton Ellis
First published in 1968
Second impression 1968
Printed in Czechoslovakia by Svoboda, Prague
T 2009

CONTENTS

FOREWORD

FOREWORD

It is of course impossible to describe all the things which go to make up the world's railways purely by an illustrated commentary. The best of photographs — and some of these are very fine — cannot describe the working of automatic warning systems, electronic computers, or even the relatively simple operation of the century-old block telegraph. So it is with some other things. This book is not a technical encyclopedia; rather it is an encyclopedic pictorial survey, in which we have endeavoured to cover as many railway ramifications in as many countries as possible. With some heartburnings I have excluded some kindred systems — aerial ropeways and passenger cable lines, for example — and have admitted only those monorail lines which worked, or have worked, for more than half a century; one in Ireland and one in Germany.

Change is upon the railway scene which your author has loved as an old sailor forever loves sail. Beautiful, heroic steam is far in retreat, a thing hard to imagine even 25 years ago except in the heavily electrified countries of Central and Southern Europe. The very function of railways is gradually changing. In sparsely populated country smaller lines are vanishing. In dense city and suburban areas new lines are having to be built, at enormous expense (wry smiles in California!) and the same happens where, for example, rich ore is found in remote places. The rail changes: the principle of the rail continues.

C.H.E.

INTRODUCTION

ORIGIN AND IMPACT OF RAILWAYS

What is a railway?

A rather inadequate dictionary we once used defined it as a 'track for steam carriages'.

Even in early Victorian times, when steam provided the only practical motive power apart from animals, that was not sufficiently exclusive. For 'steam carriages' might mean vehicles hauled by locomotives, or actual carriages with small engines driving their back axles, the ancestors of the motor-car. Moreover, both these ran on common roads as well as rails, indeed 'track for steam carriages' rather suggests the special stone curbway, expressly designed to that end, which some parties promoted as a rival to the projected Great Western Railway between London and Bristol, in the 1830s. No, that definition will not do!

Rather let us say that a railway is a prepared, confining track for vehicles moving heavy loads at relatively high speeds. Motive power is immaterial; the *rail* is the thing, the rail that both supports and guides. And the rail goes back through many generations of mankind.

At a remote time, possibly in south-western Asia, someone invented the wheel. His inspiration was doubtless the roller, formed by a piece of tree-trunk and used for moving huge blocks of stone. But the idea that the first wheels were slices of bole pierced or axled in the middle is erroneous. Such slices were most unlikely to be absolutely circular, and would have been more trouble than help. The earliest wheels, even if they were solid, were carefully built up to be balanced and symmetrical and, above all, strong.

Given the wheel, the rail was the next thing, and this may well have happened by accident. The earliest wheels gouged out ruts in the tracks they most commonly followed. It was then found that the ruts kept the primitive wheels within bounds, so in some of the earliest pavements primeval engineers made stone ruts deliberately to this end. The Sumerians probably knew all about it. Babylonians made wonderful roads in difficult places, and Isaiah marvelled. Was he thinking of those stone-rutted roads, which negotiated difficult places and safely guided their vehicles, when he wrote one of his most famous passages? *Every valley shall be exalted, and every mountain and hill laid low!* Isaiah was a very sound man, and a meticulous observer, as a good prophet needed to be (c.f. Charles E. Lee's very learned book *The Evolution of Railways*).

The Greeks in the Age of Pericles made such stone ways for the transport of heavy monumental materials, and they provided engineered passing places, the primeval points and sidings. Greek colonists took them to Sicily, and thus the Romans came to know them. One can see their grooved stone tracks in the ruins of Pompeii. Early observers thought that the grooves had been gouged out by incessant traffic, which would have thrown a dubious light on the municipal highway authorities of the first century. No! Those grooves were made, not allowed to happen. Such Roman stoneways have been found in Great Britain, not unsuitably on the site of a Victorian railway station.

In the middle of the 16th century, German miners had evolved the flanged wheel, or at

Virgula diuina — Glück rüta

Haspeler

Instrumctum Tractorium

Zerscheer — Seüberer — Hauwer

Biorin

i

any rate symmetrical flanged rollers supporting in two pairs a small wagon running on rails made of longitudinal timber poles. Wooden tramways of this sort were to be found from Transylvania to the Tyrol, and a complete, authentic relic has survived the hazards of age and war, to be preserved today in Berlin. The arrangement included very simple points or switches, an advance on the primitive *ektropoi* (turnouts) of classic Greece. The word turnout, be it remarked, is still used to describe a single set of points on a modern railway. Figure *i* is taken from Sebastian Münster's *Cosmographiae Universalis*, published in Basle in 1550. It shows a miner pushing a truck on rails in the silver mines of Leberthal in Alsace, and several other interesting things, such as the winch haulage between levels, and the diviner with his hazel rod on the top of the hill. From the miners' hoods of the period we can deduce the legends about gnomes who lived in the hills and dug precious stuff out of them. Invading barbarians doubtless took back stories of fierce and mysterious cave-dwellers.

Wooden railways were known, in certain localities, to the England of Elizabeth I. During the succeeding 17th century, they became quite common in mining districts, and early in the 18th century, where iron was to be had, the iron rail began to succeed, or at first to supplement, the wooden pole or baulk road. Iron straps could be laid on top of the latter, for flanged iron wheels, or the rails could take the form of flanged iron plates whereon

ii

Echelle de 12 Pieds

1 2 3 4   8   12 Pieds

wagons would run with ordinary small cart-wheels. Stone blocks came into use to support the iron plates, and later iron edge rails superseded these. The Battle of Prestonpans in 1745 was fought over a railway, the coal-carrying Tranent and Cockenzie Waggon-Way, in the country between Edinburgh and Dunbar. General Sir John Cope, commanding the Government forces, called it 'a narrow cartroad' and tried to hold it, as an incidental fortification, against the Jacobite army. The latter was composed of wild and bloody-minded Highlanders who delighted to chop up strange men in red coats. Cope's men were raw levies from the North of England, facing a charge for the first time in their lives. Shortly after, these poor devils, as Prince Charles Edward rather illiterately recorded, *ran like rabets.* They did not know, nor had they time to care, that their general had just become the first soldier to make strategic use of a railway.

Figure *ii* is taken from Gabriel Jars' *Voyages Métallurgiques*, published in Paris in 1765, and shows 18th century practice on some of the mining lines in Durham. The instance given had wooden rails of 4 ft. gauge. The wheels were of iron, and flanged. Incidentally, the most common world standard gauge, used in Britain and the U.S.A., is 4 ft. 8½ in. That of the Soviet Union is 5 ft. That of the ancient Roman rutways was 4 ft. 9½ in.

In County Durham, the mining railway system called the Tanfield Wagon Way was begun in or before 1671. By 1727 it included the historic Causey Arch, the world's first railway viaduct, built by Ralph Wood. Though long ago abandoned as such, it is fortunately cherished as an ancient monument. On June 9, 1758, the first railway to be built under Act of Parliament, from Middleton to Leeds, received the Royal Assent. It is still there, run by a preservation society, and under steam too.

The colour picture in Plate I is taken from a unique painting, *The Surrey Iron Railway Terminus at Wandsworth.* This was the first *public railway* in the world. It had up and down roads, allowing for continuous traffic in both directions. The permanent way consisted of iron plates on stone blocks. The painting shows, not only points, but the double-flanged plates on the outsides of these, to control the flangeless wagon wheels on the turnouts. One horse

could haul several wagons — a *train* — instead of the single one within his power on a common road. The Surrey Iron Railway was incorporated by an Act of May 1, 1801, and was opened from Wandsworth Wharf on the Thames to Croydon on July 26, 1803. The Croydon, Merstham and Godstone Railway continued its course as far as quarries at Coulsdon on July 24, 1805.

Meanwhile the locomotive — the steam railway engine that was to transform an industrial and commercial machine into a feature of worldwide life — had been invented, and built. Down the centuries, mechanical engineering had lagged far behind military and civil engineering, the building of ways and bridges. Sir Isaac Newton, purely in the way of experimental physics, had contributed an idea for a kettle on wheels, to be propelled by its own steam jet directed backwards. At the end of the 1760s, Newcomen and Watt having shown the practicability of the piston engine for stationary work, Nicolas Cugnot in France produced a very primitive sort of tractor which could indeed lumber along a road under its own power. Drive was by a pair of single-acting cylinders through rack and pinion, not by cranks. The machine was unmanageable, butted a wall, and got Cugnot into serious trouble.

Man's efforts to make a locomotive machine at this time strikingly anticipated his striving, a century later, to make a heavier-than-air craft leave the ground. Until such an engine could be really successful, railways, so old in conception, would remain minor appendages to collieries and other mines. Civil engineers were preoccupied with canals, aqueducts and turnpike roads. William Murdoch in England (to be exact, in Cornwall) and Oliver Evans in America made interesting practical experiments. But Richard Trevithick *iii*, another Cornishman, was to be the Father of the Locomotive. It was his invention of the relatively small, high-pressure, stationary engine that made the locomotive possible. Applying the same principle, he made a model, a road locomotive and a steam passenger coach, then, in 1804, a locomotive which succeeded in hauling what was then a prodigious load along the iron flanged tramroad at Penydarran, Merthyr Tydfil, South Wales.

In Figure *iv* is shown a model in the Science Museum, London. No *complete* working drawings of the original Trevithick engine seem to have survived, but the model may be taken as reasonably accurate. There was a return-flue boiler, having a single horizontal cylinder partially embedded in one end, which also contained the fire-door and chimney. The slide-bars, bearing the cross-head and the primitive gear for working the valves, projected a long way back. An immense flywheel and a set of gears helped in transmission.

Several Trevithick locomotives were built. One, which came to be known locally as *Black Billy*, went to Tyneside. There it was seen by a young enginewright, one George Stephenson, who was later to become famous. Another, called *Catch-me-who-can*, was demonstrated on a circular track in north-west London in 1808. It was attached to a landau in which the bold and daring might ride round the 'circus' at a shilling a time. A derailment, not in itself very dreadful, ended this jolly mechanical prank.

But already fare-paying passengers were riding on the horse-drawn cars of the Oystermouth Railway in South Wales, the world's first passenger line, which had begun to convey them on March 25, 1807. So both steam traction and passenger conveyance by railway were established facts eight years before the Battle of Waterloo, though scarcely so as a commercial proposition. Trevithick, like many creative workers, was no businessman, and few others believed in him. Years after, he died in penury, while George Stephenson was to grow rich and his son Robert Stephenson was to become a millionaire.

But a most important thing was the provision of a really solid road for the new machines. They knocked iron plates to pieces. Edge rails of various sections, supporting flanged wheels, were the ideal form, but not much could be done, while rails continued to be made of cast iron. It was on October 23, 1820, that John Birkinshaw of Bedlington Ironworks, Northumberland, was granted a patent for the manu-

iv

facture of rolled iron rails (steel rails were to come later in the century). Only with the coming of wrought, or rolled rails, could the way be regarded as clear. In some places, ancient usages died hard. The first railway in the Austrian Empire, though opened as late as 1832, used horse traction. Figure *v* shows Josef Hafner's charming lithograph *Arrival of their Majesties the Emperor and Empress of Austria in St Magdalena at the Opening of the Railway from Linz to Budweis.*

Horse traction, of course, lasted much longer on lighter forms of railway. The pit pony remained a familiar animal in collieries. At the beginning of the present century horse tramways were still common in many of our cities and towns; Oxford went straight from the horse tram to the motor-bus, and a solitary horse tramway along the front of Douglas, Isle of Man, remains a major tourist attraction, if nothing else.

Our following pages will unfold the structural and mechanical development of railways from the first days of steam traction to the present time, when steam is far in retreat, but before embarking on them it is opportune to review some of the practical effects of railway transport on commercial and social life. The Liverpool and Manchester Railway of 1830 was the first railway as we understand the term, with mechanical traction, up and down roads, proper stations, timetables and signalling of a sort. The last-mentioned was at first of the most primitive order; hand signals by policemen, then flags by day and lamps — possibly nothing more than a candle put in a window — at night. But signalling — or telegraphy — had been long accomplished by semaphore. Provided the weather was clear, messages could be transmitted with extraordinary speed across country, by huge pivoted boards on high masts.

The semaphore was adapted to visual railway signalling at the beginning of the '40s. For years, its rival was a vertically pivoted board, or a board and a disc pivoted at right angles. A horizontal position of the semaphore arm, or the presentation of the board, indicated *stop*! At night, red lamps were for *danger* and white lights for *clear*, with green for *caution*, though this last eventually became the *clear* signal. Yellow for *caution* belongs to our

own time. Semaphores were first interlocked with points in 1856, though four years passed before John Saxby produced complete interlocking in which the signals were absolutely governed by the position of the points.

Railway travel was thus fairly safe from the first, and though the earliest safety equipment was primitive, transport still moved at a relatively slow pace, and nothing terrible was liable to happen so long as people stuck to Rules (always spelt with a capital R!).

The social and commercial impact of railways was tremendous. This was the first mechanical form of land transport mankind had ever known. As the rails advanced, distances abruptly shrank. Motors and aircraft have only carried on the process which the railways initiated; it was the rail that changed the world. The change was the greatest since the remote beginnings of ocean navigation. Transport made new empires, and slowness in developing it broke old empires. The railway came as a finial to the industrial revolution, indeed as an inevitable complement. Rails and steam navigation gave the British a new empire, to replace the one lost when the United States was formed.

In Great Britain, and generally in Continental Europe, the new railways followed the old trade routes, linking cities which had been of more or less importance for many centuries. The position was much the same in the older, Eastern, United States, but in the West, especially beyond the Mississippi Valley, it was virgin country for pioneers. The railroads pushed west, north-west and south-west. Roaring shanty towns grew up at railheads, and then, as the rails went on advancing, either relapsed into empty prairie or survived as more or less respectable towns. Rails — and the Americans preserved the sonorous old English term 'railroad' — made the United States as we know it today. So it was in other countries previously undeveloped. The cities followed the rails.

Of course, there was speculation galore in both sorts of country. In Britain the success of the Liverpool and Manchester Railway stimulated the building of the great inter-city lines — London and Birmingham, London and Southampton, London and Bristol, Manchester and Birmingham, Edinburgh and Glasgow

PLATE I The Surrey Iron Railway, Wandsworth Wharf, 1803.

— and the success of these greater lines led to the great Railway Mania of the middle 1840s, which made some people extremely rich and ruined a good many others. One of the greatest promoters, and also the first of the great amalgamators, was George Hudson, a shrewd and unscrupulous man of York who foresaw his city as a focal point for railways in Eastern England and the Midlands. His career came to an inglorious end when an inquiry was ordered into the business of the York and North Midland Railway, but an immense and useful railway mileage had been built in the meantime.

While some countries like France, Belgium and the German States built railways on a national and geographical plan, in the English-speaking countries such a thing smelt of 'monopoly' and a free-for-all was considered socially more desirable. This sometimes had unfortunate results, as in the duplication of main routes, for which we are still paying to-day. Then companies engaged in feuds and campaigns against each other, and even resorted to pitched battles over disputed running powers. In 1858, for instance, the London, Brighton and South Coast Railway decided to prevent the London and South Western Railway from entering Portsmouth by the new direct route through Guildford. There was a

PLATE II The Stephensons' *Northumbrian*, by James Nasmyth.

17

fierce engagement at the junction just east of Havant, at the end of which the South Western forces, having at first captured a Brighton locomotive used for blocking purposes, retired with their own train to Godalming.

The scene in Figure *vi*, though a pastiche, gives a racy impression of what the Battle of Havant must have been like, and in the background the outline, at least, of the beleaguered engine is plausibly like that of London, Brighton and South Coast No. 99, that which first blocked, and then was captured by, the South Western company's 'army'. It was a relatively gentle battle — nobody got killed — and fiercer ones were yet to be fought in the States, where guns were liable to be fired in anger.

The hired ruffians who fought were recruited from the navvies who had worked on construction of the railway. They were ferocious characters, often from the Celtic portions of the British Isles which were then much depressed; their strength was tremendous, and they loved fighting. They derived their name from 'navigators', which was given to them when they were building the long canals which came before the railways.

Most of Britain's railways, with their immense embankments, cuttings and tunnels, were built by these tremendously powerful men with pick, spade, shovel and barrow.

They were usually worn out by middle age, and buried their dead with a strange, solemn ritual of their own.

Late in the 19th century, such railways as remained to be built were constructed with gradually improving mechanical aids, of which the 'steam navvy', or as we would call it, mechanical excavator, was one of the most important. An early example is shown in Figure *vii*. All the essentials of the modern machine are there, in spite of the somewhat archaic vertical steam engine with its wooden-lagged boiler at the rear.

Another tremendous mechanical aid was power drilling, introduced at the end of the 1860s during the building of the Mont Cenis Tunnel. It was this that made possible the relatively rapid construction of the other great mountain tunnels in both Europe and America.

The railways changed people's lives. They could move about as never before, and so could their goods. By 1869 much of London's beer was coming from Burton on Trent. The term 'sea-coal' became obsolete. Yorkshire coal and wool came rolling down the Midland main line in a continuous stream. Bread ceased to be a luxury in the Scottish Highlands. The pattern was repeated wherever the rails and the locomotive went.

viii Stephenson long-boiler express, 1848

PRIMEVAL STEAM

MIDDLETON, WYLAM AND KILLINGWORTH COLLIERIES

In the locomotives of the Middleton Colliery Railway [1], built by Matthew Murray with John Blenkinsop's rack-and-pinion propulsion, we see the first commercial application of motive power to land transport. Drive was entirely through a cog-wheel to a single rack on the left side only. The two cylinders were embedded in the top of the centre-flue boiler, which was lagged with wooden strips.

The first of several appeared in 1812, and they worked for some 20 years. In 1813 Christopher Blackett and William Hedley produced *Puffing Billy* [2] (the unofficial name became historic) on the Wylam Colliery Railway beside which George Stephenson had been born in 1781. Reversion was made to Trevithick's axiom, that adhesion alone was sufficient to an

1

2

engine to propel itself, and its load, without rack-and-pinion. *Puffing Billy*, now at the Science Museum, London, is the oldest steam locomotive in existence.

On the right [3] is the second of Stephenson's locomotives for the Killingworth Colliery Railway, built in 1815, and now represented by a model made by the late E.W.Twining. The two axles, though independently driven, were coupled by a pair of chains on sprockets. The engine 'went', and better than its predecessors, but steam locomotives were still an obscure form of industrial machinery. Very few people had ever seen one.

4

ARCHAIC LOCOMOTIVES

Some ancient engines lasted for an almost incredible time and others were built years after their general design had become obsolete. Two such examples are shown in this trio.

The photograph [4] taken about a century ago by R.E. Bleasdale, shows what is believed to have been George Stephenson's second locomotive on the Killingworth Colliery Railway. Bleasdale himself wrote '1820—25' on the back of the print. The engine has clearly undergone some modifications down the years, but not radical ones. The old-time engine-wright simply had — in Naval parlance — to

'make-and-mend'. There is a centre-flue boiler. The smokebox and the dome would be later additions. The four-coupled drive anticipated that of Stephenson's *Locomotion* of 1825.

Figure 5 is of a fine old model which we believe to represent one of the Stephenson locomotives of the St. Etienne and Lyons Railway, used on the Givors-Rive-de-Gier section in 1830.

Figure 6 exemplifies construction of an engine which was already archaic, for this was one of nine built by Thomas Ellis to run on a South Wales plateway at Tredegar between 1831 and 1854, with flangeless wheels. This one was the *St. David* of 1848.

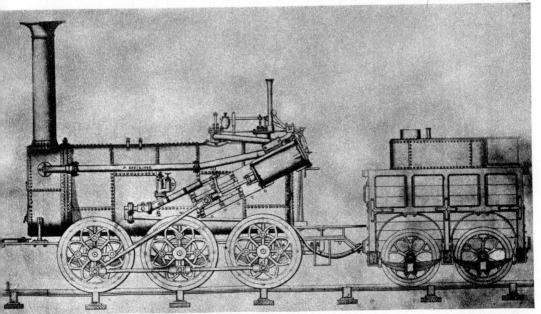

GEORGE STEPHENSON

Figure 7 shows George Stephenson (1781–1848), still called the Father of the Locomotive, though in no way did he *invent* it; the son of an engineman at Wylam Colliery, Northumberland, he was himself illiterate almost to maturity. Entirely self-taught, his virtues included perseverance, integrity and mechanical judgement. His entry to locomotive engineering may be said to have begun in 1813, when he watched *Puffing Billy* at Wylam, saw how to improve such an engine, and did so at Killingworth Colliery in the following year. His fame was founded on his abilities as both an improver and a businessman.

His engine *Locomotion* [8] was the first ever to work a steam public railway, the Stockton and Darlington in 1825. Passengers were still cautiously conveyed with horse traction in between the coal trains. *Locomotion* has been fortunately preserved. The photograph shows her mounted on a plinth but later she was placed under cover at Darlington Bank Top

7

8

S. & D. R. Nº 1. 1825.

24

Station, where she still is. The wheels, though with independent drive, were rod-coupled.

Figure 9 is from a French publication of 1829, and shows Stephenson's *Lancashire Witch*, built for the Bolton and Leigh Railway in that year. The boiler has two fireboxes and converging flues. The inclined outside cylinders show a considerable advance.

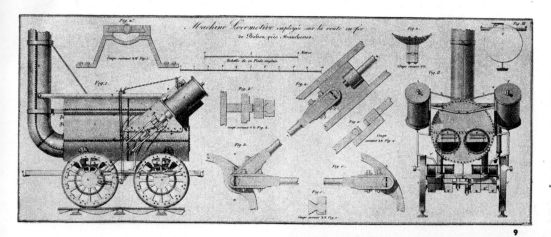

ROCKET AND NORTHUMBRIAN

The *Rocket* [11] successful joint entry of George and Robert Stephenson and Henry Booth to the competition set by the Liverpool and Manchester Railway in 1829, needs little introduction. Her worn-out shell rests in the Science Museum, London, but there are several working replicas made by Robert Stephenson and Company upwards of a century after. That shown was made for Henry Ford, and there are others in the United States.

The *Rocket* had the inclined cylinders of the *Lancashire Witch* and the multi-tubular boiler simultaneously, if not originally, invented by Marc Seguin in France. She might have been described as the world's first express engine. The firebox was outside and water-jacketed; there was no proper smokebox; the tender was the work of Nathaniel Worsdell the coach-builder, doing his best without much precedent. But at a critical time she went without failure.

Robert Stephenson [10] became the first recorded 'millionaire-engineer', though the *Rocket* alone was not responsible for that. James Nasmyth's drawing, facing page 16, of what he thought at the time to be the *Rocket*, in fact shows the Stephensons' *Northumbrian* of

1830. The sharp incline of the cylinders has been depressed, the boiler has an internal firebox as well as the firetubes of the *Rocket*, and she had a proper tender tank instead of a waterbarrel above the coal. The kneeling figure is George Stephenson, and Robert is firing. The scene was drawn on the Liverpool and Manchester Railway, shortly before its opening on September 15, 1830.

A note of the *Rocket's* colour scheme: she was painted bright yellow, picked out in black, with a white chimney.

11

ERICSSON'S NOVELTY

It was with his 'secret weapon' for the United States — the Monitor class turret battleship — that John Ericsson [12] achieved fame and fortune. But over 30 years before the American Civil War he went into partnership in England, with John Braithwaite, and entered the locomotive *Novelty* [13] for the Rainhill trials on the Liverpool and Manchester Railway in 1829.

Born in Sweden in 1803, he was one of the very greatest of the pioneering mechanical engineers of the 19th century. His locomotive was a precursor of the light motive unit, as opposed to the heavy *travelling engine*. Its weak point was in the boiler which was made like a T lying on its side. Its complexities were inaccessible in the event of breakdown, which occurred during the trials. While the boiler held, *Novelty* was the fastest of the four steam locomotives which ran in the trials, but her haulage capacity would not have been much in regular service. The boiler was fired from the top, and draught was induced by bellows. Fuel and water were carried on the main frames.

12

Some portions of the original are incorporated in this handsome replica made by the Science Museum in London. Ericsson, after many vicissitudes including imprisonment in the Marshalsea for debt, lived to the ripe age of 86.

13

TIMOTHY HACKWORTH

During 1824, just before the opening of the Stockton and Darlington Railway, Timothy Hackworth [14] was employed by George Stephenson at Forth Street Works, Newcastle-upon-Tyne, and the coupling of wheels by side rods, to increase adhesion, has been accredited to him.

To allow for the lateral displacement of coupled axles, relative to one another, he used spherical coupling-rod pins. In 1827, he built the first six-coupled locomotive, the *Royal George*, for the Stockton and Darlington Railway, and Figure 15 shows a small working

14
15

model of this engine which he made for experimental work beforehand. It must be emphasised that this was what one might call a laboratory model and not an exact replica in miniature of the full-size engine. Hence such oddities as the solid wheels which would have been very heavy in real practice, and the safety-valve loaded by a bent spring. This would not have answered in full-size construction.

In 1829 Hackworth was one of the Stephensons' most formidable rivals in the Rainhill Trials set by the Liverpool and Manchester Railway, and for this competition he built the *Sans Pareil* [16] which still exists at the Science Museum in London. She was heavier than the *Rocket*; under the set conditions, too heavy to be mounted on only four wheels. Further she was dogged by ill luck and had a breakdown, including shortage of water, in the course of the trials.

Hackworth, who when not engaged on engines was a lay-preacher, lived to the age of 64 (1786 – 1850). Many of the early engineers wore themselves out while relatively young. They had an incredulous and close-fisted world with which to contend. Both the *Royal George* and *Sans Pareil* exemplify Hackworth's early practice of using outside vertical cylinders and return-flue boilers, the latter having chimney and firedoor at the same end.

16

17

STEPHENSON'S PLANETS

The printed cotton handkerchief [17] doubtless dates from the early 1830s, for the locomotive in the middle is a Stephenson four-coupled *Planet*, of which variety the original one, *Samson*, was built in February, 1831. The inscription 'Views of the Liverpool and Manchester Railway' is repeated in French and German. The caption list is in English and French only. The ovals show: top left, the station at Water Street, Manchester; top right, Crown Street station, Liverpool; bottom left, Sankey Viaduct; bottom right, skew arch at Rainhill. In the corners are, top left, a train at Parkside; top right, Wapping Tunnel, Liverpool; bottom left, Edge Hill Arch; bottom right, cutting near Liverpool. The first-class, second-class,

livestock and goods trains round the border are from Ackermann's long prints.

Figure 18 is from an ancient photograph. It shows a *Planet* of the original single-driver type, the *Pioneer* of the Bangor and Piscataquis Railroad, U.S.A., built by Robert Stephenson in 1836; possibly the only photograph ever taken of this type in service. The smokestack, whistle on dome, and bell were doubtless later American additions.

The *Planet* type, with its inside cylinders under the smokebox driving a cranked axle, was a very notable advance. The original *Planet* was delivered in October, 1830, and was still at work on the Liverpool and Manchester Railway 10 years later. Figure 19 is from a photograph taken by R. E. Bleasdale at the Stephenson Centenary celebrations in

Newcastle-upon-Tyne, 1881. Right-to-left are Stephenson's *Invicta* (Canterbury and Whitstable, 1830); engines from Killingworth and Hetton Collieries; *Locomotion* (Stockton and Darlington, 1825); *Derwent* (a Hackworth-type engine of 1845) and *Dwarf*, a light locomotive built by George England, London, in the '50s, and the only one not still in existence.

PETER COOPER'S "TOM THUMB" 1829-30 BALTIMORE & OHIO R.R.

20

EARLY AMERICAN LOCOMOTIVES

Peter Cooper's *Tom Thumb* of 1829 was rather a scientific model than a proper locomotive, designed to convince American business that steam traction was a practical thing, and run to that end on the Baltimore and Ohio Railroad, which then used horse haulage. Figure 20 shows a small donkey engine mounted on a truck and driving one of the axles through spur-wheels. A belt-driven fan improved the draught. The boiler flues were improvised from old musket barrels.

The first successful steam line in the United States was the South Carolina Railroad, whose first locomotive, the *Best Friend of Charleston*, hauled an inaugural train on Christmas Day, 1830. Later the *Best Friend* burst her boiler, owing to monkey-business with the safety valve, but with her the railway and the locomotive had come to stay in America. Figure 21 shows a replica of the original train made by the Southern Railway Company.

By 1883 the S.C.R.R. extended from Charleston to Hamburg, 135 miles. It was then the longest railway in the world. Early American lines were often built as short feeders or connecting links between navigable waterways. Such was the Mohawk and Hudson. Figure 22 shows its locomotive *De Witt Clinton*, built by West Point Foundry, New York, in 1831, hauling a replica train at the time of the Chicago World Fair, 1893. The engine was akin to the *Best Friend of Charleston* by the same makers but had a more advanced, horizontal boiler. She made her maiden run with a train from Albany to Schenectady, 14 miles, in 46 minutes, on August 9, 1831.

PLATE III Excavating the Olive Mount Cutting, near Liverpool, from an Ackermann print.

21
22

PLATE IV Sankey Valley Viaduct, Lancashire,
from an Ackermann print.

33

THE BURY LOCOMOTIVE

Father of the traditional American locomotive was Edward Bury, a stay-at-home Englishman who was just too late to run his first locomotive in the Rainhill Trials of 1829. Norris of Philadelphia was his mechanical executor. Bury used bar frames and inside cylinders, and George Woodcock's beautiful model [23] of Eastern Counties Railway No. 18 shows his characteristic arrangement. The firebox was D-shaped, with a large dome-shaped steam space above it. This made a light locomotive and one not adaptable to much enlargement.

Bury four-coupled goods engines, which could negotiate tortuous colliery sidings, endured for a surprising time on the Furness Railway; *Old Coppernob* [24] survived both obsolescence, local preservation and enemy bombing. Built in 1846, she is now at Clapham Museum, London.

Now the firm of Bury, Curtis and Kennedy

23

24

34

early on exported engines to the United States where light axle loads were of first importance on the crazy tracks of Old America. The Norris Brothers of Philadelphia added flexibility by putting a bogie under the front end, and simplicity by mounting the cylinders outside. Then Borsig of Berlin added a trailing axle for steadiness, and the Norrises not only did this but coupled it up to the driving axle, thus producing the first of the classic American type which they built for both home consumption and for export. The much weathered relic [25] mounted under the palms of Santiago, Chile, and dating from 1850, is an example of the Bury-Norris mutation. She was built for the Copiapo and Caldera Railway.

Bury had been too sure that his primeval form was sufficient for all time; his contract with the London and Birmingham Railway was terminated, and he retired with a grievance. But the bar-framed engine lasted in America for as long as steam did.

ROBERT STEPHENSON'S PATENTEE LOCOMOTIVE

A very great advance in locomotive design was made with Robert Stephenson's Patentee, delivered to the Liverpool and Manchester Railway in 1834. Figure 26 shows its elevation, from which it can be seen that it was an elongated *Planet*, with horizontal inside cylinders and an extra axle. That trailing supporting axle, with the backward extension of the frames, not only steadied the engine but also allowed for a more adequate firebox. The frames were still of wood, strengthened by iron plates. 'Sandwich frame' was the term for them and they were to persist in certain designs, notably on the Great Western Railway, for a good half-century.

Thousands of the type were ultimately built, and the engines exported to the first railways in several European countries, including the Netherlands, the German States, Russia and Italy, were Patentees. They were steady in running, and though the early examples were very small the type was capable of considerable enlargement, as we shall see in some later pages. For goods traffic, the leading, trailing, or all three axles could be coupled.

Figure 27 shows a masterpiece of restoration, by which we mean the complete new building of an ancient locomotive from the original drawings. It was made for the German Railway Centenary celebrations of 1935 and reproduced the *Adler* (Eagle), built by Robert Stephenson for the first German public steam railway between Nuremberg and Fürth, in 1835. Figure 28 suggests something of a circus, for centennial exhibitions are like that. The engine is again the *Adler* and the view is of value in showing what a Patentee looked like to nervous passengers on a station platform, about to have their first ride in a train.

28

SANDWICH-FRAMED, SIX-WHEELED LOCOMOTIVES

Archaic though it became, the sandwich-framed six-wheeled locomotive had a long innings. These three examples, all from British works, cover a large part of the 19th century.

Figures 29 and 30 show a large Patentee built by Robert Stephenson for the Alais and Beaucaire Railway in France, in the late 1830s. It was very similar to the first engines in the Netherlands (1839). Figure 31 shows a tank engine originally built with a separate tender which the North Staffordshire Railway acquired from a contractor and converted. Little appears to be known of her origins. The date given, 1859, may refer to the conversion, and the boiler is doubtless of later date than the engine. The Great Western Railway maintained a long affection for sandwich frames and found that teak planks made a better internal core than oak, which was common in early days.

The original of Figure 32 was taken by A.G. Bristow at the beginning of the 1890s, probably soon after the abolition of the broad gauge, for the line still has mixed gauge though the outer rail shows signs of disuse. The subject is a down Great Western local train, passing through Sydney Gardens, Bath.

29
30

LONG-BOILER LOCOMOTIVES

An altogether less happy locomotive essay by Robert Stephenson was the so-called long-boiler engine, with all the wheels between smokebox and firebox. It was not that the boiler was really so long: rather that the engine wheelbase was so short in relation to the boiler. It could be dangerously unsteady at speed, particularly on the light track of the period, which was a very serious fault in a locomotive which Stephenson's firm intended specially for fast passenger haulage. When the type was matched against Gooch's great, steady, broad-gauge engines on the Great Western Railway, in what was called the 'Battle of the Gauges', there was trouble, though no member of the Royal Commission appointed to study the gauge question managed to get himself killed.

Figure 33 shows the long-boiler's primeval form, in No. 43 of the Paris-Orleans Railway, built in 1843. Later specimens were sometimes given outside cylinders which made their behaviour even worse at high speeds.

Figure 34 shows the long-boiler engine *Limmat* on the first Swiss railway, from Zürich to Baden. This again is a masterpiece of re-production, including some parts of the original engine, which was built by Emil Kessler of Esslingen in 1847. Fortunately high speeds were not attempted on the 'Spanish Bun Railway' (*Spanische Brodli Bahn*) as the citizens called it after a local delicacy.

A four-coupled version of 1849 is shown in Figure 35, just after rebuilding at Stratford, Great Eastern Railway, in 1867. She ran until 1881 upon undemanding East Anglian branch-line service. Noteworthy is the delightfully Georgian multipane side-window to the cab, the work of Robert Sinclair.

33

THE HOLLAND RAILWAY

To introduce railways to a country so well-served with waterways as the Netherlands must have required some nerve. In one case the King over-rode democracy, authorising by decree.

The first section of the Holland Railway was opened between Amsterdam and Haarlem on September 20, 1839 [36]. The drawing is charming, but the representation of a train somewhat inexperienced. The locomotives followed the Stephenson Patentee type. Opposition, as in other countries, was sometimes militant. In 1847 a small squire near Delft, Mr. Van der Gaag, stuck out against a level crossing over his carriage drive. Figure 37 is a caricature (*not* an accurate representation) of the detour which the Holland Railway made while the lawyers were enjoying themselves. In fact, they made a Y, not a loop, and the din of trains shunting and generally banging about by day and night doubtless influenced the disgruntled proprietor into agreeing terms.

It was in the late 19th century that the military value of railways began really to be appreciated, America in particular having provided an example in the '60s, though the Prussians and others were already well aware. Many old soldiers still remember the stock inscription on railway vans: 'Men 40, Horses 8', rendered in different languages. Figure 38 shows Dutch dragoons entraining at Zutphen in 1900. The occasion is not known, but at that time Dutch feeling was highly anti-British, owing to the South African War. The busbies and frogged tunics do not, however, suggest a volunteer force for service on the Veldt.

38

39

legendary. Taking advantage of the 7 ft. broad gauge, he built much larger engines than his contemporaries. A higher proportion of boiler capacity, relative to cylinders, higher working pressure, and use of the Gooch link motion, enabling the steam to be used expansively, with a variable cut-off, all told in any comparison with the locomotives of other British — or foreign — railways.

The basic design was that of Stephenson's Patentees, plus the Gothic Firebox casing of the early Stephenson Long-Boilers, but all very much enlarged. *Actaeon* [40] was one of the Firefly class — 62 express engines with 7 ft. driving wheels — which were built between 1840 and 1842. *Actaeon* herself ran for 26 years, surviving a boiler explosion in 1856.

From 1846 onwards, Gooch built eight-wheeled express engines with 8 ft. driving wheels. Figure 41 shows the *Lord of the Isles* (1851—1884) beflagged for the conveyance of couriers and dispatches at the close of the Crimean War. So successful was this design that when the old engines wore out, similar but slightly more powerful ones were built almost to the end of broad-gauge working.

G.W.R. GOOCH LOCOMOTIVES

Daniel Gooch [39] who was ultimately to be made a baronet, was one of a large engineering family from Northumberland. He was given command of the Great Western Railway's Locomotive Department just before he came of age and his bold yet simple designs became

40

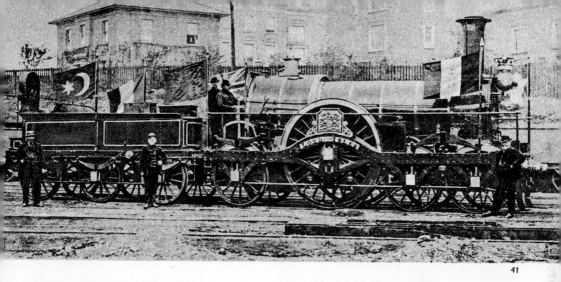

THE CRAMPTON LOCOMOTIVE

Thomas Russell Crampton (1816—1888) was an Englishman more honoured in France and Germany. The best of his engines, conceived on the lines of a stern-wheel steamer, had little ratio of adhesive to total weight but could go like the wind with light, fast passenger trains. His long-term contribution to steam practice was accessibility of working parts, sometimes with a high running platform clearing these.

The first Crampton locomotives were six built by Tulk and Ley during 1846—47. One of these was the *Kinnaird* [42] on the Dundee and Perth Junction Railway. Of many engines built abroad under Crampton's patents, most successful were those in France. The Paris-Strasbourg engine *Le Continent* [43] was in

43

service from 1852 to 1919, and is preserved in working order. *Die Pfalz* [44] was one of four very beautiful Cramptons built by Maffei of Munich for the Palatinate Railway in 1853. Joseph Hall ('Maffei's Englishman') designed the arrangement of outside cranks and gear. The photograph shows a full-size restoration made by Carl Klensch (standing on footplate), now in Nuremberg Transport Museum.

The photograph of *Kinnaird* is believed to have been taken by R.E. Bleasdale as far back as the 1850s, and is with little doubt one of the earliest photographs of a railway engine in service.

44

VICTORIAN STEAM

CLEGG AND SAMUDA ATMOSPHERIC RAILWAY

Railways were still young when we saw the first attempts to dispense with heavy locomotive haulage. Most important was the so-called atmospheric system of Clegg and Samuda, which was tried on the Dublin and Kingstown, London and Croydon, and South Devon Railways. The accompanying drawings [45, 46, 47, 48 and 49] are taken from the *Illustrated London News* of October 5, 1845, and show the Croydon outfit. It involved a continuous pipe between the rails, with a slot in the top, kept airtight by a greased leather flap. Air was exhausted from the pipe by pumping engines at

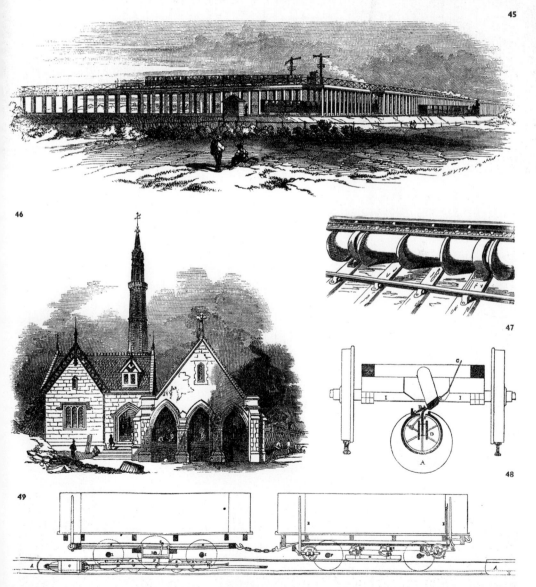

45

46

47

48

49

intervals. The leading vehicle, attached to a piston in the pipe, was thus pushed along by the atmospheric pressure in rear of it, and a second vehicle resealed the flap-valve as it passed over.

Sanguine people expected the rapid obsolescence of locomotive traction — even Brunel, who ought to have known better, but loved anything new — but junctions raised very serious problems, wear-and-tear was quite tremendous, and finally rats took to gnawing the leather flaps for the sake of the grease. The thing was a very expensive failure, after people

had briefly marvelled at the high speeds attainable. But at least the junction difficulties resulted in the building of the world's first fly-over, between Norwood and Croydon in South London.

In the 1860s, there was a brief outburst of rail-motoring. Both Robert Fairlie and James Samuel produced steam-car designs which were so alike that there were editorial sniggers in the technical papers. Figure 50 shows Samuel's version. Only one car was built, however, under Fairlie's patent. Nobody seems to have bought it.

51

LONG-BOILERS

In places where speeds were low, the unsteadiness of the long-boiler type of locomotive was of little consequence. At the same time, with its short wheelbase the engine could negotiate the most curvaceous and even crazy branches and sidings.

In Continental Europe some old veterans lasted for a tremendous time, and as shown elsewhere they still are to be seen in Spain. Portugal also musters a few, and one of these, from the old Minho-Douro Railway, is shown in Figure 51, from a photograph taken quite recently by Peter Allen in the course of travels that have several times encompassed the world.

The other two subjects exemplify the four-coupled type with outside cylinders, at one time much favoured in France. No. 428 [52] of the Eastern Railway of France was, we believe, photographed in the 1890s, but was then little altered from her original state, nearly half a century before. The chimney is original; a cannister-shaped sandbox has been mounted on top of the Crampton-type domeless boiler.

An Italian specimen, somewhat rebuilt, is shown in Figure 53. The photograph cannot be positively dated, but as the engine carries the Italian State Railways' initials and number (she was an old Italian Southern engine), it cannot have been earlier than 1907. Observe the wine casks on the leading wagon.

52

53

ALEXANDER ALLAN
LOCOMOTIVES

Persistent breakage of crank axles on the Grand Junction Railway in the early 1840s induced Alexander Allan to design engines with outside inclined cylinders, which he mounted on massive double frames, some existing locomotives being thus modified for a start. Allan went to Crewe, and the arrangement became so characteristic of the London and North Western Railway's Northern Division that it was for years known as the 'Crewe Type'. William Buddicom took it to France, where it became equally widely known as *Le Buddicom*. Illustrations of it will recur, but these four figures show its general development.

One of the original Crewe engines of the L.N.W.R. is shown in Figure 54, unaltered save by addition of a Webb chimney in the '70s. The *Columbine*, first of these, and still preserved, was built in 1845, but already in 1844 Buddicom was building Allan's type at

56

Chartreux, near Rouen. Figure 55 shows a typical example of a Buddicom version, built for the Paris and Rouen Railway. Robert Sinclair modified the type, and one of his engines, built rather surprisingly by Schneider of Creusot for the Great Eastern Railway, is shown with some contemporary rolling stock in Figure 56. (The chimney is a later form, as in the L.N.W.R. engine.)

The last engines of the classic Allan form were built by David Jones for the Highland Railway over a period of 18 years, from 1874 to 1892. That shown in Figure 57 is *Atholl*, built in 1886. Jones' engines were of course much heavier and more advanced than their forerunners, and had Adams bogies, but the deep, slotted frame at the front entirely preserved the original form.

57

THE HAWKSHAW TYPE

Quite a favourite in the mid-19th century was a steam locomotive type originated by Sir John Hawkshaw in the 1840s, having outside cylinders with all axles in rear of these and the trailing one about the back of the firebox, with a distinctly low-pitched boiler. In spite of the overhang in front, such engines were remarkably steady at high speeds, of which they were indeed capable when lightly loaded.

The very elegant *Cossack* [58] was one of the many built for the London and South Western Railway to the designs of Joseph Beattie between 1855 and 1875, and was equipped with his patent double firebox ('coal-burning without smoke') which had two fire-doors and a water-filled midfeather.

Below the Beattie engine, in Figure 59, is our oldest example of the type, which was one of a series built by Beyer, Peacock and Company of Manchester for the first lines of the Swedish State Railways in 1856. The somewhat grandiose station was the original Gothen-

58
59

60
61

burg Central, not entirely vanished. The Swedish carriages of the period do not look very luxurious, but — wonder of wonders for 1860 — the leading one appears to have a lavatory. It has also some sort of heating apparatus whose chimney is just visible to the right of the intermediate pillar supporting the end-screen to the station roof.

Next, in Figure 60, comes a Danish example of this type, the *Skade*, built for the Zealand Railway by Beyer, Peacock and Company in 1870. The family resemblance between the London and South Western, Swedish and Danish State engines is remarkable, and not inexplicable. Joseph Beattie, who was Irish, and Charles Beyer, who was German, were close personal friends. Both worked in England.

Lastly, in Figure 61, is the Holland Railway Company's *Xanthippe*, built by Borsig of Berlin in 1881. This engine, named after the sharp-tonged Mrs. Socrates, was in service for 53 years.

LONGEVITY OF STEAM LOCOMOTIVES

Subject to renewals and the maintenance of patterns and spare parts, a steam locomotive could last and work for a tremendous time. In Spain and Austria, centenarians could be seen still earning revenue as late as the 1960s.

The *Lion* of the Liverpool and Manchester Railway was built by Todd, Kitson and Laird in 1838. 21 years later her then owners, the London and North Western Railway, sold her to the Mersey Docks and Harbour Board, which latterly mounted her as a stationary pumping engine. When aged about 90, she was retired and restored as a locomotive relic, still well able to steam after some necessary operations. Figure 62 shows her in 1930 with a replica of a Liverpool and Man-

62
63

chester train (observe open coaches in the rear).

Figure 63 shows London Midland and Scottish Railway No. 20002, originally Midland Railway No. 158, built at Derby by Matthew Kirtley in 1866. Apart from overhauls she was continuously in service for 81 years, being finally withdrawn (and preserved) in August, 1947.

The engaging little 3 ft. 6 in. gauge New Zealand tank engine in Figure 64 was built in Glasgow by Dübs and Company in 1873. In the service of the Canterbury Frozen Meat Company she steamed until a diesel replaced her in 1962 — after 89 years.

Lastly, Figure 65 shows a strange contrast at Andover, in May, 1955. The diesel-hauled express (1.30 p.m. Waterloo to Exeter) is passing a Beattie tank engine built for the London and South Western in 1874, and here heading an enthusiasts' special.

64

65

OLD EUROPEAN MOUNTAIN ENGINES

Originating in Austria on the Semmering Railway, the Engerth locomotive was articulated to its tender so that it bore part of the latter's weight, thus improving its own adhesion. The original arrangement included coupling of the tender wheels also, with derived drive from the engine, but this complication was speedily dropped. Thus simplified, the type was much used in the Alpine countries a century ago, and *Genf* (Geneva) was one of a series built by Kessler of Esslingen for the Swiss Central Railway in 1858. She worked for 40 years, then served as a stationary boiler at Olten Works, and is now preserved [66] at the Verkehrshaus in Lucerne.

Though outwardly rather resembling an Engerth locomotive, *Le Rubicon* [67] was built under Eduard Beugniot's patents, involving sideplay and horizontal lever control of the coupled axles. The articulated tender was incidental, and contrary to Engerth's principle which took some of the engine's weight at the rear, thus sparing the light track of the period. In 1862 *Le Rubicon* and her sister engine *L'Apennin* were delivered from Koechlin of Mulhouse to the Austrian Southern Railway at Trieste.

The latter company had a grand scheme for swallowing the Lombard-Venetian and Italian Central Railways, hence the engines' names. The takeover was politically scotched, but to Italy the engines soon went, and with six more sisters they worked the very difficult Porretana line over the Apennines from Bologna to Pistoja, now replaced as an international route by the great Apennine Tunnel. They were giants of their day, as they needed to be on such a line.

ROMAN RAILWAYS

The five modern lithographs in colour, facing pages 64 and 65, were based on drawings in the Roman Railways' diagram book of 1878. The green tank engine [V] was built by William Bridges Adams of Bow, London, in 1850. Plate VI, showing an archaic American-type locomotive, is a curiosity. The tender is as early-Victorian-English as the engine is pre-Civil-War-American, being of a type built up to the early 1850s by Norris of Philadelphia. Each may have come to Italy under quite different contracts, to be united in later years.

Jones and Potts of Warrington built the Stephensonian long-boiler 2-4-0 passenger engine in Plate VII. Built in 1848, she ran until the 1880s. In 1859, Ansaldo of Sampierderena (Genoa) built the neat little 0-4-2 mixed-traffic engine [VIII], the design of which shows strong British influence. The stylish single-wheel passenger engine [IX] built by Peto, Brassey and Betts of Canada Works, Birkenhead, is characteristic of that firm's practice, and ran for about 20 years from 1863.

68

DEVELOPMENT IN THE 1860s

The 1860s saw the production of many good, solid, enlarged versions of what already were classic types of locomotive. The 'Jenny Lind' type, dating from the late '40s and owing its origin to James Fenton and David Joy, was a single-driver passenger engine with inside cylinders and double frames, but with inside bearings only to the driving axle. It was a steady, manageable locomotive, and capable of enlargement, as shown in two examples of the general type, built in 1862.

Dom Luiz [68] was built for the Portuguese South Eastern Railway by Beyer, Peacock and Company. The designer is believed to have been Charles Beyer himself, sometime an immigrant Saxon from Plauen, and a stickler for neat design as well as for sound mechanical engineering. The engine ran for very many years, and has been preserved.

Very similar, but with a domed boiler, was the engine shown in Figure 69, built and shown at the 1862 Exhibition in London by Lilleshall Company. The shape of the cab, and a similarity to locomotives built later for the Great Northern Railway, suggests that Patrick Stirling (then on the Glasgow and South Western) may have had more than something to do with the design. This Lilleshall engine was probably sold abroad after the exhibition. There is no further record of her in England. Engines of the same general type were to be found on the North British Railway local services right into the present century, one lasting until 1912. The first of these had appeared in 1856.

In Figure 70 is a specimen of what for years was the standard British goods engine (in many varieties, forms and dimensions), exemplified here in a locomotive built for the East Indian Railway by the Yorkshire Engine Company in 1867. The cab framework was intended to support a covering which should be a sunshade or an umbrella, according to the season.

58

OLD FRENCH LOCOMOTIVES

Jules Petiet, Chief Engineer of the Northern Railway of France from 1845 to 1872, designed a form of cylindrical steam dryer [71] which he mounted on top of the boiler. It was in open communication with the boiler steam space, and through it passed flues carrying the products of combustion from the smokebox in front to a chimney at the rear. The dried steam was led to the cylinders from a Crampton style regulator-box on top. In principle, the apparatus anticipated that of the Franco-Crosti boiler, extensively employed in Italy, and to a limited extent in Great Britain, from the late 1940s onwards. Figure 72 shows an Eastern of France engine, a de Glehn compound of 1891, with the Flaman boiler, also having a cylindrical steam-space on top, but without the flues passing through it.

71

72

UNDERGROUND STEAM I

It is not always realised that a century and more ago, London had an internal traffic problem. Getting from the City to the West End, or from the northern termini to the southern and western was a long business, and no joke as the cabs and carriages crawled between immense carts, or stood long immovable at jammed intersections where a policeman or two

73

74

strove to sort things out. Hence the world's first schemes for city underground railways.

Many considered the project impossible, but by the beginning of the 1860s the first section of the Metropolitan Railway was under construction, by cut-and-cover methods, following the line of the streets from Paddington (Bishop's Road) to Farringdon near High Holborn. Sir John Fowler was Engineer, and one of his headaches was the production of a fireless, or at any rate smokeless, locomotive. Practical electric traction was unborn: 'atmospheric' propulsion was discredited. Hence the engine later known as 'Fowler's Ghost' [73]. She was a fine, sturdy creation, but the trouble was that her boiler not only refrained from producing smoke, it produced very little steam either. From a very small firebox there extended nearly to the front of the barrel a cylindrical chamber filled with firebricks, which were intended to be brought to a white heat and thus to deputise for the real fire. To adapt Lewis Carroll: *Bold, heroic was the notion, but the boiler failed entirely.* The unique photograph

shows the engine near Edgware Road, on trial in 1862.

The line was opened on January 10, 1863, on broad gauge and worked by the Great Western Railway. In place of the 'Ghost', Daniel Gooch had produced a set of tank engines with surface condensers, which looked after the exhaust steam while the smoke looked after itself in the tunnels. At the end of each trip the nearly boiling water was run off, enveloping the engine in a huge cloud, to be replaced by cold water in readiness for the next adventure.

Figure 74 shows one of Gooch's engines heading a westbound train between Edgware Road and Paddington, later to become the western portion of the 'Circle'. The carriages were lit by coal gas (an innovation) which was carried in collapsible rubber bags enclosed in boxes on the roofs. Observe the mixed-gauge lines. Provision of the extra rail was indeed fortunate, for soon after, the Great Western quarrelled with the Metropolitan company and withdrew its broad-gauge trains.

UNDERGROUND STEAM II

Following the quarrel, the Great Northern Railway lent the Metropolitan engines and carriages to enable it to carry on until it had sufficient of its own. A new design for a standard underground locomotive was produced by Beyer, Peacock and Company in 1864, this time on standard gauge, and this class was to work the trains of the Metropolitan, and its younger neighbour the District Railway, right down to the completion of electrification in 1905.

Condensing was achieved by leading the exhaust into the side tanks and periodically changing the water as before. Figure 75 shows one of the standard Metropolitan engines with a New Cross-Hammersmith train on the junction at Aldgate, vigorously exhausting through

her chimney on leaving the tunnel, much as a whale spouts after being long submerged. The atmosphere in the tunnels was often frightful, but the trains worked and the passengers survived. Some indeed made underground trips for the sake of their health; the sulphur fumes were supposed to be good for respiratory complaints.

The Metropolitan and District companies steadily expanded their systems, co-existing with periodic quarrels, until they served a great part of London and had numerous connections with the main lines. Figure 76 shows the so-called 'Widened Lines' of the Metropolitan in 1868, just east of the burrowing junction and the Clerkenwell Tunnels. The train in the foreground has come through from the Great Northern Railway via York Road, Kings Cross. Above it, and receding, is a train on the origi-

75

nal line, possibly running through to the Great Western. Somewhere concealed, but not far off, is the great Fleet Sewer, which had to be diverted for the railway and burst during the process, a noisome accident which also caused enormous damage at this place, bringing down the retaining walls and flooding the tunnels. The second set of tracks forming the 'Widened Lines' never was electrified. It is used by diesel trains to and from the main lines today, having previously had steam traction between Kings Cross and Moorgate.

76

UNDERGROUND LOCOMOTIVES

Figure 77 shows one of the standard District Railway locomotives in London, No. 34, which at the electrification of 1905 was reprieved for working breakdown and ballast trains. Originally all of this type, both District and Metropolitan, had the dome on the first ring of the boiler, as shown, and the surviving District locomotives carried it to the end. This classic Beyer-Peacock design was itself based on one for the Tudela and Bilbao Railway in Spain, made by the same firm in 1862 and apparently the joint work of Herman Lange and John Ramsbottom. The latter was Locomotive Engineer to the London and North Western Railway, which clearly had no objection to his working for other people as a consultant.

This District engine, photographed in her old age with the 'UndergrounD' symbol on her tank sides, very clearly shows the main features of the design. The breeches pipe at the back allowed steam to escape from the tanks when they became really hot from condensing. Above the cylinders can be seen the gear for working the two-way valve which directed the exhaust into the tanks while in the tunnel, and up the chimney when in the open. The four-wheel truck under the front end was not a bogie but a Bissell radial arrangement, perpetuated for much longer in the United States. One of the Metropolitan engines, built in 1866, is preserved in Clapham Museum, London.

The first provincial underground line was in the Mersey Railway, passing under the river between Liverpool and Birkenhead (February 1, 1886), closely followed on March 15 by the

PLATE V Bridges Adams' light tank engine, 1850.
PLATE VI Norris-type locomotive with English tender.

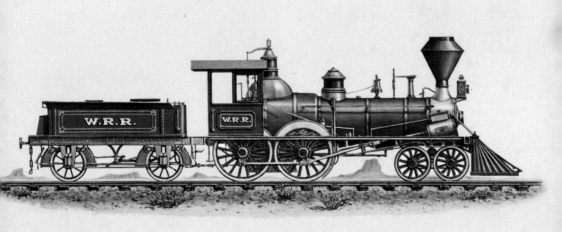

Glasgow City and District Railway, which was worked by the North British company. On the former, the under-water passage within a short linear distance involved very heavy gradients, entailing the use of suitably massive and powerful locomotives. The *Fox* is shown in Figure 78. This line, steam-worked until May, 1903, was reputed even more foul than the worst sections of the Metropolitan in London. From our own recollections, the Glasgow Central underground line (opened in 1896) must have run them both close.

PLATE VII Jones and Potts 'long boiler' engine, 1848.

PLATE VIII Ansaldo mixed-traffic engine, 1859.

PLATE IX An Italian 'Birkenhead', 1863.

THE ELEVATED RAILWAY

While London, in the second half of the 19th century, favoured underground railways for intramural passenger traffic, several American cities used elevated railways, trestled over the streets. Compared with earlier modes of transport, they were noisy and most destructive of amenities, but they were cheap and useful, and were widely used from the 1870s onwards, particularly in New York City where the serpentine rock forming Manhattan Island was scarcely inviting to those who might otherwise have promoted the introduction of underground lines.

Steam traction was used until early in the present century, when legislation forbade the emission of smoke by locomotives in the cen-

tral city area. Figure 79 shows a train on the Third Avenue Elevated in the '90s. The locomotive is a Forney 0-4-4 tank engine, which became the commonest type on the elevated lines. The Eames vacuum brake was used, for so short was the distance between each stop that there was no time to keep up the pressure of air brakes.

Of the two engravings, Figure 80 shows one of the earlier, four-wheeled engines in New York, with saddle tank. The Metropolitan Elevated engine in Figure 81 is generally similar, though its aspect is rather altered by the elaborate all-over cab and the leading and trailing radial trucks, which were intended to ease its passage round the inevitable sharp curves of lines built above, and following, the city streets.

80

81

THE NEW YORK ELEVATED R.R.

CURIOSITIES

As in all mechanical engineering, locomotive design that went into service, quite apart from that describable as crackpot, had many oddities. The most normal of the four engines shown is that in Figure 82. It is an example of the work of Stephen Lewin, who from the late 1860s to the early '80s built locomotives, traction engines, steam launches and agricultural machinery at Poole in Dorset. The little engine, shown mounted on rollers for street transport to station or docks, was probably for a gasworks or quarry, and the imposing number she carries is an invention for it seems unlikely that Lewin, who was rich and ran his works for enthusiasm's sweet sake, built nearly 700 locomotives.

Lartigue's monorail [83] was expected to revolutionise rural mechanical transport, and did not. Engines and vehicles were made double, and straddled a trestle rail. All the same, the Listowel and Ballybunion Railway worked on this system from 1888 to 1924. It

82

83

had been preceded by experimental lines in Belgium and France, and in the latter country the results were singularly unfortunate. But it took severe damage in the Irish Civil War to finish the Ballybunion line, one of whose engines, by Hunslet Engine Company, is here shown on turntable (the sole means of getting locomotives and vehicles from one track to another).

John Fowler of Leeds was particularly interested in agricultural locomotion, thus influenced by his partnership with David Greig, a food producer whose name is still famous. For traction on very light railways he produced little locomotives with a form of jack-shaft drive. One is shown in service on a sugar-cane plantation during the '80s [84]. Cane-trash was the usual, very economical fuel. The other [85] on the Powyan Steam Tramway in India, has her interesting motion covered with hinged side-sheeting, probably to save inquisitive children from injury and possibly to protect buffalo, and other wandering creatures, from alarm.

86

87

THE BRITISH 4-4-0

A type of express passenger locomotive which was to be built over several generations was that with four-coupled wheels, inside cylinders and a leading bogie, the classic British 4-4-0. Outside Great Britain, it was to be much used in Scandinavia, the Low Countries and parts of Australia. It was akin to the ancient American 'inside-connected' 4-4-0 engine, though this was not properly describable also as 'inside cylindered', the cylinders being generally between the narrow smokebox and the frames. Figure 86 shows a very elegant example, and also one of the earliest, built by Slaughter, Gruning and Company, Bristol, for the Barcelona-Granollers Railway and the Barcelona, Tarragona and France Railway from 1859 to 1861. The photograph shows one in later years, on the Madrid, Zaragoza and

Alicante Railway, where she ended her days.

The first for home service were two designed by Thomas Wheatley for the North British Railway (Nos. 224 and 264) in 1871. Figure 87 shows No. 224 rather the worse for wear. She had just been fished out of the Firth of Tay, about three months after the first Tay Bridge had fallen under her, and her train, on December 28, 1879 (see page 396). Repaired and twice rebuilt, she ran until 1919. First of the type for major British express service were built by James Stirling for the Glasgow and South Western Railway between 1873 and 1877 [88]. Three of them were still at work in 1930, and in their earlier days they handled the heavy Pullman trains north of Carlisle, following completion of the Midland-Scottish route in 1876. It was a very robust design. Hit hard, it could still manage to limp home under its own steam.

LOCOMOTIVES
FOR THE EMPIRE

In 1862, Sharp, Stewart and Company built the first of some very massive tank locomotives for work on the Ghat inclines of the Great Indian Peninsula Railway. One of these, in her later years, is shown by Figure 89. They were among the very first of the 4-6-0 type to be built in British works. All three driving axles were compensated, and the bogie pin had side-play controlled by inclined planes. During their mountain service the engines also had skid brakes, to be applied to the rails during descent. Observe the proprietorial English driver, the fireman (probably a Parsee) on the footplate, and the Hindu assistant fireman or *augwalla* proudly but irresponsibly dangling the oil-can by its spout.

Figure 90 shows an old Indian colliery locomotive undoubtedly built by either E. B. Wilson or Manning Wardle at Leeds, and probably about 1860. The fluted dome-casing was once the hallmark of these, but the plain chimney bespeaks the later firm, which took over the old Wilson drawings with the rest of the property.

The beautiful little *Snake* [91] exemplifies Robert Fairlie's double-bogie, double-boiler patent locomotive, and was built for New Zealand (3 ft. 6 in. gauge) by the Avonside Engine Company, Bristol, in 1864. Interesting is the early form of Walschaert radial valve gear. The picture was taken at Auckland in 1877, with Driver Withers in the cab and Mr. Hargraves, leading painter, with his hand lovingly laid on the platform. Few people can nowadays realise how important to early settlers was the almost metropolitan blessing of a new steam railway.

89
90

'BIG WHEELS'

Essentially British in the mid-Victorian years was the express engine with very large single driving wheels combined with outside cylinders. The latter were essential; the low-pitched boilers then in favour would not clear the throw of inside cranks.

Benjamin Conner's Caledonian engines [92]

and John Ramsbottom's London and North Western Problems [93] both began to appear in 1859. The former class in shown with a somewhat modified boiler. The engine was, of its period, a large and heavy version of Allan's Crewe type, but with horizontal instead of inclined cylinders. The driving wheels were 8 ft. 2 in. in diameter, and when these first appeared they were among the heaviest and most powerful express engines on any British main

91
92

line. The L.N.W.R. engine *Lady of the Lake*
[93] is shown in her original state. Her class
was lighter than the Scottish engine, with 7 ft.
7½ in. drivers. Both classes hauled the West
Coast expresses for many years. The Ramsbottom design was an enlarged version of one
made by Patrick Stirling for the Glasgow and
South Western Railway in 1857, and the
'Lady' shown won a gold medal at the 1862
Exhibition in London (see small replica over
the number on the side-sheets).

In 1870 Patrick Stirling produced the ultimate of this type in his splendid 8 ft. bogie
singles on the Great Northern Railway, to
which he had gone from Scotland. G.N.R.
No. 1 of this class has survived, and has often
been photographed. Figure 94 shows one of her
sisters, No. 22, in service with the big tender
of later days. The bogie was not so much to
assist on curves (it had a rigid pin) as to 'roll
out the track' as the engine advanced; more
accurately, to steady her.

93

94

BRITISH LOCOMOTIVES ABROAD

As early as the 1850s British works were building an anglicised version of what in the United States was already regarded as the classic American locomotive, with outside cylinders and a leading bogie, and this appeared on the Stockton and Darlington in 1860.

Most early examples, however, were for export. Those in Figures 95 and 96 were for the Americas. The engine with two domes and a large headlamp was an early example of many built for South America. This was made by the Yorkshire Engine Company for the Buenos Aires Great Southern Railway ('Bags') in the '70s. In Figure 96 is shown one of the passenger engines built for the Windsor and Annapolis Railway, Nova Scotia, by Fox, Walker and Company's Atlas Works, Bristol, in 1868. (The works subsequently belonged to Peckett and Sons, whose brass plate has been faked into this extremely rare photograph.) The en-

75

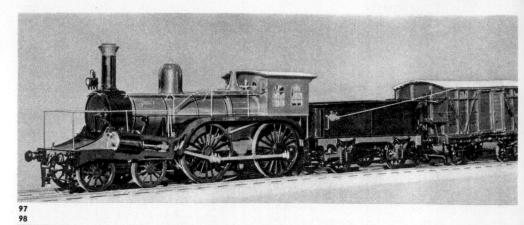

97
98

gines had North American bells, chime whist-les and large wooden cabs; otherwise they were of entirely English style which was highly unusual for Canada, even in the middle of last century.

In 1860, Peto, Brassey and Betts of Canada Works, Birkenhead built the first locomotive for the Finland State Railways, and a slightly heavier example, *Pilvi*, built in 1865, is shown by the model in Figure 97. The characteristic Allan supplementary framing below the out-side cylinders was much favoured by Canada Works; (compare the Italian locomotive in Plate IX, facing page 65).

Lastly, in Figure 98, is shown one of the old 'mail engines' of the sometime Bobadilla and Algeçiras Railway in the extreme south of Spain, built by Beyer, Peacock and Company in the 1880s. Spanish engines have often at-tained great ages. This one was photographed at Alicante in the 1960s; still useful, though a long way from Gibraltar by then.

EARLY AMERICAN STEAM

An early example of what was for years the standard American locomotive for all ordinary work was the *Bob Ellis* [99] first engine of what became the Chicago, Milwaukee, St. Paul and Pacific Railroad, 'the first engine to turn a wheel in the State of Wisconsin'. Built by Norris of Philadelphia in 1848, this had the bar frames and haycock boiler initiated by Edward Bury in England and exported, but the four-coupled wheels and leading bogie were Norris's improvements.

From this developed the classic American Type of the 19th century, well exemplified in the *William Crooks* of the St. Paul and Pacific Railroad [100], built by Smith and Jackson of Paterson N.J. and shipped up the Mississippi to St. Paul in 1861. The engine is shown at Elk River, Minnesota, in 1864, and is preserved today in mint condition by the Great Northern Railway. Boston and Albany No. 214 *Dukes* [101] was most unusual in American practice through having a domeless boiler with a perforated steampipe. She was built by Wilson Eddy in 1872. Exemplary reliability earned

99
100

the class the name of 'The Eddy Clocks'. The design belonged characteristically to the New England states.

Ross Winans' engines, inevitably named 'Camels' [102] were designed for heavy coal haulage on the Baltimore and Ohio Railroad; they went back to 1848, and were in service for many years. Low-grade anthracite was the fuel in a swallowtail firebox. They were slow and sombre-looking engines while contemporary American express locomotives were frequenty ornate. The 'Camel' type was later perpetuated by Samuel Hayes, still on the B. & O.

101
102

LOCOMOTIVES FOR SPECIAL JOBS

Mid-19th century America, having already spanned the Rockies, presented country far beyond the ability of her traditional four-coupled locomotive. *Uncle Dick* [103] was a heavy banking engine for helping trains over the temporary Raton Zigzag of the New Mexico and Southern Pacific Railroad, pending completion of a tunnel. Baldwins built her in 1879, their largest engine yet, and her owners named her for a Western old-timer who had declared a shooting war against them, they being invaders on his territory.

103
104

On the eastern slopes of the Sierra Nevada, A. J. Stevens of the Central Pacific Railroad designed what were then immense locomotives, for the climb from the Pacific Coast. His 12-wheeler of 1882 [104] was intended for coping with traffic on a rise of 2,800 ft. in 25 miles, and did it very well, on the local timber. Her 19 in. cylinders had the very long stroke of 30 in. A 10-coupled version (*El Gobernador*) remained an isolated prodigy, but Stevens' eight- and six-coupled engines were on the job for many years. Figure 105 shows a very early 12-wheeler locomotive for Pennsylvania coal traffic, obviously designed by James Milholland of the Philadelphia and Reading Railroad and built in 1863.

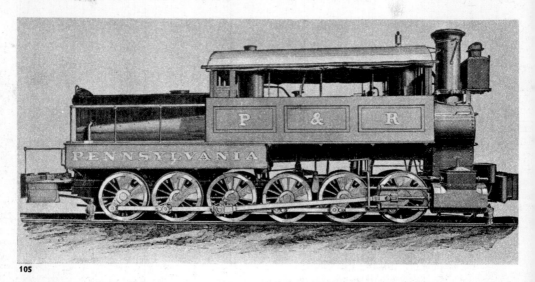

105

WELSH NARROW GAUGE

Oldest of the world's public narrow-gauge lines, the Festiniog Railway (1 ft. 11½ in. gauge) was opened on April 20, 1836. While the distance between Portmadoc, Caernarvonshire, and Blaenau-Festiniog in Merioneth is but 9½ miles, a difference of 700 ft. in altitude entailed a route of 13¼ miles as the line wound about the mountainside. In early days, horses took the empty slate wagons up and gravity brought the loaded ones down. A steep section at first worked by cable traction was later avoided by tunnelling. About 1850 there was a 'tram fitted for visitors'. Steam traction came in 1863, regular passenger services in 1865, and from 1869 new engines were nearly all of Fairlie's double-bogie, double-boiler type.

For many years *y Tren Bach* — the Little Train — toiled up into the mountains, or gently coasted down. But with the decline of the slate industry came that of the railway. By 1950 it was not only silent but completely overgrown in places. The enterprise of devot-

ed people led to the formation of the present Festiniog Railway Company. Fortunately some of the equipment survived, and it has been supplemented by stock from other lines now closed down. Figure 106 shows *Merddin Emrys*, a Fairlie engine built in 1879, with a full train at the present upper terminus, Tan-y-bwlch. The second carriage is new. The third, a buffet car, was rebuilt from an old Lynton and Barnstaple carriage.

Though junior to the Festiniog Railway — it was opened in 1865 — the Talyllyn Railway from Towyn to Abergynolwyn, Merioneth, has adopted the proud motto: *We never closed*. Strictly, the meaning is: 'We never closed down'. For many years, this 2 ft. 3 in. gauge line was worked with its original equipment, and even in 1945, many of the 80-year-old rails were still bearing its trains. Traffic had fallen almost to token movements, but the venerable Sir Haydn Jones kept it going, rather as a personal, private business. So it was until he died. Then the Talyllyn Railway Preservation Society was formed in 1950. Once decrepit, the

PLATE x Talyllin Railway, Merionethshire: engine *Talyllin*, 1865, running today.

railway was rescued by dedicated men, who worked long, and for love alone.

Now its permanent way is sound; its equipment has increased from the original two locomotives and five carriages to five steam locomotives (including the two ancients and two from the Corris Railway), one light diesel, and 17 carriages including a quite sumptuous and elegant saloon, also from the Corris Railway. At the same time, the present Talyllyn Railway company musters but 25 wagons compared with the 114 used in the great days of slate.

Figure 107 shows the original 0-4-2 tank engine *Talyllyn* banking a heavy summer train out of Rhydyronen station.

106
107

PLATE XI American express locomotive, with a river steamboat in the background, from a Currier and Ives print.

MID-VICTORIAN SCOTTISH LOCOMOTIVES

From 1842 to 1908, subject to brief intervals, all trains leaving Glasgow Queen Street Station were assisted up the steep gradient to Cowlairs by a big stationary engine working a continuous cable, to which locomotives were attached by chain and messenger rope. Figure 108 shows a local, headed by an old Forth and Clyde Junction engine, being hoisted up in the '90s. City-bound trains went down the incline without locomotives, but special brake-wagons were used for the 1 in 45 descent.

Figure 109 shows the Caledonian Railway's inspection train, probably in the early '80s.

108
109

The engine was ancient and unique. Her outside link motion was most unusual in British practice, though it was a common arrangement in France and several other Continental countries. The Caledonian Railway always worked the Callander and Oban Railway, built in slow stages from the middle '60s onwards, and not reaching Oban on the West Coast until 1880.

Figure 110 shows a train from Oban to Edinburgh, with one of George Brittain's 'Oban Bogie' locomotives, which worked most of the trains through the mountains from 1882 to 1902, and lingered for many years longer on lighter loads. The place is in Glen Ogle, at the head of which bleak and savage valley the railhead stayed for some time (1870).

110

ENGINES LARGE AND SMALL

In his travel diary, under the date of June 28, 1896, J. P. Pearson recorded of a journey from Brussels to Bruges: 'We had engine No. 1988 for this journey, a huge 2-4-2 type — altogether too big for the tiny train of 80 tons.' The engine would have been a Belgian State Type 12, dating from the end of the '80s, and capable of taking really heavy international trains, as Pearson was doubtless aware. What is interesting is that 70 years ago this was a 'huge' engine to English eyes [111]. Belpaire's influence — and he was a great engineer — is very strong in this design. It is probable that he too thought up the square chimney. This rugged form was still to be seen on a few old Belgian engines in our young days.

Our other two views are both from Sweden in those same 1890s, and certainly the locomotives are of more modest sort. Figure 112 shows a train from the port of Luleå to the military station of Boden in 1898. The little single-driver express engine was No. 35 *Muspell*, Swedish State Railways, which was built in Manchester by Beyer, Peacock and Company in 1863, and rebuilt in Sweden in 1885. Captivated artists may paint her in holly-green with black bands and double red lines, and a bright brass dome. Figure 113 shows the old Swedish-Gothic station at Uppsala, copperplated roofs and all, with the morning slow train about to leave for Stockholm. The engine is a 2-4-0, basically of the old Hawkshaw type and of Swedish State Railways class Db, built at Motala in 1891.

111
112

84

114

115

HISTORICAL AMERICAN LOCOMOTIVES

Through the '80s into the '90s of the last century, the classic American 4-4-0 locomotive continued to be built in immense numbers. On some lines, notably the New York, New Haven and Hartford, an extended smokebox rather altered the lines, and possibly improved the steaming of the engines [114].

Styling became plainer; the 'straight stack' succeeded the ornate capped chimney in Figure 115, which portrays a New Haven locomotive, this time with a characteristic four-car train. This must be one of the very earliest photographs of a moving train, though one doubts that the speed was very high. Otherwise the exuberantly petticoated girl on the embankment probably would have made her-

self scarcer. She seems not to have been frightened by the steam hissing from the drain-cocks. After the tender, the train consists of a baggage-and-express car, a very old day-coach (probably the 'smoker') and two early wooden Pullman cars.

American citizens have long had a passionate devotion to everything *new*, but side by side with this novelty-for-novelty's sake there is a powerful minority-worship of the American past. Hence the charming little train [116] quite recently built for the pleasure line in the Disneyland Park, California (first opened in 1955). One might have found the *E.P. Ripley*, or her clerestoried wooden train, not to mention the fine American-Gothic station, on some narrow-gauge line in the Adirondacks — or for that matter in Colorado — 80 years ago.

116

INFLUENCES IN SWEDEN

In Sweden, during the latter part of the 19th century, both British and German influences were at work in standard-gauge locomotive design, with a seasoning of American also. Out of these evolved what became the characteristic Swedish engine. Figure 117 shows three standard Beyer Peacock goods engines of the '70s, triple-heading a heavy iron ore train at Gällivare in 1895.

The Lapland line had been begun by a British concern, the Swedish and Norwegian Railway which, however, went into liquidation. The Swedish State Railways took over and completed and extended the line. Some American influence is apparent in the little 2-6-0 passenger engine of the Uppsala-Gefle-Ockelbo Railway [118] though she was Swedish-built, by Motala Engine Works in 1895. The company worked an important main line from junction with the Swedish State Railways at Uppsala out to the East Coast.

In Figure 119 is the handsome *Svana* of the Swedish State Railways, built by Borsig of Berlin in 1875 for the expresses between Stockholm, Malmö and Gothenburg. Later enlarged forms (Classes Cb and Cc), with leading bogies, appeared in the 1880s and '90s, and the second-named were on the best trains down to 1906. All the engines shown have the almost unique form of Swedish spark-arresting chimney, (there were isolated examples in Norway). It contained spiral baffles as well as a cone in the 'collar', and the blastpipe nozzle was above these, in the base of the stack.

117
118

119

SCANDINAVIAN NARROW GAUGE

In the early days of Norwegian railway construction, it was believed that the 3 ft. 6 in. gauge would be not only more economical than the European standard gauge, but the only one practicable for internal lines. At one stage, indeed, the through service to Trondhjem was worked on narrow gauge, with small Pullman-type sleeping cars on the night trains. Figure

120 shows one of the earliest Norwegian State narrow gauge engines, many of which were built in British works. This, the *Alf*, was built by Beyer, Peacock and Company, and was akin to the 3 ft. gauge engines of the Isle of Man Railway.

In Sweden, while standard gauge was adopted for main lines, local lines were built to narrow gauges. The commonest was .891 m. (three Swedish feet), while in the South there

120

was a considerable mileage of 3 ft. 6 in. gauge (now mostly converted to standard gauge). Figure 121 shows No. 3 of the Gothland Railway (one of three on the island) in 1955 after restoration to her original state.

The scene in Figure 122 suggests a railway picnic party in the 1890s according to the costumes of the older persons. It is on the 3 ft. 6 in. gauge Blekinge Coast Railway. All three locomotives date from the '70s.

121
122

WILLIAM STROUDLEY

William Stroudley, an Oxfordshire man who first made a name in Scotland and then came to serve the London, Brighton and South Coast Railway for the rest of his life, attracted even lay attention by the elegance of his locomotives, to which was added efficiency from mechanical judgement in design. His little local-line tank engines known as Terriers

numbered 50, built between 1872 and 1880. *Boxhill*, built in the latter year, is shown in Figure 123. The engine is now preserved at Clapham Museum, London, and the photograph shows her on her last visit to Brighton, with her rods removed for conveyance. (*Waddon*, of 1875, is now in Canada; *Stepney*, built at the same time, now works on the Bluebell Railway in her native Sussex.)

Stroudley perpetuated single driving wheels for express engines for some time. His *Sutherland* [124] ran from 1880 to 1908. Wiseacres' heads wagged when, in 1878, Stroudley began to build express engines with the coupled wheels leading, as in his tank engines for suburban and local services. The heads wagged vainly, for the Stroudley 0-4-2, instead of bursting the road or doing something equally unsuitable, made a fast and steady engine. The *Gladstone* [125] was built in 1882, ran until 1927, and is now preserved.

From boyhood memories, we retain a vivid impression of the quite enormous Pullman trains these little engines could take in their stride between London and Brighton. As for steadiness, when *Hayling* was derailed at full speed by the failure of an old cast-iron bridge near Norwood Junction, she was safely brought to a stand, quite upright, with the train also upright and in line.

125

DUGALD DRUMMOND

An able — and alarming — personality in later Victorian years was Dugald Drummond (1840–1912). Before returning to his native Scotland in the '70s, he had been works manager to William Stroudley on the London, Brighton and South Coast Railway, and he perpetuated many mechanical features of Stroudley's practice, together with his own.

He liked making strong and capable locomotives. Unlike Stroudley, he also favoured leading bogies. His engines could steam well at high speeds. Figure 126 shows his *Abbotsford*, built for the North British in 1876, and Figure 127 shows the same engine, rebuilt with a larger boiler in 1902. In this form the engines lasted into the early and middle 1920s.

Drummond's standard goods engines lasted even longer. Figure 128 shows one somewhat,

126

127
128

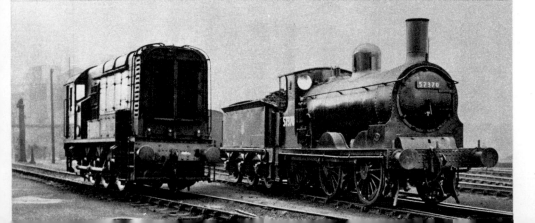

though not radically, rebuilt, standing beside a diesel shunter in the 1950s. This was a Caledonian design, dating back to the middle '80s, and at one time a persistent feature of the landscape from Carlisle to Aberdeen and Oban.

Drummond's front-coupled passenger tank engines, of markedly Stroudleyan inspiration, also first appeared on the North British Railway in the '70s, but the largest, London and South Western class M 7, were built between 1897 and 1911. Edward Griffith's photograph [129] shows one in old age on the Petersfield-Pulborough line in 1950. The last of the class ran until 1964.

129

EXTENSIONS OF THE DRUMMOND STYLE

As suggested elsewhere, the great increase of train weights in the '90s and early 1900s had its effect on locomotive design. Boilers were becoming less and less adequate. In 1896, the year after the 'Race to Aberdeen', John F. McIntosh of the Caledonian Railway considerably increased the boiler/cylinder ratio in his famous Dunalastair class [130] which otherwise was the basic Drummond express engine

which Scotland had known since 1876. Success was immediate. James Holden on the Great Eastern did the same sort of thing with his *Claud Hamilton* of 1900 [131] though in this case the engine differed markedly from the 2-4-0 T 19 class which it was to supersede.

As early as 1894, David Jones on the Highland Railway built the first British 4-6-0 tender locomotives for home service, beginning with No. 103 [132] which is preserved, and still steams. Of its day, this was a very big engine, and though the class was known as 'Big Goods', it was to be seen on all sorts of traffic north of Perth, over many years.

Down on the Caledonian Railway, McIntosh also adopted the 4-6-0 type, for both goods and passenger service, early in the century, but unlike Jones he did not use outside cylinders, keeping to the basic Drummond style which he had already perpetuated in the Dunalastair class. Figure 133 shows the famous *Cardean*, built in 1906, and at the time the most powerful express locomotive in Great Britain. Painted sky-blue, she was for years on the 2.00 p.m. Anglo-Scottish express between Glasgow and Carlisle.

132
133

PLATE XII *Greater Britain* heading the West Coast royal train, 1897, from a painting by the author.

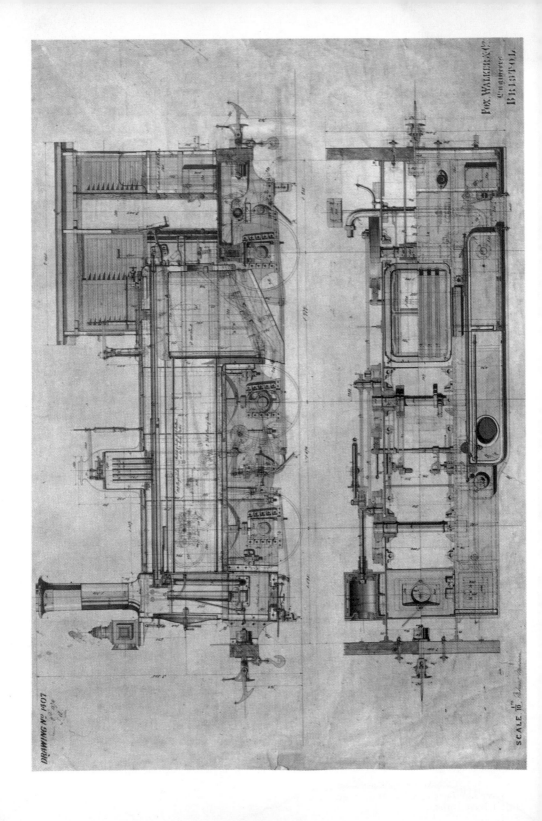

FOX WALKER & Cº

Engineers

BRISTOL

SCALE $\frac{1^{in}}{16}$

WEBB COMPOUND ENGINES

Francis William Webb, Chief Mechanical Engineer of the London and North Western Railway from 1871 to 1904, was the British apostle of compound expansion. His first system to be widely applied involved three cylinders, two outside using high-pressure steam straight from the boiler, and one very large inside cylinder fed by a receiver from the high-pressure exhaust. In passenger engines, there were two driving axles which were not coupled, the trailing pair being driven by the high-pressure cylinders, with Joy's radial valve gear, while the single low-pressure cylinder drove the leading drivers.

Early examples suffered from insufficient boiler power, but the Teutonic class of 1889 [134] was, when driven by a real artist, quite adequate. During the competitive running between London and Aberdeen in 1895, *Adriatic* made a start-to-stop speed of 64 m.p.h.

from Euston, London, to Crewe (158¼ miles).

Webb's designs of 1893 had a considerably longer boiler, with a combustion chamber, and the engine supported on eight wheels. The drivers were still uncoupled. Of these, *Greater Britain* is shown in Plate XII, facing page 96, specially painted for hauling the royal train in the year of Queen Victoria's diamond jubilee, 1897. The sister engine *Queen Empress*, which had been to America for the Chicago World Fair of 1893, was painted white (not cream, as has been stated), and as the Caledonian engines north of Carlisle were in any case blue, haulage was by a sort of tricolour.

Webb's last compound engines differed markedly in having four cylinders, coupled wheels, and in the case of the expresses, a four-wheeled radial truck under the front end, not a bogie but outwardly resembling one. Figure 135 shows *Victorious*, of the final Alfred the Great class, leaving Manchester London Road with a London express about 60 years ago.

PLATE XIII 19th-century mechanical drawing by Fox, Walker & Co., of Bristol; engine for the Dutch East Indies.

136

OLD RUSSIA

In the second half of the 19th century Russia became a Tom-Tiddler's-Ground for foreign locomotive builders, with the British and German firms particularly in competition. Figure 136 shows a Class G freight engine of the old Poti-Tiflis Railway in Georgia. It was of the French Bourbonnais type, stemming from the ancient Stephenson 'long-boilers', but its clean lines suggest other-than-French origins. So it was. The builders were the Yorkshire Engine Company in Sheffield. The high rails on the tender and the coned, spark-arresting chimney both bespeak woodburning, but also noteworthy is the well-lagged outside steampipe from the side of the smokebox to the cylinders on each side.

Yorkshire Engine also built a series of 0-4-4 passenger tank engines for the Poti-Tiflis line. Beyond a remote resemblance to something on the Caledonian, they were distinctly un-British apart from their unencumbered outlines. Figure 137 is from a more recent, though still old photograph, showing how the engines worked in pairs, back to back, on local passenger traffic. That on the left is one of the Yorkshire Engine lot, plus later Russian accessories. Her partner, though basically the same, appears to have a German, or Russo-German, boiler. The shape of the dome strongly recalls the practice of such firms as Borsig of Berlin, or Hartmann of Chemnitz. Both engines have been equipped for oil burning, though the right-hand example still retains the old woodfuel rails round the top of the bunker.

137

AUSTRALIAN VETERANS

Australia of 1864 saw the first of what England knew as the Metropolitan type of locomotive. New South Wales docked the tanks, added a tender, and made of it an express engine.

Figure 138 is from a recent photograph, showing two of the last survivors heading an enthusiasts' special. Goodness knows how many boilers the engines have worn out, but the Belpaire fireboxes and the electric head-lamps with their generators (behind the domes) sit lightly on these energetic old ladies.

Figure 139: very similar in general design, but on a smaller scale, were the Class A 4-4-0 express engines on the Tasmanian Government Railways (3 ft. 6 in. gauge). They were plainer of aspect, and had bogies instead of the Bissell radial trucks used in New South Wales (and, for that matter, on the ancestral engines of the London underground lines). For many years they worked the principal mail and passenger trains between Launceston and Hobart, and one has been fortunately preserved.

No better value in locomotives for money spent on them could have been found than in the New South Wales P 6 class 4-6-0 [140]. Beyer, Peacock and Company built fifty during 1892—3. The class eventually numbered 191, and 55 years after the first were built all these were still in service. Further, the design was copied when the Commonwealth Government needed engines to work the Trans-Australian Railway between Port Augusta, S.A., and Kalgoorlie, W.A., a quarter-century after the first had appeared. Basically, the design was akin to the Indian class L of 1883, whereof another development was David Jones' 'Big Goods' on the Highland Railway in 1894. One did not expect high speeds with a 5 ft. driving wheel, but on the Newcastle and Albury expresses, N.S.W. class P 6 (later C 32) could nevertheless loaf along at a respectable 70 miles an hour.

140

ITALIAN, FRENCH AND AUSTRIAN EXPRESSES

In 1884, Cesare Frescot, Mechanical Engineer to the Upper Italian Railway at Turin, produced the first 4-6-0 main-line locomotive in Europe, the *Vittorio Emanuele II*. The arrangement of the engine, which was to have many sisters, was somewhat French. Figure 141 is additionally interesting in that it shows the original company's brass plate on the dome casing, with its coat of arms, the initials S.F.A.I., and the date. British works produced 4-6-0 engines almost simultaneously, but they were for India (the North Western Railway).

Certain French railways favoured the 2-4-2 express engine at this time. It was really a development of the old 'long-boiler' type, being steadied by the addition of an extra axle, in rather cramped-looking quarters at the rear. Figure 142 shows an example of a once very numerous class on the Paris-Orleans Railway. The boiler, dome, sandbox and cylinder casings were all of unpainted brass, which in the engines' prime was kept highly polished. As in the Italian locomotive, the link motion was outside with the excentrics mounted on a return crank each side.

141

142

Figure 143 shows the Paris-Milan express of the P.L.M. company, somewhat embarrassed by snow in the station at Andelot-en-Montagne, Jura, on the morning of February 2, 1907. The train engine is an early 4-6-0 and the snowplough engine in front is an ancient Bourbonnais (0-6-0 long-boiler goods).

At the other end of the Alps, both the Austrian State and the Austrian Southern Railways built during the 1880s some remarkable 4-4-0 express engines which perpetuated Joseph Hall's old arrangement of cranks and valve-gear outside frames which were also outside. Figure 144 shows a veteran which we remember from the middle 1930s. Lignite was often the fuel, and the immense external spark arrester was a feature of thousands of Austrian locomotives, right up to their retreat before the advance of electric traction. The cylindrical mounting just in front of the cab was the exhaust from the Hardy vacuum brake apparatus once much favoured on Austrian railways. One of this class has been partly sectioned to show its internal features, and thus installed in the Vienna Railway Museum. Several somewhat similar engines remained at work on the Graz-Köflach Railway in Styria until 1965.

LOW COUNTRIES LOCOMOTIVES

Many influences were at work on locomotive design in the Low Countries. Belpaire's generous, flat-topped firebox was Belgian, while much of both design and construction was in the hands of British or German builders, between whom there was severe competition.

The 2-4-0 passenger engine [145] was built by Beyer, Peacock and Company in Manchester for the Mechlin-Terneuzen Railway in 1872, and was one of the first British-built locomotives to have the Belpaire firebox. The railway linked north-eastern Belgium with the Dutch coast south of the Scheldt, and was independent of the Governments in both kingdoms.

The same famous Manchester firm built hundreds of engines for the Dutch State Railway, and two of its 7 ft. bogie engines, dating from the beginning of the century, are shown outside the sheds at Utrecht in the 1920s [146]. The Kingdom of the Netherlands for long supported several railway companies — even the Dutch State Railway was run by a company — and of the others the principal one, the Holland Railway, for long favoured German locomotive builders.

103

When it divided with the State Railway the old Dutch Rhenish Railway, it acquired some very fine bogie express engines which had been built in Glasgow by Sharp, Stewart and Company in 1889 [147] and was so pleased with them that there was an abrupt and far-reaching change of custom. Some examples of both these Dutch classes survived war and pillage from 1940 to 1944, and one of the Rhenish engines, beautifully restored, now stands in the Utrecht Railway Museum. That shown here has acquired the Knorr feedwater-heater and pump, a German accessory, but is otherwise substantially in its original condition.

147

THE PACIFIC

The Pacific type locomotive — 4 6-2 — came by accident. It began in the United States with Strong's patent firebox, a double cylindrical arrangement, which Americans quickly termed the 'pant-leg' firebox. To support it, on a Lehigh Valley six-coupled bogie engine, there was a rearward extension of the frames with a supporting axle, as shown in Strong's engine of 1887 [148].

Then in 1889 the Chicago, Milwaukee and St. Paul Railroad produced a heavy locomotive of the conventional six-coupled-bogie type, and to ease the axle-loads put in an extra carrying axle right at the rear [149].

The classic Pacific, which was to serve five continents, was simply an elongated Atlantic, with a second pair of coupled wheels and the final axle supporting the big broad firebox. It was built first for New Zealand in the early 1900s. Soon it was to be seen all over America.

Figure 150 shows a later one heading a milk train on the Rutland Railroad, near Burlington, Vermont, in 1951. The type first appeared in England in 1908, with the Great Western engine The Great Bear, but it was left to (Sir) Nigel Gresley, on the Great Northern in 1922, to produce a home design which went into large-scale building. Continental European examples will be found on other pages.

151
152

OLD SOUTH AFRICA

In the country that was later to become the Union of South Africa, the first railway was built from Cape Town to Wellington during the years 1859—63, but the first actually in operation was a very short two-mile stretch at Durban, opened in 1860. Railway construction was naturally much stimulated by the Kimberley diamond rush of the early '70s and the opening of the Witwatersrand goldfield in 1886. Dutch and British interests were both at work, with both State and company sponsorships. A powerful early enterprise was the Netherlands South African Railway Company, while the British pushed inland with the Natal Government Railway. Both lines saw heavy wear and tear in the South African War.

From an early stage 3 ft. 6 in. had been agreed upon as the standard gauge of South Africa. Figure 151 is from the Transvaal (in 1899) and shows a train of the Pretoria and Pietersburg Railway. The locomotive is a British-built 2-6-4 tank engine, and the train is made up of a van, two first- and second-class coaches, and three 'Natives'. In Figure 152 is a train of the Natal Government Railways in the early 1900s. Like the Dutch lines, the N.G.R. favoured tank-engine haulage. Its coaches were distinctly good of their period; observe the hooded ventilators in the clerestory decks. Down in the South were the Cape Government Railways, and Figure 153 shows a northbound express in 1905. After the war, the former Dutch lines became the Central South African Railways, and the general amalgamation into South African Railways followed in 1910.

OLD NEW ZEALAND

In spite of a false start with the European standard gauge of 4 ft. 8½ in. in the 1860s, New Zealand, like South Africa, developed an efficient and very fascinating railway system on the 3 ft. 6 in. gauge, necessarily divided into two parts, North Island and South Island respectively.

Figure 154 shows a mixed train at Invercargill, South Island, late in the '80s. The locomotive is a class J 2-6-0, No. 118 built by Neilson of Glasgow. Others of the class were built also by Avonside of Bristol, Dübs of Glasgow, Robert Stephenson, and Vulcan Foundry, all between 1874 and 1883. The Neilson engine shown has a fine spark arrester. Fuel at Invercargill was incalculable, but with a chimney (Australian funnel, American stack)

like that, an engine could burn some of the forest inside without setting fire to the rest outside. Apart from this funnel, and from the fine Continental European headlamp, the engine was well describable as Anglo-Irish, a good blend in spite of a few invidious opinions in such cities as Birmingham and Cork. How odd! Southern South Island remains more Scotch than Glasgow, by far.

The great wonder of old New Zealand was the Rimutaka Incline, a mountain crossing on J. B. Fell's centre-rail-adhesion system (briefly employed over the Mont Cenis Pass while the tunnel was being built) and in commission from 1878 to 1955. Figure 155 shows a Fell train on the climb (a heavy train might have three locomotives, one at the head and the others marshalled intermediately to spread the load). Figure 156 shows the deviation opened in 1955, just north of Upper Hutt, with the remains of the old embankment in the foreground. Six Fell engines were built, by Avonside and Neilson.

155
156

LOGGING ROADS

The lumber railroad or 'logging road' was a feature of North American forestry from the 1880s onwards. They followed the contour of the ground, with consequent violent gradients.

In early days the track was often made of trimmed poles, like the primeval mining lines of Central Europe. Locomotives had geared transmission. Figure 157 shows a 'pole-road' chain-driven locomotive by Adams and Price, about 1885. The Shay geared locomotive, with

157
158

159

its boiler off-centre to balance vertical cylinders and a propulsion shaft at the side, was in use on logging roads for more than half a century.

In Figure 158 is a Lima-built 'Shay' of 1927 on the 3 ft. gauge line of the West Side Lumber Company. Figure 159 was taken on the Meadow River Lumber line in the mountains of West Virginia in 1953. In the foreground a Shay engine heaves her load over a hump. On the upper level are bunk cars for the lumbermen.

110

AMERICAN LOCOMOTIVES, 1890s

Stimulated by the World's Fair in Chicago, in 1893, several lines in the United States went in for locomotives with large driving wheels, intended to haul light, competitive trains at what were then very high speeds. Probably the most famous of these was No. 999 of the New York Central Railroad, designed by William Buchanan. Figure 160 shows her in her later days, with smaller driving wheels for ordinary service. When new, on May 10, 1893, she hauled the Empire State Express at 112 m.p.h., pass-to-pass over a measured mile west of Batavia, N.Y., making a world land-speed record that endured for some years. It was the first responsibly recorded instance of speed exceeding the sought-after 100 m.p.h.

In the same year of 1893, with a view to having big driving wheels and a generous fire-box, engines were built with trailing carrying axles, the wheels being arranged either 2-4-2 or 4-4-2. The latter form prevailed under service conditions, but a very stylish example of the former is shown in No. 590 of the Chicago, Burlington and Quincy, built by Baldwin Locomotive Works in 1895, and very rarely illustrated [161]. Not least remarkable is the European-style six-wheeled tender with slotted outside frames.

Engines with leading bogies were more steady at very high speeds, and of the 4-4-2, or Atlantic type engine, we show No. 1027 on the Atlantic City line of the Philadelphia and

160

161
162

Reading Railroad, also built in 1895 [162]. Here, full advantage was taken of the room allowed for a very large firebox. The engine was a Vauclain compound, with the high- and low-pressure cylinders mounted together each side, driving on a common cross-head. The engineer had a large cab saddling the boiler; the fireman toiled out in the rain at the rear. The nickname they acquired was 'The Mother Hubbards'.

PLATE XIV Mid-Victorian Running Shed at Nine Elms, London, from a painting by the author. Beattie locomotives *Havelock*, *Medusa* and *Ajax*.

C. Hamilton Ellis

ADAMS BOGIES

One of the more likeable characters among Victorian mechanical engineers, and certainly one of the most accomplished, was William Adams. His beginnings were in marine engineering, with which he grew up on London River, and he had been an Engineer-Officer in the Sardinian Navy during the Garibaldi wars before he took to locomotive engineering and command, serving successively the North London, Great Eastern, and the London and South Western Railways. Adams was sound on front-end design and produced the once-famous Adams Vortex blastpipe. He knew the value of generous bearing surfaces. But his most important contribution to locomotive design was the Adams bogie, which was to be used throughout the world and made him a lot of well-deserved money.

Early bogies were mere pivoted trucks, which assisted suspension but did not follow a true curve. The Adams bogie had a laterally-sliding pin, controlled by check springs, and thus all wheels of a four-coupled bogie locomotive truly followed the curve they traversed. At the same time, on many of his engines, Adams compensated the coupled axle springs with pivoted connecting levers, thus giving the locomotive a three-point suspension. The engines were extraordinarily steady, easy runners.

Figure 163 shows an Adams bogie tank engine of the North London Railway, somewhat rebuilt, but substantially in her original

163
164

PLATE XV Lancashire and Yorkshire locomotive No. 1008, built in 1889; now preserved.

form of 1868. In Figure 164 is the ultimate form, designed by Thomas Whitelegg and built for the London Tilbury and Southend Railway in 1909, but essentially an enlargement of Adams' Tilbury design of 1880, with a trailing radial truck. In Figure 165 is one of Adams' splendid designs for express engines on the London and South Western Railway. This engine, built in 1893, is now at Clapham Museum, London.

165

STEAM LOCOMOTIVES OF THE 1880s AND '90s

By the 1880s and '90s many British railways were firmly committed to large-diameter four-coupled wheels for fast passenger locomotives, though the engines themselves might considerably differ in general design, as in detail. Figure 166 shows the first of Thomas W. Worsdell's two-cylinder compound express engines for the North Eastern Railway, built in 1886. In the case of the N.E.R. a reversion was soon made to the use of large single driving wheels, in conjunction with a leading bogie, though the compounding arrangement was in fact perpetuated for several years longer.

On the Great Eastern Railway James Holden made an interesting and successful experiment in the use of liquid fuel, which had been used for some time already in the oil-producing parts of Russia. Holden's fuel was of a very economical sort, namely the waste from the oil-gas producing plant used for charging the old gaslit carriages. The Great Eastern company had got into trouble for river-pollution, and a good way of getting rid of the effluent was to burn it in the engines. That shown in Figure 167 is the original oil-fired express engine *Petrolea*, G.E.R. class T 19, built in 1890.

On the London and South Western Railway

114

Dugald Drummond's class T 9 [168] was an enlargement of the very successful designs which he had made for the North British and the Caledonian Railways during the '70s and '80s.

Though not apparently big engines, they steamed extremely well, one of the supposed secrets being in the use of a very long, deep firebox. L.S.W.R. No. 120 is shown decorated for the return of General Sir Redvers Buller, and his ceremonial conveyance from Southampton, after the South African War. The official photograph, we admit, was not an outstanding success. Drummond's comment, when he saw it, was: 'Och, ay! In a fog, like Buller himself!'

168

EAST COAST EXPRESSES

Both these extraordinarily fine speed shots of East Coast expresses in the late 19th century recall the days of the railway 'races' to Scotland, more especially those of 1895 between London and Aberdeen. We have illustrated Patrick Stirling's eight-foot bogie single on page 74, but the class deserves inclusion of one of the later ones, heading out of London on the Great Northern Railway's main line [169]. The original photograph was taken nearly 70 years ago by R. W. King. In Figure 170 (photograph by Dr. Tice Budden) the northbound Flying Scotsman is leaving York, North Eastern Railway, behind two Worsdell 7 ft. coupled bogie engines, which did outstanding work in the later competitive running between the East Coast and West Coast companies. Nobody called this 'racing', except enthusiasts of the period, but that was what it amounted to.

The earlier race was a day-to-day one between London and Edinburgh, in 1888. In 1895 racing broke out again, between London and Aberdeen. In each case it was begun by the West Coast companies (London and North Western, and Caledonian) cutting their schedules and the East Coast retaliating. In the running of 1895 it entailed a race from London to Kinnaber Junction, north of which the northern East Coast partner, the North British Railway, exercised running powers over the Caledonian Railway along the coast to Aberdeen. Sometimes one train got in first, some-

times the other. Arrivals at Aberdeen became earlier, and earlier, which must (like the motion of the old light carriages) have been less than tolerably comfortable for the passengers. The fastest East Coast train covered the distance of 523½ miles from Kings Cross to Aberdeen Joint in 518 minutes.

Then the West Coast companies staged what they called an exhibition run, with the racing train reduced to a featherweight, and covered the 541 miles from Euston to Aberdeen in 518 minutes. An average speed of 67.2 m.p.h. was maintained twice, from Crewe to Carlisle on the London and North Western and from Perth to Aberdeen on the Caledonian (engines, L.N.W.R. *Hardwicke* and Caledonian No. 17 respectively). The sporting element hoped for a resumption of racing next year, but before it could begin, the London and North Western had an accident of the apparently more reckless sort, and public opinion went against the idea of trains racing round curves in the night.

WEST COAST LOCOMOTIVES

In 1886, Neilson and Company built a locomotive for the Glasgow Exhibition of that year and sold her, probably by prearrangement, to the Caledonian Railway. This was the famous, and still surviving, C.R. No. 123 [171]. Though unique, the design was characteristic of the practice of Dugald Drummond on the Caledonian (and before that on the North British) and he in his turn was strongly influenced by William Stroudley under whom he had served on the London, Brighton and South Coast Railway. Almost the first of the late-Victorian bogie single drivers, the engine did well in the 'Race to the North' in 1888, maintaining a mile-a-minute average, day after day, over the heavily graded route between Carlisle and Edinburgh. Later, she was generally employed as the royal train pilot engine, and for hauling the officers' saloon, as shown.

In the Race to Aberdeen, 1895, the finest work was done by Webb's little 2-4-0 'Jumbo' class on the London and North Western, and by Drummond's and Lambie's almost identical 4-4-0 engines on the Caledonian. Figure 172 shows a London and North Western Scottish express in the '90s beginning the descent from Shap. The leading engine is a 6 ft. 'Jumbo' and the second is of the more famous 6 ft. 6 in. class of which the racing engine *Hardwicke* has survived.

The other view, in Figure 173, shows one of the Drummond engines in old age, heading a local train from Arbroath near Perth about 1923. She is little changed, save that she carries a Lambie boiler with closed dome and safety-valves in rear (compare with the first figure). Both the Caledonian engines are shown in 'sky blue', which resulted simply from a greater admixture of lead white with the standard Caledonian Prussian blue.

171

HIGHFLIERS

At the end of the 19th century, more people were travelling over longer distances — mid-Victorian journeys were often arranged weeks in advance — and rolling-stock had become much more elaborate. These factors caused a startling increase in tons behind the tender. When John Aspinall (later knighted) brought out his 7 ft. 4-4-2 express engines for the Lancashire and Yorkshire Railway in 1899, it was widely believed that this represented the maximum dimensions possible within the British loading gauge.

The engines were very successful after some teething troubles. Figure 174 shows one of them, somewhat modified though not radically, after about a quarter of a century in service, and bearing the London Midland and Scottish number of her later years. The men called them 'Highfliers'. Visible alterations included, most importantly, a supplementary frame and outside bearings to the trailing axle. The original inside bearings, so close to the firebox, had tended to run hot. There was now a superheater, in the use of which Aspinall was a British pioneer. The chimney was wider than originally, and the smokebox saddle was also a later feature. Some of the engines lasted into the early 1930s. Aspinall himself lived from 1851 to 1937; no mean span.

While the Atlantic (4-4-2) type engine had

appeared in England the year before Aspinall took it up, under Harry Ivatt on the Great Northern Railway, it was in 1902 that the latter exploited its possibilities to the full, and those possibilities included not only a large boiler, but a big firebox with a wide grate, exemplified in his G.N.R. No. 272 [175]. The first engine of the class, No. 251, is preserved. Superheating was a later improvement, but down to the early 1920s these engines hauled all the heavy East Coast expresses south of York, including the grossly overloaded wartime ones, single-handed.

In the late 1890s, W.M. Smith on the North Eastern Railway produced a new and admirable compound locomotive, with one high-pressure cylinder inside and two outside low-pressure cylinders. On the Midland Railway in 1901 Samuel W. Johnson produced an enlarged version [176], and with some important improvements by Richard Deeley in 1905 the type was to be built for at least twenty years more.

In Figure 177 is an Atlantic-type form of the original Smith type, built by J. G. Robinson for the Great Central Railway in 1905. One of four, she had the somewhat ponderous name of *The Rt. Hon. Viscount Cross, G.C.B., G.C.S.I.* Robinson's Great Central locomotives were esteemed by many as having the most beautiful lines of any in the early 20th century British tradition.

AUSTRALIAN INTERSTATE EXPRESSES, 1890

Australian railway development was bedevilled by inter-state suspicion which led to the most ridiculous breaks-of-gauge on state boundaries. People new to the country and travelling between Sydney and Melbourne were sometimes disagreeably surprised when they were turned out at the admittedly handsome border station of Albury. The Interstate Express, they found, was not one train but two, running respectively on the 4 ft. 8½ in. gauge in New South Wales and on the 5 ft. 3 in. gauge of Victoria. The broad gauge went on into South Australia which also had a further network on 3 ft. 6 in. gauge (also the standard gauge of Queensland and Western Australia).

Figure 178 shows the New South Wales interstate train at Albury towards the end of last century. The engine, No. 255, was one of six built by Beyer, Peacock and Company in

1882. Next to the tender is a Travelling Post Office, followed in order by a non-corridor second-class coach, a lavatory-first (non-corridor, first class, with lavatories), a Pullman sleeping car and a passenger brake van.

The photograph was probably taken after the departure of the connecting Victorian train from the other side of the long island platform. Figure 179 shows this broad-gauge train on its way, headed by a V.G.R. class A 4-4-0 and an old class B 2-4-0. The train, like so many in Europe at that time (1889), was austerely non-corridor, with not even a Pullman car for those who might pay extra.

Larger engines, and more comfortable carriages, came and went with the succeeding years (Figure 180 shows the Victorian train in 1914, with an A2 4-6-0), but it was not until 1962 that one could travel through from Sydney to Melbourne without that often inopportune turnout at Albury.

178

179
180

181

EARLY SERVICES

As far as the passengers were concerned, mid-Victorian trains offered rather cold comfort. The coaches were small and flimsy. There was no intercommunication of any sort. We had no real sleeping cars until 1873. Local train stock was peculiarly pokey.

The view shown in Figure 181 was taken at the long vanished terminus of the Great North of Scotland Railway, Waterloo Quay, Aberdeen. Passengers from the South had to cross the city from the Caledonian terminus, and as the Great North company started their train the moment the mail-bags were aboard, many of the unfortunate passengers missed the alleged connection. The engine shown is one of a pair of 0-4-0 tank locomotives, built by Beyer, Peacock and Company in 1856. Later rebuilt, they lasted at least half a century, and were then sold to the Government for war service in 1915.

Figure 182 shows a London suburban train

about a century ago. The locomotive is one of Joseph Beattie's little 2-4-0 tank engines for the London and South Western Railway (No. 190, built in 1863) and the carriages form a close-coupled set of the London and North Western Railway. The scene is the old Addison Road station, Kensington, and the train would be on its way round West London from Euston to Waterloo, one of many services that have long since vanished.

Indeed, in the days before there were deep-level underground lines and motor buses on the streets, there were some extraordinary through services in and about London. Trains ran from Southall to Victoria, from Wimbledon to Ludgate Hill via Herne Hill (a route revived in much later years), from the South Eastern to the Great Northern via Blackfriars and Snow Hill, from Broad Street to Mansion House via Willesden and Earl's Court (that was the 'Outer Circle') and even, at one time, there was a service linking Liverpool Street and Brighton.

STEAM TRAMWAYS

Steam tramways never attained in England the popularity they enjoyed in some other countries, notably in the Netherlands and Belgium, but they enjoyed a passing vogue in the Midland and Northern English cities.

In London they were rare, but Figure 183 shows an engine and car of the North London Tramways Company, in service from 1885 – 1889. The engine shown was by Merryweather and Sons, best known for their fire-appliances; (in late Victorian speech, 'a Merryweather' meant a steam fire-engine just as, some 30 years later, 'a Ford' was synonymous with a mass-produced motor-car). A condenser on the cab roof took care of the exhaust. The four wheels were aproned all round to save wandering dogs, romping children and incapable

drunks from inadvertently rolling under them.

Fireless steam locomotives, charged with steam from central boilers at regular intervals, made an early appearance on the Crescent City Railroad, a street tramway in New Orleans [184]. They were designed by Theodore Sheffler, and eight were built in 1876. To retain heat as long as possible, the steam drum was partly filled with boiling water.

In the present century, more advanced fireless steam locomotives were built in great numbers for works and other installations where naked fires and the possible emission of sparks were dangerous. Several builders, both British and German, specialised in them. Figure 185 shows a very neat little specimen built in 1932 by W. G. Bagnall of Castle Engine Works, Stafford, for a famous biscuit factory in Reading.

183

RAILWAY
CONQUEST

AMERICAN CIVIL WAR

From Ohio down into Georgia, the States fought a war of rapid movement, and it was the efficiency of United States Military Railroads in the west, finally supporting Sherman's Atlanta campaign in 1864, that really broke the back of the Confederacy in the South.

Back in 1862 Captain Andrews and a party of saboteurs from the North captured the Confederates' locomotive *General* [Plate XVI, opposite] near Marietta, Georgia, and drove her north on a wrecking jaunt. Hotly pursued over many miles, it was captured short of the State line, and several of the saboteurs were afterwards hanged as spies.

The other scenes show the Cumberland River Bridge [186] and the station at Nashville, Tennessee [187]. The former, with its gun-turrets, was built in June 1862, replacing one destroyed by the Confederates. The station scene, from 1864, shows a line of Sherman's military locomotives with, in the foreground, one that has clearly been in the wars.

186

PLATE XVI The American War engine *General*, steamed for recent exhibition.

PLATE XVII Mount Washington Cog Railway
engine, *Old Peppersass*, as preserved.

THATCHER PERKINS

Baltimore and Ohio Railroad No. 117, ultimately named 'Thatcher Perkins' after her designer, was built in 1863, and furnishes an early example of the 4-6-0 engine, later to be widely used for both freight and passenger service all over the world [188]. This one was at first too heavy for light — and additionally war-worn — tracks. The B. and O. Railroad was fiercely fought over. So *Thatcher Perkins* was laid up for some time before beginning a useful career. She is now preserved.

A much later American 'big engine' is exemplified by the 'Decapod' [189]. This was built by Baldwin for the Dom Pedro II Railway in Brazil (5 ft. 3 in gauge) in the early 1880s.

188
189

FIRST AMERICAN TRANSCONTINENTAL RAILROAD

In 1865, at the cost of a million lives in four years of war most bloody, the entirety of the United States was maintained. Now was the time for the wild American interior to be tamed by a railroad to the Pacific. From the Mississippi basin the Union Pacific Railroad built westward. From Sacramento [190] the Central Pacific built into the mountains. On May 10, 1869, after a wondrous striving towards one another, Irishmen laying track against Chinamen, Union Pacific and Central Pacific were formally joined at Promontory Point, Utah [191]. Indeed they had met, and had built over-lapping lines, some time before this, ere Big Business decided where the real meeting point ought to be. Then the Union Pacific's No. 119 drew slowly forward to meet the Central Pacific's *Jupiter* (left, with the big smokestack). The keystone in the arch of the

131

great republic was at last firmly in place. Our view is the famous 'bottle photograph', but Collis P. Huntington of the Central Pacific thought it a rather improper sort of memorial, and caused a vast and inaccurate canvas to be painted of the alleged scene, with ladies and a parson around, and everybody looking very solemn and saintly. But the passing of the bottle (Californian wine, one hopes) was the true, immortal gesture. The last spikes had just been driven, one of Californian gold and the other of Comstock silver. The way was open for the passage of the *steam cars*, whether Pullman, immigrants' or freight. Robert Louis Stevenson sampled the second-named, while on his travels, and survived the experience: 'I must say, the car of the Chinese was notably the least offensive'. Figure 192 shows a Central Pacific train threading the Nevada Palisades.

192

CITIES FOLLOW THE RAILROAD

In the middle 19th century, a basic difference between the European and American civilisations — the races being much the same — was in the relation of mechanical transport to the communities.

In Europe the then new railways followed the old trade routes and linked cities many of which, from Falkirk (Camelon) to Brindisi (Brundusium), Imperial Rome had known. In North America speculators first introduced steamboats on the great rivers, and then built railroads out into the blue, which migrant populations followed, to make settlements which, surprisingly rapidly, grew into cities.

In the great Mississippi basin, for nearly half a century the flat-bottomed side-wheel steamboat reigned supreme. She was a floating palace, though perhaps inclined to blow up several of her eight boilers and then blaze furiously on a mud-bank. Then came the railroad, and what Mark Twain recalled wistfully as a solid mile of steamboats along the levee dwindled to half a dozen sound-asleep ones, with an occasional packet passing them by.

Figure 193 shows, at Louisville, Kentucky, the changing phase. The bridge shown was opened on March 1, 1870, and though the trusses look rather perilous, it killed the ferry traffic dead.

In the West, the railroad came more than ever as conqueror, with millions of camp-followers. Figure 194 was taken from the top of a Central Pacific locomotive cab, with the train halted for the photograph at Cape Horn, just east of Colfax, California, in or soon after 1869. The enormous smokestack caught as many as it could of the cinders thrown out by the woodburning engine, the big whistle in the right foreground scared the local big game or mountaineers' children off the track, the brass bell clanged vehemently through the mountains.

AMERICAN RIGHT-OF-WAY

Oldest and most venerable of railway viaducts in the United States is the Thomas Viaduct of the Baltimore and Ohio Railroad in Maryland, nearly as old as the Stephensons' Sankey Viaduct between Liverpool and Manchester, which is the patriarch of European multi-arch railway bridges. It is shown [195] as it was when it approached its centenary, still under steam; a view of singular beauty.

A second old American classic is the famous horse-shoe curve on the Pennsylvania Railroad near Altoona [196]. This is a more recent view. The trains threading the Alleghanies are diesel-hauled freights, and each appears to be upwards of a mile long from locomotive to caboose. The summit level here is 1,594 ft. above sea level and the rise to it is at 91 ft. per mile.

On the other side of the Continent, we see in Figure 197 the railroad approaches to Spokane — still in steam days. From left to right, the lines are those of the Spokane, Portland and Seattle, the Union Pacific (with Milwaukee running powers), and the Northern Pacific companies.

196

CONSTRUCTION OF THE GREAT NORTHERN

While British interests were pushing on with the Canadian Pacific Railway, the Americans were busy with the Great Northern; indeed, in the early 1880s it was feared in Canadian quarters that with prior completion of the latter, and possible failure of the former, the United States would annex British Columbia. The railway was a weapon, and Anglo-American relations were not of the best at the time. Figures 198 and 199 both show construction of the Minneapolis and Manitoba, forerunner of the Great Northern, in North Dakota.

On August 11, 1887, nearly 8½ miles of track were laid in the day, which was a world record.

It was done without any sort of mechanical track-laying, by armies of roustabouts housed in the grim-looking bunk cars shown. But not until 1892 were the Cascade Mountains crossed. Figure 200 shows the old four-terrace switchback by which trains hoisted themselves up before the building of the first Cascade Tunnel in 1900. A train of seven old wooden cars, engines fore-and-aft, is approaching the third V-switch. Above it can be seen the uppermost line of the switchback, with a water-tank and a short trestle. The longer trestle in the foreground has been cut from the immediately surrounding forest, indeed tree-cutting has been carried out with reckless and untidy disregard for probable rapid erosion of the denuded mountainside.

201

SOUTH-EAST RUSSIA

Russian railway construction in Central Asia, under the Tsars, was often strategic rather than economic. Figure 201 is officially dated 1897—1898, though one might not judge that from the rolling stock. It shows a ballast train in a place as remote as any in North America at that time. The ancient locomotive is an oil burner, and conveys an additional supply of water for working in desert country on an aged

flat-car between herself and the ballast brake. Somewhere away to the south-east are India and China.

How lush, by comparison, is the view in Figure 202! It might be on an Austrian narrow-gauge line in Styria; the inverted bow-string span, the two little tank engines, and the end platform coaches all suggest Austria, but in fact it is in the Georgian Soviet Republic, not far from the delightful holiday resort of Tsagveri.

THE LUCIN CUT-OFF

When the first American transcontinental line was built in North America, a natural obstacle was the Great Salt Lake, Utah, as was Lake Baikal when the Trans-Siberian Railway was built by the Russian Government. But there the resemblance ended. The Americans built a circuitous line round the lake and then, years later, built a trestle across it. The water was quite shallow, and American railroad builders were trestle-minded. The Lucin Cut-Off, as it was called, was nearly 12 miles long, and was opened on March 8, 1904. Though unimposing as a bridge, it was certainly the longest in the world by a very great way.

During the 1950s its replacement was undertaken, not by another bridge but by a rock-fill causeway through the shallow brine in which a man cannot sink but must not drink. Figure 203 of these two aerial views shows the new causeway (right) deviating from the line of the old trestle formation and rejoining its approach embankment several miles away. Figure 204 gives a closer view of the new fill, with a transcontinental freight train heading east.

PLATE XVIII Canadian National three-unit
diesel-electric locomotive.

PLATE XIX Canadian Pacific diesel
freight locomotives.

TRANS-SIBERIAN

When the Russians encountered Lake Baikal on their way to the Far East, they put on a train ferry; and when the ice became too thick even for icebreaking bows (of which they knew something) they laid rails on the lake itself. But Baikal was not in the least like the Great Salt Lake. One could not make trestles across it.

So while the Americans cut out their devia-

tion in Utah, the Russians built one in Eastern Siberia, threading it through mountainous country on the southern shore of the great lake, a passage of singular beauty, especially in spring. Yet another difference [205]: double track and electric traction, instead of single track, train orders and diesels. Figure 206 shows a Russian mixed-freight train on the Trans-Siberian Railway near Sludiansk, in the Irkutsk Region. Observe the older and more recent tunnels.

PLATE XX Norwegian electric locomotive crossing the high snows.

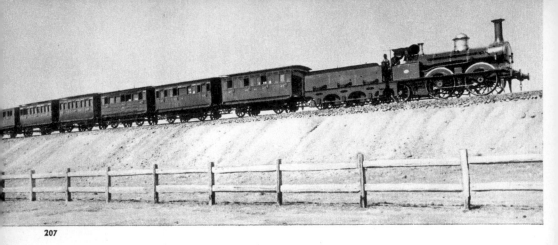

207

HISTORIC AUSTRALIAN LINES

Australia's first steam line was the Melbourne and Hobson's Bay Railway in Victoria, opened on September 12, 1854 (see Figure 209, opposite). It was preceded by a horse-worked line in South Australia, earlier in the same year, and followed by the Sydney and Paramatta Railway, the first in New South Wales, which was opened on September 26, 1855. Figure 207 shows the original locomotive of the Sydney line, designed by J. E. McConnell of the London and North Western Railway, Southern Division, and built by Robert Stephenson and Company. The coaching stock of the period includes both compartment and saloon-type vehicles.

In Figure 208 is an old photograph of the famous Lithgow Zigzag in the Blue Mountains, on what later became the north-western line out of Sydney to Bourke. This early, and very difficult section reached Bathurst early in 1876, having been over 10 years in construction from Penrith. A new alignment, cutting out the great Zigzag, with 10 short tunnels and a ruling gradient of 1 in 90, was decided upon in 1908, to be rapidly carried out. Figure 209 shows the pier of the Melbourne and Hobson's Bay Railway, the first steam line in Australia. The little engine in the middle of our scene was called the 'Pier Donkey'.

Of later date is the scene in Figure 210. The day is October 1, 1889, and the occasion is the opening of the Palmerston and Pine Creek Railway, earliest section of the North Australian Railway.

208

INDUSTRIAL TRAFFIC IN SWEDEN

Not everybody expects to find heavy haulage on a gauge of 2 ft. 11 in., but there is something very near it on the narrow-gauge lines of Central Sweden. Both these views are from the Nordmark-Klarälven Railway, which works 104 miles of route in the Karlstad-Munkfors area, with headquarters at Hagfors. The great John Ericsson came from these parts, early in the last century (see page 27).

Figure 211 shows a timber train headed by a locomotive with side-rod drive. Most of the railway was electrified in 1920, and the short branch to Skoghall was converted in 1941. The 15,000 Volt $16\frac{2}{3}$ cycles single-phase system is used, as on the Swedish State Railways and the Grängesberg-Oxelösund Railway. Like these, the Nordmark-Klarälven Railway handles iron ore, for it is one of the lines serving the great Bergslag mining region. In Figure 212 is a bogie hopper car on roller bearings.

212

COUNTESS OF DUFFERIN

Steam railway traction in the Canadian West began with the *Countess of Dufferin*, which now stands as a mechanical national monument in Sir William Whyte Park, Winnipeg [213]. Since many Canadians and nearly every stranger in Winnipeg believe her to be the original No. 1 of the Canadian Pacific Railway, brevities of her true history had better be given here.

She was built by the Baldwin Locomotive Works, Philadelphia (Baldwin No. 2660) in 1872 and became No. 56 of the Northern Pacific Railroad, U.S.A. Late in the '70s, she was bought by the contractor Joseph Whitehead, who used her on Government contracts in Manitoba. In 1881 the Canadian Pacific Railway was incorporated, and Whitehead steamboated her up river to Winnipeg, as shown in Figure 214.

Quite arbitrarily, but apparently without any disapproval, he lettered her 'Canadian Pacific' on the tender; she had already his own number, which was 1. As the Canadian Pacific Railway was the dream and the hope of Winnipeg and all the vast prairie region, everybody was happy. The 'Countess' was indeed bought by the Canadian Pacific company for $5,800 in 1883, and thenceforward until 1897 she was C.P.R. No. 151. She then went to a lumber company in British Columbia, and was at last bought back by the C.P.R. in 1910. Then and thereafter she became the monumental engine she still is.

Any idea that she still wholly represents the original Baldwin design or not, must be respectfully disputed. The parallel boiler, as opposed to the semi-conical or 'wagon-top' type, and the shape of the spark-arresting stack both bespeak Canadian rather than United States practice. The general arrangement of the engine, the shape of the cross-heads, slide bars and steamchests, with the valves worked through rockers from inside motion, are, of course, classic American, and so is the tender. In any case, from the middle years onwards, Canadian locomotive practice followed that of the United States very closely, just as that of Australia followed that of Great Britain. But there were ever subtle differences, as there were, in Europe, between English and Scottish design, or French and Swiss, or Saxon and Bavarian. The *Countess of Dufferin* may be properly accepted, after all these years, as Canadian Pacific Honorary Number One.

213

CANADIAN PACIFIC RAILWAY

It was to make a great country, an ocean-to-ocean country, that the Canadian Pacific Railway was built. Without it, British Columbia faced American annexation. So for British Columbia a technically bloodless war was fought with railroads as weapons. The combatants fought not each other, they fought the immense distances and enormous mountains of the Canadian Rockies.

The story of the railroad was the story of men, and money, and men, and money, and men and money again. There were pioneers like Rogers (people sometimes wonder vaguely about the naming of Rogers Pass). There were politicians like Disraeli in England, who was sympathetic but old, and Sir John MacDonald who was first Prime Minister of Canada. There was the tremendously powerful Hudson's Bay Company, personified in Donald Smith (very rich, he backed it to the last penny of a staggering overdraft, and ultimately became Lord Strathcona, and richer still). There was the old pioneer Canadian, Sandford Fleming; there was Van Horne, the American contractor who ironically won a British knighthood (he had the gift of sleeping in odd naps like a cat, and could work round the clock for a week).

Before the passage of the Rockies, there was the very difficult passage of the wild country north of Lake Superior; some of it rock-bound shores, some of it waterlogged muskeg or spruce-swamp. Figure 215 shows the original Red Sucker timber trestle. Steel spans could come later. At one stage of apparent financial ruin, Smith sent a telegram with the single word *Craigellachie*, the name of a great rock by the Spey in his native Scotland. For the Clan Grant's war-cry had been 'Stand fast, Craigellachie!' So the railway was built, and when the eastern and western rails met in the Selkirks, in 1885, the spot was named Craigellachie. There, in Figure 216, Smith is driving the ceremonial last spike. Behind him, in ulster and top hat, is Fleming. On his right is Van Horne. That was on November 7, 1885. On June 28, 1886, the first through train to the Pacific Coast left Montreal, to reach Port Moody, British Columbia, on July 4, after 139 hours.

215
216

CANADIAN PACIFIC II

Following the slow passage of the inaugural transcontinental train, a regular through service over the C.P.R. from Montreal to Port Moody began in July, 1886, to be extended to the final terminus at Vancouver in May of the following year. Back in England *Punch*, usually more inclined to jeer at the railways, published a majestic cartoon of Britannia making one of her grand gestures, with a Canadian Pacific train behind her and declaiming verses indicative of British commercial conquest in the Far East by way of this true North-West Passage: '... around Cathay and old Zipangu's shore, my course is clear; what could I wish for more?'

As we have already indicated, the great thing had been to get the railway through. The company's contract had bound it to complete the line within 10 years; that was, by May 1, 1891. By dint of violent grading over the Kicking Horse Pass and down the Yoho Valley, and the bridging of gaps by groaning wooden trestles, completion came several years ahead of the deadline. Figure 217 shows the original wooden Stoney Creek Bridge in the Selkirks, the highest bridge on the C.P.R., soon after the opening. The locomotive appears to have been a modest 4-6-0 heading, in order, two baggage cars, two colonist cars (hard sleepers) and a Pullman sleeping car.

By way of contrast, Figure 218 shows the present steel arch at the same place, with the westbound Canadian crossing over. Behind the diesels are 16 steel cars, including a 12-car set with a 'dome' at each end. The Canadian runs daily between Montreal and Toronto, and Vancouver.

217

219

220

RAILWAYS IN GREECE

Greece was the last major country in Continental Europe to be physically connected by rail with the international network, though internal lines were quite old. The south-to-north longitudinal line was not complete until 1916. The Hellenic State Railways took over in 1920. It traverses country of singular grandeur, including the classic Vale of Tempe and the Pass of Thermopylae. All Greek lines suffered very severely from war. Gorgopotamos Viaduct [219] had five of its seven spans blown up in 1944. Only the two inverted bowstrings and their piers are original.

Greek motive power ranges from the colossal to the droll. Of the former, we show in Figure 220 one of the enormous 10-coupled locomotives built by Breda of Milan during the post-war reconstruction. Among the largest steam locomotives ever built in Europe, they work all classes of traffic between Athens and Salonika. For a contrast, Figure 221 shows the squat outlines of a little 2-6-0 tank engine running on the 0.6-metre-gauge line between Volos and Milee.

222

FIRST RAILWAYS IN INDIA

If India had already had an adequate railway system in 1857 the great Army Mutiny would have fizzed, at most, like a damp firework. But it was not so. In the middle and late '50s, the Indian railway mileage was still paltry.

The first railway in India had been the Bombay-Thana line of the Great Indian Peninsula Railway, opened on April 16, 1853, and Figure 222 shows an early train crossing the Thana Bridge, 21 miles from Bombay. The photograph has been described as showing the first train in India, but the locomotive is clearly one of those built by Kitsons of Leeds for the same railway in 1856, one of which, the *Sindh*, was preserved at Parel Locomotive

Works, Bombay, after many years in service.

Far away in the Calcutta area were the first beginnings of what later would become the mighty East Indian Railway. The *Fawn* [223] was one of a series of 2-2-2 passenger tank engines built variously by Kitsons and by Stothert and Slaughter of Bristol for local traffic between Howrah and Raneegunge, during 1856—57.

Nostalgia, though an unmentionable weakness in Victorian Englishmen, was nevertheless there. One could not make Bombay a part of England, but somehow the old Churchgate Station [224] of the Bombay, Baroda and Central India Railway acquired a Victorian-Alpine look. We have seen something very like it in Austria.

223
224

159

DARJEELING–HIMALAYAN

Nowhere else in the world has there ever been a railway quite like the old Darjeeling-Himalayan, climbing partly about and partly on the old road through the immense foothills of the Himalayas, foothills which in most other countries would be substantial mountains in their own right. Perhaps, long ago, the Mount Tamalpais line in California was something like it, but on a small scale. The American line's famous *double-bow-knot* was but a single specimen of the sort of thing the Darjeeling-Himalayan did at fairly short intervals on its original main line of 51 miles on 2 ft. gauge.

The original company was formed in 1879, and the D.H.R. Extensions Company, having 96 miles of route, was formed in 1913. Figure 225 shows some of the looping at Ghoom, the summit of the old line. What might have been called the standard locomotive of the D.H.R. is shown in Figure 226. A coolie would squat in front, sanding the rails by hand from the box behind him. If the engine happened to be derailed on the way, there was always the big lever carried for first-aid purposes, just above the tanks, to be unshipped when needed.

Figure 227 shows what must have been one of the world's smallest Pacifics, apart from miniatures. She was one of two which worked on the Extension lines, which might have been called the D.H.R.'s 'Plains' section, and ended her days on the Siliguri-Sukna branch in the 1960s. Both engines were built by the North British Locomotive Company, Glasgow, early in the present century.

225

226
227

GERMAN TRAINS IN EAST AFRICA

While the British built inland from Mombasa, the Germans built inland from Dar-es-Salaam and, fortunately for later developments, also on the metre-gauge. While Uganda equipment came chiefly from India, that for the German East African lines came straight from their homeland. Photographs of trains during the German regime are unfortunately scarce. The highly mobile campaigning between Generals Smuts and Van Deventer, and the German General von Lettov-Vorbeck, lasted until the Armistice in 1918.

In the meantime the Germans had very systematically destroyed much of their railway, 743 miles long between Dar-es-Salaam and Ujiji, to embarrass the invaders. Bridges were blown up and all available locomotives and vehicles were driven into the gaps to form huge piles of wreckage.

Particular interest therefore attaches to Figure 228, showing a German ballast train of side-discharging hoppers in the years before 1914. The engine appears to be a Mallet built by Henschel and Son of Kassel in or about 1908. But for the extra water-tank car with its pile of wood fuel on top, it might have come straight out of the Harz Mountains. The snake-like coils on top belong to a massive hose for taking water from a lower level when, as often, occasion demanded. Observe also the typically German steam bell behind the chimney. Figure 229 is more recent, showing a natural 'tunnel' near Mwanza on what had been the Ostafrikanische Centralbahn.

228

UGANDA RAILWAY

'The Uganda Railway' was a legend amongst British youth in the years before 1914. Indian officials and equipment had been shipped across to Africa, and a classic chestnut was the signal telegraphed by a Babu stationmaster: 'Lions eating clerk in booking office. Kindly advise!' In East Africa both the British and the Germans were pushing inland from the coast, as fast as they could go against each other. India, by virtue of distance, was a great help to the British; Bombay was a much nearer port to Mombasa than was Hamburg to Dar-es-Salaam.

Figure 230 was taken at Limuru more than half a century ago, a railway scene of great charm. Observe the hand-car in front of the old Indian engine with its girl passenger, and the auxiliary water tank behind the tender.

The engine, a little 2-6-0, is characteristic of minor lines during the time of Kipling's stories, and so are the sunshaded carriages, not to mention the two-horse gharry on the extreme right. Figure 231 shows a freight train (with passengers both on a flat and over the cow-catcher) on a temporary trestle between El Burgon and Molo. As in North America, the main thing was to get the railway through; trestles could be made from timber out of the bush, and more permanent structures could come later.

The Uganda Railway was opened from Mombasa to Kisumu on December 26, 1901. Its ex-Indian equipment was responsible for the metre-gauge having been chosen instead of the Cape gauge of 3 ft. 6 in. Had Cecil Rhodes' dream of a Cape-to-Cairo Railway been realised, the route would have suffered several bothersome breaks of gauge.

230

MAU ESCARPMENT

In building the original Uganda Railway, such obstacles as the Mau Escarpment could not be quickly surmounted. The first thing was to get some sort of a railway route between the Indian Ocean and Lake Victoria, and a truly continuous course could come later.

These early views of the Central Rift show one of the artifices: railheads with an intervening steep-grade funicular line, with interlaced tracks and a passing place in the middle. Figure 232 shows the bottom of an incline, with an old sunshaded Indian metre-gauge carriage on the funicular transporter car, at the beginning of its translation to higher levels. Observe the clearing of the scrub on each side of the line, and the modest water-pipe weaving over the earth from top to bottom, on the left side of the track. Figure 233 shows several consecutive inclines in another place. The little locomotive in the right foreground is not a derelict. She is destined for higher things, or at any rate, higher places, and has been lightened for her ascent. The front of the main frame, the cylinder heads, pistons, motion and the driving axle and wheels have all been removed, but she still proudly bears her headlamps; the two regulation ones over the steamchests, and the big one, for discovery and possible scaring of elephants and rhinoceroses, in front of the chimney. Like those shown elsewhere, the engine is a standard metre-gauge type of the late 19th century.

233

234

VICTORIA FALLS

Cecil Rhodes said: 'Let the spray from the falling Zambesi River fall on the trains as they pass.' Long after, in 1910, J. P. Pearson wrote in his impassive travelling Englishman's style: 'At 2.55 p.m. exactly, when still a good way from our journey's end, the spray of the Victoria Falls, mounting high in the air, was first seen by me on the left. On the same side, just about 10 minutes later, a most wonderful display of wooded country was disclosed — this also being seen on our right, where indeed the view was more extensive still, but less rich. After this came a glimpse down the great rocky gorge of the Zambesi (my first sight of this great river), with a huge bastion-like rock standing out at a point where the stream abruptly changed its direction, and then we ran into the station of Victoria Falls and the long journey was over.'

The bridge has a clear span of 500 ft. at a height of 420 ft. above the river. In Figure 235 it is shown in the 1950s, with a mixed train from Zambia crossing southwards behind a Beyer-Garratt locomotive. It carries a single-track railway with a single-carriageway motor road added in the '20s.

From the sublime to the bucolic: Figure 234 shows an out-of-window view from a Rhodesia Railways train in Zambia. As in many parts of the world, the passage of the daily mail train is something for which every township knocks off. There are many besides passengers on the platform. One may see the same sort of thing from Australia to Lapland, where the rail is the lifeline.

BENGUELA RAILWAY, ANGOLA

In 1902 the Benguela Railway Company was incorporated in Portugal under a concession granted to Sir Robert Williams, most of the capital being British and the balance held by the Portuguese Government. Its object was to give an outlet from the Katanga (Belgian Congo) copper-mines to the sea at Lobito in Angola. The undertaking having begun purely

as a colonial line running inland, it was in 1928 that Williams' object was achieved and the railhead reached the Belgian Congo frontier, 838 miles from Lobito.

Three years later it was linked up with the Belgian lines which in turn were already linked with the Rhodesia Railways, and thus for the first time there was an unbroken African transcontinental route from the South Atlantic to the Indian Ocean, on 3 ft. 6 in. gauge, and

thus in physical connection with the railways in the Union of South Africa and the sister Portuguese system far away to the east in Mozambique.

From its completion the line has been successful without any 'planned obsolescence' absurdities, for the equipment is on the old side with obvious South African affinities.

Many of the engines are woodburning, like the 4-8-2 standing in the rain at Lobito [236].

In the foreground is the little *General Machado*, preserved on a short stretch of track (also in the rain) as a memorial to Lobito's first experience of railway transport. In Figure 237, an oil-burning Beyer-Garratt of patrician Manchester origin heads a transcontinental passenger train of mixed gaslit wooden and electrically-lit steel coaches, all but the leading van having the classic clerestory of old South Africa.

237

238
239

NORWEGIAN MOUNTAIN LINES

On the great Norwegian mountain lines — the Dovre and the Bergen-Oslo routes — the snow-plough works in summer. Figures 238 and 239 show steam-snowploughing with both the ordinary locomotive plough and the rotary plough near Finse on the Bergen line, which reaches a summit of 4,265 ft. beside Tauge-vatn Lake. The colour view, in Plate XX facing page 145, shows a Norwegian electric train crossing the high snows which lie banked up after clearance on either side of the track. As is customary in these conditions, the headlamp is permanently lit for the perpetual chain of tunnels and snowsheds.

HEDJAZ RAILWAY

Construction of the old Imperial Ottoman Hedjaz Railway, on 3 ft. 5¼ in. gauge, was begun in 1901, in the interest of pilgrim traffic between the Near East and Mecca. Strategic considerations also entered the picture. Amman was reached in August 1904, Tebuk in the Hedjaz in 1906, and Medina, the railhead for Mecca, on August 31, 1908. Ownership was Turkish and equipment German. So destructive were the attentions of Colonel T. E. Lawrence and his Arabs that after the 1914—18 war the southern section of 523 miles to Medina remained derelict. Stranded and overturned locomotives lay about the desert for over 45 years [240 and 241]; everything, indeed, which the wandering Bedouin found neither useful nor portable. One could not carry off the shell of a Krauss locomotive, however good the iron and steel it contained.

Not until 1963 was a tender accepted from British interest for the clearing and reconstruction of the line. The northern portions had passed into the hands of the Syrian State Railways and, successively, the Palestine Railways and the Jordan Hedjaz Railways, with a southern terminus at Maan. Now we have the singular spectacle of the railway which died receiving artificial respiration plus blood transfusion after nearly half a century.

240
241

242
243

CHILE

There is no other country in the world like Chile. From east to west it ranges from 58 miles to, at most, 273 miles across; from north to south it is 2,661 miles long, from 17 deg. 57 min. south nearly to Cape Horn. It has thus an immense littoral, backed by some of the highest mountains in the world. Up and down this is a far-reaching modern main-line railway system of 4,408 route miles, nearly half of it on the South American (Indian) broad gauge of 5 ft. 6 in. but including nearly 2,000 miles of metre-gauge line and smaller systems on the European and the 2 ft. gauges.

The atmosphere in what might be called Metropolitan Chile recalls in some respects Southern Europe, far more than does California in the Northern Continent. The handsome electric inter-city train in Figure 242 might almost be something in the neighbourhood of Rapallo. Far otherwise are those of the Andean lines. On the metre-gauge, a diesel set of the Chilean Transandine line [244] looks curiously modest and tame, down in the coastal area. Figure 243, on the other hand, suggests that a mountain railway has invaded some place out of Dante or Milton. This is the western approach to the summit naturally dividing Chile from Argentina, with its triple rack rail in the middle of the sterile single track. In steam days, locomotives came from Great Britain and Germany. Electric traction superseded them later on the Chilean side.

244

RAILWAY
BUILDINGS

WATER STREET, MANCHESTER

Though long since abandoned as a passenger station, the original eastern terminus of the Liverpool and Manchester Railway, at Water Street, Manchester, lasted into our own time. At first it had a passenger station on one side and a goods dock, with warehouses on the other, as shown in the rather bad drawing which, aesthetic considerations apart, nevertheless has the virtue of authenticity [245].

In Figure 246 is what once was a passenger platform with its awning supported by massive timbers. The gable-ends of the warehouse roof are still clearly recognisable across the tracks. Figure 247 shows the old booking office, possibly dating back to 1830 like the other buildings. In the early days it was customary to write out the tickets, as in stage-coaching practice.

245

BRIDGE OVER WATER-STREET, MANCHESTER,
With the Offices and Warehouses of the Railway Company

248
249

IMPOSING STATIONS

From the beginning of regular passenger traffic, railway companies aimed at creating an impression of solidity combined with elegance, partly out of natural pride in commerce but also to reassure nervous people who never before had travelled by train. Philip Hardwick's famous Doric Propylaeum, forming the entrance to the London and Birmingham Railway's terminus at Euston Square, was designed and built with both these ends in view [248]. When new, it quite dwarfed the modest station beyond, but made a centrepiece to a fine vista from Euston Square. Long before its ultimate demolition in the early 1960s, that effect had been lost through the portico being surrounded by buildings on all sides. Moore's lithograph shows how it was originally meant to be seen.

Tunnel portals likewise were often made as imposing as possible, for here, more than ever, novice passengers had to be convinced that the fearsome passage was solidly safe. Figure 249 shows Ipswich Tunnel in an early Victorian watercolour.

Elsewhere we show the 'cottage' style of English country station, but in some places the small station house took on an elegant 'pavilion' form, more akin to the lodge of some great house in the Italianate manner. Figure 250 shows what we consider a very neat example, Francis Thompson's Wingfield on the original North Midland main line between Derby and Chesterfield, opened in 1840 and thus but little junior to the London and Birmingham.

The recent railway policy of 'cutting out the dead wood' (which means intermediate country stations as well as small branch lines) has resulted in a sad mortality among some of our best Post-Regency buildings, and the days of others are numbered, though some survive as railwaymen's dwellings.

250

251

252

HISTORIC SCENES FROM ITALY

Although the first railway in Italy dated back to 1839 (Naples to Portici), political disunion and hostilities delayed construction for a considerable time. Roman lines received the guarded blessing of the Vatican, and Figure 251 shows the solemn dedication of the Rome to Civita Vecchia Railway in April, 1859. While the artist's efforts are somewhat quaint — the soldiers and others in the foreground appear as midgets — he has done his conscientious best to draw a long-boiler 2-4-0 engine. One should bear in mind that quite possibly he had never seen a train before. There are no levers between the safety valves and the springs supposed to be loading them.

In 1871 several things happened. The Papal temporal power ceased, Italy became a united kingdom, and the first train passed through the great Alpine tunnel to the west of the Mont Cenis Pass. The old Sardinian State tank engine carries a bouquet from France on her right-hand tank [252], an unusual tribute from sticky neighbours!

Even early Italian city stations were often grandiose, as are their successors today. Figures 253 and 254 show the exterior and interior of the old station in Florence. In the view of the train hall, the artist has somewhat shrunken his engine and coaches, to lend greater magnificence to the structure surrounding them. The engine appears to be a Bury, Curtis and Kennedy six-wheeler.

253
254

GREAT WESTERN STATIONS

About the larger stations of Brunel's Great Western Railway there was an unprecedented splendour of architecture. Of its kind there was nothing more beautiful than the magnificent hammer-beam timber roof of the old station at Bristol, Temple Meads [255], covering five broad-gauge roads which converged on a sector-table at the terminal end. Opened in stages, the Great Western Railway had been completed throughout from London (Paddington old station) to Bristol Temple Meads on June 14, 1841. Its splendid western terminal building is still there, though latterly it was used much more for the storage of vehicles than for traffic, which passes through a great curved station built many years later.

As suggested, the original London terminus was something of a make-shift, and its site lies west-by-north of the present terminus. Paddington, another superb example of Brunel's realised ideas, was completed in 1854. Figure 256 shows it in a photograph taken 110 years later. A diesel Pullman train stands at Platform 7, motors throng the carriage drive, and the porters are of obvious Eastern birth. But the magnificent Brunel roofs are unchanged — they are even now painted in the original colour scheme of grey and red. Noteworthy are the transepts, originally designed to allow for the quick transfer, by horse haulage, of carriages from one road to another by means of transverse tracks and turntables, a practice long past and almost forgotten. Apart from the foreground, the station is much as Frith painted it in his picture *The Railway Station*, and one hopes that it may long remain so.

255

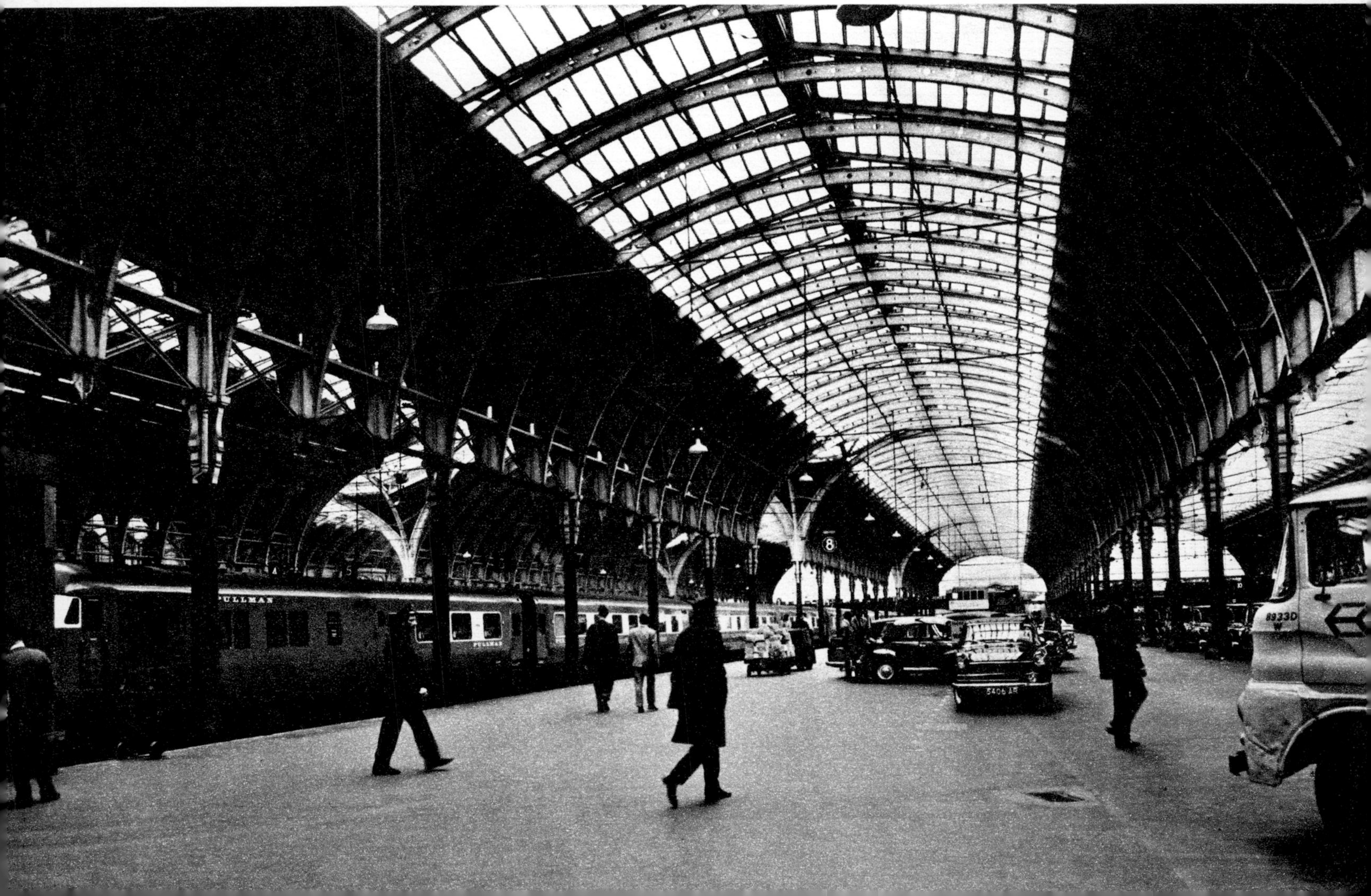
PULLMAN
PULLMAN
8
5406 AR
8933D

EUSTON STATION

Euston's great hall in London [257] was unique in England and outstanding by world architectural standards. Designed by P. G. Hardwick, together with the beautiful Shareholders' and Directors' Rooms [259] beyond the stair at the far end, it was completed in 1847, a decade after the opening of the station. Inadequacy and obsolescence of the ancient teminus led to the destruction of all the buildings in the middle 1960s. That of these great chambers, and of Philip Hardwick's Doric portico outside, was bitterly deplored by lovers of splendid buildings. The battle was to the Philistines, and there were those who said that perhaps after all it was just as well in view of the rot that lurked in the Great Hall's roof. The statue below the stair in Figure 257 is that of George Stephenson. It was saved. Figure 258 shows a corner detail of the superb ceiling, which was decorated thus with allegorical panels of the principal cities on the London and North Western Railway, in high relief.

258
259

260
261

19TH CENTURY TERMINALS

Delftsche Poort Station, Rotterdam [260], from a watercolour by H. W. Last, c. 1848, exemplified the idea of having a new sort of city gateway, suited to the dignity and importance of the new Holland Iron Railway Company, linking the city with Delft, the Hague, Leyden, Haarlem and Amsterdam, one of the closest succession of rich and respected cities in Europe. It has long vanished, but the present Rotterdam Central, a creation of the 1950s, stands on its site, although the new building is not a terminal.

Also from the late '40s dated the great old Main Station of Munich [261], destroyed by bombing nearly a century later. The large central pavilion was originally the train hall, but in more recent times became the main circulating area, with the platforms under the much larger roofs visible beyond. Its style was describable as Ludwig-Romanesque with later Bankers'-Renaissance beyond.

Imitation was still a major aim in commercial architecture. Yet as early as 1852, entirely new ground was broken in Lewis Cubitt's Kings Cross [262], the terminus of the then new Great Northern Railway in London. Only the clock tower resembled anything that had been seen before. Alone of these three, it has survived the years. Observe the influence of the great new railway viaducts in the façade and wings. Kings Cross was the first important attempt to build a large railway station which should look just that, without disguise. Later generations would have called it 'functional', and rightly, though the word has been much abused. The two great naves originally provided under-cover storage space for carriages, as well as shelter for passengers.

262

BRITISH COUNTRY STATIONS

Local vernacular styles distinguished British village and country town stations in many places, and the old railway companies showed many individual peculiarities of Victorian design. An architectural feature almost exclusive to the railway station down the years has been the cantilevered platform canopy, owing something to the veranda and something to its contemporary, the seaside awning.

Splendid examples occur in this view of Llandrindod Wells, London and North Western Railway, in 1905 [263]. On the right is the original station building with its Victorian Gothic chimneys visible over the canopy and its rather low, brick fronted platform. On the left is a more recent canopy, glass-topped and taking a flat umbrella form. Observe the variation in the wooden valences. Such seemed to

be infinite. The mail train is just entering, and the postman can be seen waiting for it with his wickerwork trolley. Observe the one-legged man and the girl, among others, apparently enjoying a warm updraught on the foot-bridge.

The view of Wickham Bishop Station on the Maldon branch in Essex is comparatively recent [264]. The station house, separate from the very modest platform, exemplifies the Victorian liking for the *cottage ornée*. It was much used for railway stations in country places, as it was for the lodge gates of large houses built about the same time.

Stations with all-over timber roofs were for long characteristic of the Great Western Railway and its associated lines. Some were of great charm, such as Cheddar in Somerset [265], though they gave rather meagre platform protection for all their important appearance. The style was a legacy of I. K. Brunel.

263

264
265

ST. PANCRAS I

A new grandiosity, in all the exuberance of late Gothic Revival, distinguished English public and commercial architecture in the 1860s. The austere functionalism of Kings Cross, only a decade before, was now rejected and when the Midland Railway Company built its own main line into London, Gilbert Scott was given his head in the making of a tremendously ornate terminal building, containing not only railway offices (the company's headquarters were at Derby) but a vast hotel and a clock tower which should effectively dwarf the Great Northern Railway's establishment next door. Gothic, Gothic, and yet more Gothic! Further, let it be in blood-red brick with red sandstone pillars!

So St. Pancras reared its terrific pile above the drab commonplaces of the Euston Road. Its contemporaries marvelled and delighted in it. Their sons derided it as something too Victorian to be borne, but they could not knock it down. Taste and fashion are ever mutable. Today many of us treasure St. Pancras as did our forefathers in 1868. The general view [266] was taken in the late 1920s (observe the NS type bus, the archaic cabs and the horse-drawn carts); the view from under the arch [267] is later. The station has not changed.

266

190

268
269

ST. PANCRAS II

While Gilbert Scott enjoyed himself with the façade and offices, W.H. Barlow was entrusted with the great train hall of St. Pancras and he, too, produced something that was at the time unique. The station was built with high-level tracks, and beneath these was a vast range of catacombs, designed and used for storing beer, which the Midland company brought to London, in vast quantities, from Burton on Trent.

Figure 268 shows construction at an early stage, with the massive steel decking which later would support the tracks, and the first of the roof girders in course of erection. With a span of 240 ft., the roof was at the time the largest in the world without intermediate support, having a parabolic arch. The internal and external aspects of this noble roof are shown in Figures 269 and 270, both fairly recent. In the former, the clock tower of Kings Cross is visible above the emergent Pullman.

270

MELBOURNE FLINDERS STREET

Flinders Street Station, beside the Yarra in Melbourne, was a busy place with formidable rush-hours even in the 1890s, as shown in Figure 271, taken about 1892. While the inter-state expresses ran in and out of Spencer Street, Flinders Street handled Melbourne's already considerable suburban business traffic. It was to become the busiest city railway station in the world.

An Englishman, arriving in Melbourne at the end of last century, might have been more forgiving in the making of comparisons than he would be nowadays. Had he been observant of railways, he might have remarked that the brass-domed engines recalled the Great Western, as did the deep clerestories on some of the coaches; that the flat sides of the latter recalled the District in London, that the 'somersault' (French's) semaphores were pure Great Northern, and that the segmental canopies over the middle platforms had come straight off the London and South Western Railway. At the

271

same time, the shape of the lookout lanterns on the passenger brake vans were almost London, Chatham and Dover. The plastering of structures with bald commercial exhortations was, alas, peculiarly Anglo-Saxon, and only to be expected.

Let us take a possibly disastrous header in commenting on Flinders Street as it is today [272]. As a railway station, like Waterloo in London, it is admirable. As a piece of architecture it is equally comparable with Waterloo in London, and that is less of a compliment.

However, J. P. Pearson wrote in 1907: 'As for Flinders Street Station . . . it was in course of transformation. The existing station had 11 platform faces arranged as one main and five island platforms, which were covered by zinc roofs. The new station promised to be a good one and an excellent new subway in enamelled tiles, staircases, signboards and lavatories were already in evidence, as also were part of the exterior walls. These, in the lower part, were in red brick with relief in a blue-tinted stone.'

272

273
274

RIGHT-OF-WAY

Rivalry betweeen British railway companies during the 19th century could be bad enough, when it came to unconnected terminals or main through stations occupying the same city, as in Sheffield and Nottingham. In the United States, things sometimes went beyond the borders of absurdity. Each company was jealous of its own 'right-of-way'. Use of that expression to denote railway tracks has always been peculiarly and typically American.

In Figure 273, from a view taken in the early part of the present century, we have the highly picturesque, yet ludicrous, spectacle of the Chesapeake and Ohio Railroad (top), the Seaboard Air Line and the Southern Railway not knowing each other socially. The Southern alone has a passenger station at this three-level intersection, which is at Richmond, Virginia. Incidentally, the visible portion of a Seaboard car on the middle level shows the somewhat rough-and-ready American apparatus — a swinging arm — for picking up mail-pouches at speed.

Still, as the years advanced, there was a growing movement for the establishment of Union Stations, centrally placed and used by several companies, in large cities. Sometimes there would be a specially constituted terminal company owning the station, sometimes the major user company built and worked it. British equivalents could be cited in York, Carlisle Citadel, and Aberdeen Joint. Figure 274 shows the late 19th century magnificence of the Union Station at St. Louis, Missouri, where Western, Middle-Western and Southern lines converged. Its architecture is difficult to define in European terms. The round corner towers of the main hall were of a sort much esteemed for public buildings in the Middle West during the '90s. At the 1893 World's Fair, Chicago, they fairly blossomed among the State pavilions.

It is easy to laugh at American architecture in the years of ostentation. One could see things just as preposterous — or more so — from Scotland to China, wherever money in the bank exceeded architectural talent in any given field. Certainly, however, the American Middle West had its full allowance.

275

276

NORTH AMERICA:
CITY AND MOUNTAIN

Over many years, the Golden Clock on the
concourse of the Grand Central Terminal,
New York [278] has been a rendezvous for
citizens of all sorts, irrespective of their travel
habits. Many meet there daily without having
any immediate business with the trains down
below. Here, it is a dusty morning, and the
sunbeams from the station's huge clerestory
take on an all-pervading, solid quality. The
rococo clock in Figure 277 adorns the station's
façade, with Mercury decently draped, accompanied by the American Eagle and other
allegorical figures. Both shots date from the
1930s; the façade is now dwarfed by a neighbouring skyscraper.

For complete contrast, Figure 276 shows
Canadian Pacific Railway's station at Banff,
Alberta. The second man on the diesel is about
to pick up his train order on the looped cane.
In front of the Canadian-Scottish chalet building stands a double semaphore to indicate a
station stop, a signal to be seen all over North

America at roadside stations (and very occasionally encountered in the Scottish Highlands). To unaccustomed eyes, it seems a peculiarly equivocal sort of signal for a single-
track railway, but the line is quite safe. To the
left, an old passenger car awaits the call to
service.

277

279
280

281

COPENHAGEN AND HELSINKI MAIN STATIONS

Northern Europe in the early 20th century saw a new 'national' movement in architecture, and this was very apparent in several new railway station buildings. The Main Station at Copenhagen on the Danish State Railways involved a use of rosy bricks and timber that undoubtedly *belonged* [279], as did the enormous chandeliers in the great hall [280]. The arrangement of the principal offices being built above the tracks forms a through station.

Finland, about this time, was a Grand-Duchy of the old Russian Empire. Nationalist feeling was strong, and inspired Eliel Saarinen's remarkable Central Station at Helsinki, completed in 1918 during the troubles. Figure 281 shows the great hall floodlit, with the top of the clock tower beyond.

AUCKLAND AND WELLINGTON STATIONS

A globe-trotter once described city railway-station architecture in New Zealand as 'Bankers' Classical'. He meant this as a pejorative, but the style, much favoured in the 1920s and '30s, has much to commend it, and doubtless will return to public esteem as has, after many vicissitudes, the best of Victorian Gothic.

Further — and this can be said for few great railway stations in the British Isles — the placing and surroundings of these two examples, unhampered by any severe consideration of space, are incomparably fine.

Figure 282 shows the fine Doric front of the terminus at Wellington, with its drive-in and parking space separating it from a beautifully gardened square. The building contains not only lavish passenger facilities but also the

282

head offices of New Zealand Railways. Not least interesting is the tiered penthouse construction above the main façade. All too often, a building presenting a brave front looks quite deplorable from the air, as we have occasionally noticed with dismay when airborne. That is not so at Wellington.

Figure 283 shows the terminal at Auckland, with some of the platforms and passenger roads visible on the right. There is a fine, high central hall, with an extremely good road approach. The combination of sunken garden and low-level roadway for commercial and other motors is as handsome as it is ingenious. The railway goods depot is situated beside and to the left of the main block.

Of the two stations featured on these pages, Auckland is slightly the older. It was opened in 1930. The new station at Wellington followed in 1937.

283

STATIONS: GWALIOR, DELHI AND NOVOSIBIRSK

Gwalior Station in India [284], describable as Neo-Mogul, has decency and elegance. It belongs to its place as the stations in Copenhagen and Helsinki, mentioned earlier, have belonged in theirs, now for many years.

The Eastern Punjab Railway's Delhi Junction [285] on the other hand exemplifies the nastiest of what might be called Eurasian redbrick Gothic, the worst of all worlds. Yet it is basically the same sort of station as Gwalior, an arrangement of connected pavilions with a portière for the carriages of sahibs, in the high days when it was built. It is, of course, scarcely helped by its mean forecourt and by the vertical display of the railway's title down the octagonal tower.

Of quite another sort is the Main Station at Novosibirsk, serving an important city in its own right and marking the junction of the Trans-Siberian and Turkestan-Siberian lines [286]. In style one might call it Soviet-Doric. As a railway station *per se* it has several good points, though a bad one is the lack of canopies, which has proved a common Russian failing down the years.

284

285
286

МОСКОВСКИЙ МЕТРОПОЛИТЕН ИМЕНИ В.И.ЛЕНИНА
СТАНЦИЯ МЕТРО БЕЛОРУССКАЯ
СООРУЖЕНА 1949-1951

287
288

MOSCOW UNDERGROUND RAILWAY

With the coming of underground railway transport to Russia in the 1930s, it was decided that the system should be a prestige-feature as well as a conveyance. Ornate architectural treatment was favoured, in absolute contrast to the austerity (sometimes good, but often dull) fashionable in western countries. The style has been described by some joker as Proletarian-Baroque.

Figure 287 shows the outside of Byelorusskaya Station, and in Figure 288 is the hall and escalator head of Komsomolskaya Station. The chandelier is often favoured in Northern Europe (compare with Copenhagen, page 200). Byelorusskaya Station was built during 1949 to 1951. The two little girls pondering the world (the standing one appears to have her finger on Moscow), form a detail adornment, one of many, to the Revolution Square Station [289]. For the rest, there is a splendid profusion of marble.

289

STATIONS: DUBLIN HEUSTON, AMSTEL AND SEEFELD

Contrasts: Heuston Station (old Kingsbridge), Dublin, headquarters of the old Great Southern and Western Railway in days before the Great Southern, let alone Coras Iompair Eireann, were known to men, still presents its magnificent 'great house' to the public eye [290]. It remains — all Early Victorian-Renaissance as it is — one of the most meritorious railway buldings in Europe. The same can be said neither for many of its contemporaries nor for many of the objects which have gone up, not least in England, in the last two decades.

In the middle 19th century, expanding railway transport caused a rush of building. In the middle 20th, replacement of buildings destroyed by war did the same. Of considerable merit, however, is the Amstel Station in Amsterdam, of which the main hall is shown in Figure 291. Is the mural a mistake, or will it date decently? Perhaps the latter, for it records contemporary winds of change in railway transport. There is a certain irony, too, in the portrayal of East and West; certainly for Dutchmen.

In Austria earnest efforts were made to spare the towns and pulverise the railways while war still lasted, and Austria seems to abound in lovely old towns with new railway stations. Seefeld in the Tirol [292] is not bad. The penthouse shape is rather self-conscious by appearances, but may have been inspired by natural configurations and events in country where steep one-sided slopes — and to be sure spring avalanches — are familiar things.

290

NEW EUROPEAN STATIONS

After the destruction of war, and with Marshall Aid from the United States, ruined railway stations in Western and Central Europe were replaced by structures which some of the citizens may have pipe-dreamed in less unhappy days. In Figure 293 is the front and cab-drive of the new Munich Main Station. Nothing is recognisable from the old days except the corner-house in the background. The old station is entirely gone (see Figure 261, page 186). Great cantilevered awnings stretch out to cover the motor vehicles and transferring passengers; it *can* rain in Munich!

From Austria, where, more than in Germany, Allied bombers tried to spare the cities while mauling the railways, we have a view of the Main Station at Innsbruck in the 1950s

[294]. Again there is an entirely new railway station. The trolleybus is new. The trams are old. The mountains were just so before mechanical transport was dreamt of.

The Netherlands suffered sorely with their railways. Figure 295 shows the present station at Venlo, meeting point of lines going west into the Low Countries, south to Roermond and east into Germany.

Noteworthy in all three of these European stations is the mid-20th century preoccupation with parallelograms, with perpendicular and horizontal lines and gently sloped roofing. Le Corbusier might have called a railway station 'a machine for buying tickets and entraining-from', but the styling is rather more genial than such an austere description would convey. While 19th century floridity has gone, bright colours are often apparent.

293

294
295

STATIONS: ROME AND MILAN

The great station at Milan [296], begun in the 1920s, exemplifies the heavy exuberance of what might be called the Mussolini-marble style, but considered as a railway station, it is certainly admirable. Utterly different is the great new Rome Termini [297], with its austerely spacious entrance and excellent road approach. Observe the tramway and (extreme right) trolleybus stations on the square, also the piece of ancient Roman wall on the left.

HISTORY BESIDE THE LINE

The railway's bridging of a gap in the centuries is emphasised not only by its penetration of primeval mountains, but by the buildings of former civilisations and cultures which can crop up close to the line. Railway companies and contractors of the 19th century were no more respecters of historic scenes than have been the builders of motorways in the succeeding one. The route would be cut through, but then as now there would be what current planners' jargon calls 'the preserved amenity'.

298

299

In the angle of the famous junction at the west end of Central Station, Newcastle upon Tyne [298], blackened by the soot of locomotives that have now passed into history, stands the keep built by Henry II in the 1170s, part of a castle which dated back to 1080. In the foreground are the famous diamond crossings whose aspect occasionally terrified nervous passengers as they passed over. These, of course, were junction crossings. Right-angled crossings on the level between different routes were, however, very rare in England. Even so, there were several on the East Coast Route, including that at Retford, and that of the old Stockton and Darlington Railway with the North Eastern at Darlington.

A famous landmark at Moghal Pura, me-chanical headquarters of the old North Western, now the Pakistan Western Railway, is the venerable mosque visible above the roofs of a set of diesel railcars delivered by Ganz of Budapest. Although it is, as Americans would say, 'right on the tracks', it remains a holy place. The N.W.R. never dreamed of disturbing it, nor would the W. P. R. today [299].

Back to Europe: Down the Rhine stand the more or less preserved remains of the robber-barons' castles, and the German trains of our time — and of the late Emperors' — thread their way between and under them. In Figure 300 an electric train headed by an E 10 class locomotive, between Mayence and Coblence, slides almost respectfully under the Ox Tower near Oberwesel.

214

CARRIAGE
DESIGN

BED-CARRIAGE AND MAIL

Bed-carriages, precursors of the sleeping car, appeared as far back as 1838, when they ran on the London and Birmingham and the Grand Junction Railways between London and Lancashire. An example survives in the special carriage built for the Dowager Queen Adelaide in 1842, and now in Clapham Museum. Figure 301 shows the exterior and Figure 302 the sleeping compartment made up for the night. The feet of the sleeper were extended into a boot at the end of the vehicle, as the distance between partitions did not, at the time, allow full-length recumbency, fore-and-aft.

At the same time there appeared the first

Travelling Post Offices, equipped not only for sorting but for the picking up and dropping of mail-pouches at speed. Figure 303 shows a replica made, a century after, by the London Midland and Scottish Railway. F. Karstadt first suggested sorting *en route*, John Ramsay produced the exchange apparatus, and John Dicker improved it into the form that still adequately serves our mail trains. The illustration shows Ramsay's arrangement, with a chute for delivery.

Reverting to Queen Adelaide, it is not widely known that the King of Hannover, having sampled his sister-in-law's carriage, required a similar one to be made for his German journeys.

301

302
303

304

CENTRAL EUROPEAN CARRIAGES

In general, throughout Europe, Mid-Victorian railway carriages were unimaginative things, ranging from the fairly comfortable to the extremely uncomfortable, according to the class of travel. Side-door compartments were the usual rule, except in vehicles for special purposes, but in Central Europe there was an early appearance of the carriage with end entrances and open gangways, such as America already favoured, but with regional differences, some of them for the better.

Figure 304 shows a masterly restoration of a carriage on the oldest Swiss railway from Zürich to Baden, opened on August 9, 1847. This first-class accommodation is extraordinarily 'modern' in conception, though lacking in convenience and headroom, and is lined in claret-red Utrecht velvet.

The old Central European type of carriage achieved its most grandiose interpretation in the Bavarian royal train [305] built for Maximilian II in 1860, though generally associated with Ludwig II ('Mad Ludwig') who succeeded him in 1864. The King's saloon [306], originally a rigid eight-wheeler, was rebuilt with bogies in the early '90s, and though little used latterly it was officially in commission until the revolution of 1918. It is an example of rolling baroque which even the American tycoons of the late 19th century could not match for sheer exuberant ornateness. As to its less visible appointments, the King's water-closet is cushioned in swansdown. The riot of colours and gilding unfortunately must be imagined here, but the carriage may be seen in the Nuremberg Transport Museum. The external style is in royal blue, heavily gilded. End-on to it is the King's balcony carriage which served for the wayside reception of local bigwigs.

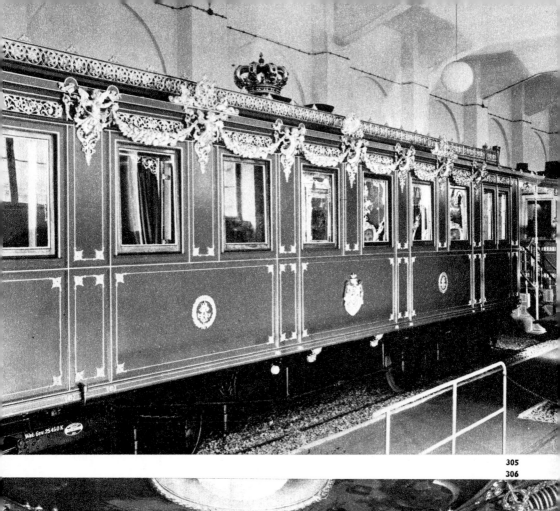

QUEEN VICTORIA

During her long reign Queen Victoria had many special carriages built for her, but without doubt the most famous were two six-wheelers, connected by bellows, built by the London and North Western Railway in 1869. In their last years they were united as a single coach on one long frame, with six-wheeled bogies, and as such are preserved today in the British Railways Museum at Clapham.

Half the double unit contained the Queen's day saloon [Plate XXI, facing page 224] and the quarters of her personal servant (for many years the fearsome John Brown). The other was made up of the royal bedroom, with two beds, and a compartment for her dressers. Double floors lined with cork, and quilting on the sides and ceiling, all helped to deaden the noise, which cannot have been very great, for the Queen objected most strongly to travelling at more than 40 m.p.h.

Figure 307 shows the external aspect. The furniture was of high Victorian style, with much watered silk. Lighting was by oil lamps and candles, and although, towards the end, electric lamps were added, Victoria never would use them. There were no gangways to the rest of the train. If the Queen requested or dismissed her dressers in some bleak place like Beattock Summit, the embarrassed girls had to descend to the permanent way and then be lifted up by the tactful officers of the train. One officer had quite a job with Lady Augusta Bruce, a large lady.

Little known at home was the pair of saloons which the Queen used in Continental Europe. They were very similar to those on the L.N. W.R., and were kept at Calais. Figure 308 shows them in the station at Nice, about 1900.

307
308

'THE STANHOPES'

In the early days of railways, some quite staggering vehicles were offered to the travelling public. 'Stanhope' was a delicately punning nickname for a 'stand-up' carriage, a box on wheels without seats, usually with hundreds of holes in the floor to let out the rain and keep the inmates' feet cool.

The thing shown in Figure 309 was at least superior to this in that it had seats. Possibly dating back to the 1830s, it ran for many years on the Bodmin and Wadebridge Railway in Cornwall, and is now preserved as a relic of those days.

Even in Mid-Victorian times, the subject of Figure 310 was not the sort of railway carriage one saw every day of the week. It was built for the Port Carlisle branch of the North British, in 1863, and the Port Carlisle line's motive power, right down to April 1914, was furnished by horses!

Altogether of a grimmer sort was the vehicle shown in Figure 311. It was for conveying political prisoners and convicts under the Czars from Russia into more or less remote Siberia — a journey of many days — and one regrets to record that it was built in Gloucester, a less spectacular portion of whose skyline so improbably appears in the background of our photograph.

221

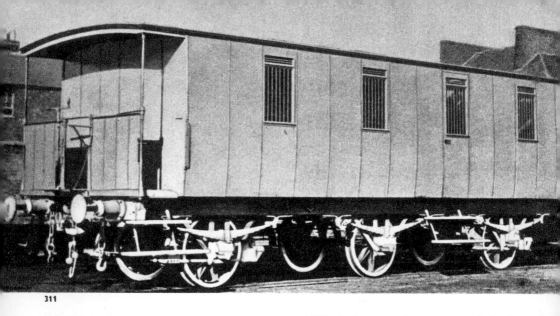

BRITISH AND AMERICAN COACHBUILDING

These four illustrate the divergence of British and American railway coachbuilding in the mid-19th century. Figure 312 shows a typical British three-compartment first-class coach at the beginning of the period. It was built by Wright and Son of Saltley for Sweden in 1854. In its later years on the Swedish State Railways, it was a third-class coach with mail compartment for remoter country branch-line service. It is now preserved. Figure 313 shows a Midland Railway four-wheeled composite of

1874. Only a year later appeared the first of the stately coaches on the Midland which were the first British 12-wheelers, with clerestory roofs and equalised bogies [314].

Then in 1874 came the Pullmans from America. Figure 315 shows one which was converted into the first British dining car in regular service, between Leeds and London in 1879. The narrow vestibule and gangway at the kitchen end were a still later addition. It was successively the Pullman parlour car *Ohio*, the Pullman diner *Prince of Wales*, and the Great Northern diner No. 2992. The photograph probably dates from the 1890s.

312

313

314
315

316
317

MAJESTY ABROAD

All the reigning monarchs of Europe before 1914 used elaborate rolling stock for their travels about the Continent, as well as in their own realms. King Edward VII, while still Prince of Wales, made many journeys in the carriage shown by Figures 316 and 317.

It was built to the design of Thomas Parker, Carriage Superintendent of the Manchester, Sheffield and Lincolnshire Railway, by Cravens of Sheffield in 1883. Ownership was vested in the South Eastern Railway, and it was kept with Queen Victoria's twin Continental saloons in a special shed at Calais Maritime. It was entirely self-contained, arranged for day or night travel, and had a pantry and quarters for personal servants. The style of furnishing was rather that of a ship; the interior view shows ship's balanced lamps as well as electric lamps (a later addition) in the upper and lower decks. The same sort of ship's lamps appear in the interior of one of the royal saloons used by the German Emperor William II [318].

PLATE XXI Queen Victoria's day saloon, London and North Western Railway, 1869.

Both carriages were of the 12-wheeled, wooden-bodied type favoured for superior rolling stock in the late 19th century. Both, too, were the scenes of uncomfortable occasions in the lives of their exalted passengers. Edward VII was shot at in Brussels while riding in the English vehicle. The photograph was taken just afterwards and the folding table looks as if the King had hurriedly pushed it aside with his feet when the bang came. More painful was the experience of the German Emperor. At Eysden on the Dutch frontier in

November, 1918, he spent in his train the last night before seeking political asylum in the Netherlands, while Queen Wilhelmina and a hastily summoned Dutch Cabinet decided what they were to do about him.

For a post-script: in 1959 the author found the imperial dining car in use as a composite carriage on the Westphalian Provincial Railway. It was outwardly little changed but the inside had been gutted long ago, to receive new partitions and ordinary hard and soft furnishings.

PLATE XXII Belgian first-class compartment of 1885, from a painting by Constant Cap.

225

OPEN CARS

Almost from the first, North American travellers favoured the long, open car, as opposed to the European compartment system. It gave easy lavatory access, which was a *sine-qua-non* over the immense distances covered by American trains; it also assisted sociability, and Americans loved to talk to strangers wherever they went. Charles Dickens, visiting and making notes, was less enamoured of the American car, which he likened to 'a shabby omnibus'. But even a century ago, the better class railroads had handsome, comfortable equipment.

Figure 319 shows an ordinary day coach of the Baltimore and Ohio Railroad, built in 1865, the same year as that of the first real Pullman car. It had reversible plush seats, a high clerestory roof containing brass kerosene lamps, and, at the end, a stove and a small lavatory.

The exterior of a veteran American car of similar type, but on narrow gauge, is shown in Figure 320. This belonged to the former East Broad Top Railroad, a line largely concerned with the Pennsylvania coalfields, and was in service at least into the 1930s. The line conjured for us the railroad described in Conan Doyle's Sherlock Holmes story, *The Valley of Fear*, though we heard nothing sinister about the locality in our own time.

Grandiosity distinguished the better-class sleeping cars in North America to the end of the century. Figure 321 shows a Pullman-type first-class sleeper built for the Canadian Pacific Railway in 1886, in all its pride of pillars and plush. The upper berths are folded up for daytime travel. The pillared portion contained a recess, with small sofas, where passengers could sit while the beds were being made up, but like the other sections it could be made up to contain four sleeping berths when the car was fully occupied.

319

322

EARLY PULLMANS

George Mortimer Pullman experimented with the fitting of upper and lower sleeping berths — an old idea in itself — as far back as the late 1850s, and three converted coaches were successfully run in the United States on the Chicago and Alton Railroad during 1858—59.

The Civil War held up development, but in 1865 he produced the prototype of the standard Pullman sleeper which was to serve the United States for generations to come. By day, the upper berths were folded against the deck-rail of the clerestory [322]. At night, they were

323

swung down and the day seats were brought forward to form lower berths, while thick curtains enabled the travellers, of both sexes, somehow to struggle out of their clothes in bed and compose themselves for the long, hot night [323].

The first real Pullman sleeper was the *Pioneer*

of 1865, and these two woodcuts are probably contemporary, for they show that the only night-time lighting was by candle-lamps. Big kerosene lamps followed soon after. Note on comportment: American males of that period favoured keeping their hats on until it was time to go to bed.

COACHING CURIOSITIES

Compartment-type side-door coaches were scarcely used in the United States after the first pioneering days, but in New England during the late 1860s and for a while after, the Old Colony Railroad had two and the Boston and Providence Railroad had a third, shown in Figure 324. At that time, many people liked to travel by overnight steamer on their journeys between Boston and New York, and the 'English cars' were used on the short-run boat trains by both companies. A serious accident, in which one was very badly smashed, put an end to their ephemeral popularity with the American public.

Figure 325 shows two very old Indian narrow-gauge carriages, third- and first-class respectively, at the Indian Railway Centenary Exhibition, New Delhi, March 1953. The third-class came from the Bengal and North Western Railway (metre gauge) and dates back to its beginnings in the 1880s. Double-decked railway carriages, though rare, have been built almost from the beginning of railways, and examples from modern times are illustrated on pages 478-9.

Figure 326 shows a much earlier specimen, formerly belonging to the Northern Railway of Spain, and still to be found, in the 1960s, on local trains in the Valencia area. Access to the open-sided upper section is by tram-car staircases and railed side gangways. The hole-and-corner lavatory on the lower deck is a later refinement. In old Spain, such things were unknown except on the best long distance train, or, sometimes, tucked away for emergencies in the guard's van.

324

325

SPECIAL CARRIAGES

In the late 19th century the short-bodied, rigid wheelbase railway carriage remained the commonest form outside the Americas. Of the two French examples here, probably dating from the early 1870s, the handsome little Travelling Post Office [327] with its clerestory roof, end gangways and admirable symmetry was for many years on the expresses between Paris and Bordeaux. Noteworthy is the position of the letterbox in the middle of the door. The pigeonholes are visible through the wired windows. The van [328] of fairly obvious P.L.M. design, was for conveying Indian Mail, already sorted, from Calais to Brindisi in connection

327
328

with the P. and O. company's steamers. The brakesman's box was once a common feature of Continental coaching stock.

The Ceylon Government first-class coach [329] was built by Gloucester Carriage and Wagon as late as 1894. Inside were ordinary compartments of the traditional Victorian sort, but structural work giving protection against the heavy tropic sun was notably elaborate.

The 'carriage' for the Pretoria and Pietersburg Railway (3 ft. 6 in. gauge), also by the Gloucester company, may be said to exemplify *apartheid* applied to coachbuilding [330]. It might have been given the courtesy qualification of 'third-class', but the inscription *Kleurlingen* simply means 'Natives'

329

330

SPECIAL SALOONS

Almost since the beginning of railways, special saloon carriages have been provided for both company's business and private hire. The anciently plushy example in Figure 331 belonged to the North Eastern Railway, which had rebuilt it from a rather smaller carriage belonging to the Stockton and Darlington Railway. The observation windows shown were at one end only. This carriage was used by the Chief Mechanical Engineer of the N.E.R., and was normally hauled singly by the little tank engine *Aerolite*, now at York Museum.

Observation windows, with a gangway door between, also distinguish the more recent saloon in Figure 332. This was built by the Great Western Railway in 1930 for use either by the company's officers on tours of inspection or for hire by private parties of the wealthier sort. The corner arm-chairs closely follow standard British Pullman style of the period.

In Figure 333 is the office compartment of the carriage always used by Lord Stamp when he was President of the Executive on the London Midland and Scottish Railway. In style it closely followed late London and North Western practice, and like the private and business cars of North America it contained complete living quarters with a full-size bathroom. Stamp sometimes lent it to King Edward VIII for northern journeys during his brief reign in 1936. The King greatly preferred it to the stately splendours of his grandfather's royal train.

331

FIRST-CLASS COMPARTMENT

For all the rigours of inferior-class travel, the European first-class compartment followed a traditional form — that of the pre-railway coach — with such improvements as fashion and comfort demanded, and experience caused to evolve. These chiefly concerned better lighting, warming apparatus, intercommunication, sanitation and greater space.

The sprightly painting by C. Cap of Antwerp [Plate XXII, facing page 225] shows a Belgian compartment of 1885. Upholstery was more substantial than resilient and the seats appear to have been rather high, but in mild weather, with good intervals at important stations for ease and refreshment, such conveyance could be pleasant enough, especially with such company as that of the agreeable girl in the picture.

The London and North Western first-class shown in Figure 334, though in stodgily stereotyped decorative style, was a remarkably comfortable carriage with especially well-designed seating. Its date was about a quarter of a century later than that of the Belgian carriage. It was spacious, steam-heated and electrically-lit, though without the partition lamps of more recent designs.

By this time the best expresses had internal communication by side corridors and usually one or more dining cars, for all classes of passenger. Class distinctions were much more marked than nowadays on most foreign trains and on the Continent the third-class could be very grim indeed, even though the days of the open wagon were long past.

334

TRAIN LAVATORIES

This most important accessory to a railway
carriage running over any appreciable distance
goes back, to our knowledge, to 1850, when
Queen Victoria, on the Great Western, was
provided with the picturesque fixture shown
in Figure 336. The lavatory basin was almost
modern but the pedestal, heavily upholstered
to protect Her Majesty's knees should she
stumble, contained but a humble pot.

For many years any such provision was dis-
gracefully rare for the commonalty, and at first
was general, in Great Britain, only on sleeping
cars from 1873. Family saloons got it from the
1860s onwards. It reached second- and third-
class passengers in the late '80s.

Quite majestic, however, is the London and
North Western lavatory of 1906, shown in
Figure 335, with hot and cold water laid on.
The floral decorations of the w.c. are what we
still would call Victorian.

POST-BROAD GAUGE, GREAT WESTERN

In 1891 William Dean on the Great Western Railway produced the prototype of the British side-corridor train, and put it on the Paddington-Birkenhead service. Figure 337 shows it, straight out of shops, posed on mixed gauge track at Shrivenham. There was no diner, but the corridors gave through passage for the guard and complete lavatory access for first-, second- and third-class passengers. Even the last-named had well-upholstered seats, and the train was liberally provided with communications. There was an electric bell service to the guard, and a pull-wire, in the same position as the old communication cord, enabled the passengers in an emergency to make a partial application of the automatic vacuum brake. The principle is the same today, only the 'cord', as we continue to call it, is a piped chain inside the compartments. The locomotive is one of William Dean's famous 7 ft. 8 in. single-drivers. Following an accident through breakage of a leading axle (fortunately without really terrible results), a bogie was substituted for this [338].

This view is of a down South Wales express near Twyford about 65 years ago. The first four coaches have corridors, some along the sides and others in the form of gangways through saloon compartments, which in those days were considered proper for people who smoked on the railway. In the foreground is the big crossover from the fast to the slow lines, governed by stop signals (upper) and splitting distant signals (with fishtail ends) for the main line and the Henley branch, which bears off to the north beyond the station.

337

AMERICAN PRIVATE CARS

In the late 19th and early 20th centuries no American businessman of the grander sort felt himself properly furnished unless he had at least one, or better still two private railroad cars in which he could live, independent of possibly doubtful small town hotels, and enter-

tain on a scale which, he felt, ought to make European emperors themselves feel provincial.

Every possible luxury was laid on; the owner could live lavishly on the rails for weeks if he wished. Gorgeous saloons, dining rooms, bathrooms and bedrooms, and a dream of a kitchen, filled some 80 feet of Pullman-Standard equipment. Pullman further built such cars for hire.

PLATE XXIII *Rain, Steam, Speed*, by
J.M.W. Turner (National Gallery, London).

If sufficiently rich, one could charter an entire train of them, with a barber-shop included for good measure.

In the master bedroom [339] the Chicago corned-beef millionaire and his lady could be thoroughly cosy as they rolled the prairie through the night, or creaked round the feet of invisible mountains. The second view [340] shows what might have been called, in later language, a sumptuous bed-sitter in the two-car private train built by Pullman for the then President of Mexico in 1898. Both interiors show the false-arched clerestory, known as the 'empire roof', which for a decade and more was a recognized hall-mark of Pullman-Standard practice.

340

PLATE XXV *Le pont de l'Europe, Gare St Lazare*
by Claude Monet (Musée Marmottan, Paris)

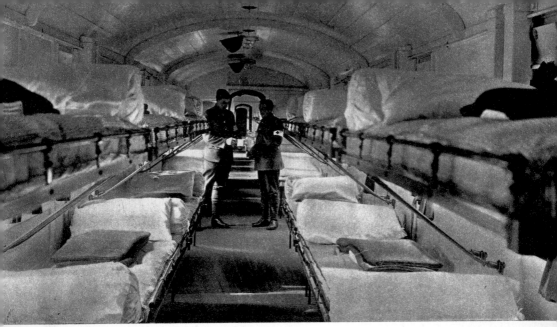

341
342

INVALID AND AMBULANCE CARS

Although we have traced the building of properly designed military ambulance trains back to the American Civil War, for many years they were improvised for the unfortunate wounded, often from the most deplorable rolling stock. In later years they were still often improvised, but from the most suitable carriages available, and their equipment was of the highest order, including fully equipped operating theatres for dealing with emergency cases.

It was in the war of 1914—18 that we first saw them on a grand scale. Figure 341 shows a ward car on one of these trains, which contained as many as 15 vehicles. This train was furnished by the Great Eastern Railway, and Figure 342 shows part of one of the staff cars, an ex-diner converted into a dormitory.

Observe the berths stowed by day against the lower roof decks, while the sumptuous leather upholstery remains from the day when it sustained dining passengers on the first lap of their way to the Continent via Harwich.

Of very different sort were the invalid saloons, the first of which were known as far back as the 1850s. These could be hired, at a handsome price, by rich valetudinarians, who could be safely put to bed with nurse and the relations all round them, and whirled away to whatever pleasant place they had chosen for their recovery. The example shown [343] was one of several on the London and North Western Railway, c. 1907. Such vehicles, available at much more reasonable rates, and of clinical plainness compared with the Old English ornateness, still serve a useful purpose in Sweden, for Scandinavia is bigger than some realise, and many live remote from hospitals.

343

344

STEAM RAIL-MOTORS

At intervals in the history of steam traction attempts have been made to produce combined vehicles — rail-motors was the term in Edward VII's England — for branch line working. Figure 344 shows a London and North Western specimen. In this a small 0-4-0 tank engine with inside cylinders was totally enclosed in the coach body, to which it was articulated. The motion, as we remember it, was very violent at any speed; further, the enclosure of the engine, with connection doors through the luggage compartment, made the coach part of the unit abominably hot in summer; the hotter the weather, the more likely the enginemen were to open those doors, for their own sake.

The little Great North of Scotland rail-motor in Figure 345, built by Andrew Barclay of Kilmarnock in 1905, was one of two. The design was unique in its incorporation of a Cochran boiler, normally used for stationary engines. The engine was a single driver, the driving wheels leading. These engine units were scarcely a success, and were scrapped rather soon. The coach bodies, however, lasted

for many years, chiefly in local service. They had been lengthened, and of course given additional bogies. We even recall seeing one thus improved — even to the extent of gangways and a solitary lavatory on an East Coast express in the 1940s, when anything that would run was made to do so.

The trouble with rail-motors was that on market days and holidays their capacity was insufficient, even with trailers cautiously attached, and ordinary trains had to be put on instead. In the 1920s, however, they were revived in an attempt to meet local motor bus competition. This time, instead of a small version of the orthodox steam locomotive, a high-speed, high pressure steam engine was mounted in the car and geared down to the driving axles.

The commonest form was the Sentinel engine, which for years gave very satisfactory service in heavy road haulage until it was killed by punitive taxation. Figure 346 shows a Sentinel steam rail-car (the new term) on the Zafra-Huelva Railway, one of the few British-owned lines in Spain. The photograph was taken by L. G. Marshall in 1963, by which time no 'Sentinels' remained in Britain.

244

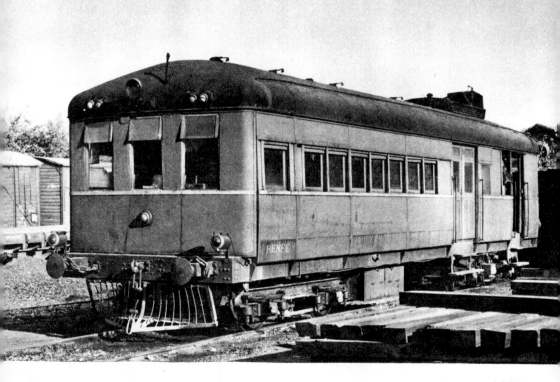

ROYAL TRAINS, EARLY 20TH CENTURY

When the London and North Western Railway, immediately after Victoria's death, asked King Edward VII how he would like the new royal train, which they had been waiting rather a long time to build, that very great man said: 'Make it like a yacht'. Figure 347 shows the smoking room — King Edward was a classic smoker — and this was the compartment in which his son and daughter-in-law, George V and Queen Mary, travelled by day when George became King. George had the baths put in [348] when he was obliged to live in the train for several days at a time during the 1914—18 war. George VI eventually had the silver-plated tubs replaced by pottery ones. The two main saloons of the train were built in 1903, and are now in Clapham Museum. They exemplify the best of C. A. Park's style on the London and North Western Railway.

Figure 349 shows one of the saloons in two royal coaches built respectively by the Great Northern and the North Eastern Railways in 1907. They were somewhat rearranged, though not radically altered, in the 1920s, and were still in service, most often between London and Sandringham, during the '60s.

347

348

351

BRITISH THIRD CLASS

In the middle 1870s the Midland Railway made what was considered an extraordinary — and to some, outrageous — *démarche*. The company abolished second-class carriages and henceforward cushioned the seats of the third class. Neighbour companies were sooner or later obliged to copy the Midland, some of them reluctantly, and as a result the British third class at a penny a mile astonished foreign visitors. British travellers, however, soon took it for granted and grumbled as of yore.

The compartment view in Figure 350 is from a Great Eastern coach of 1900. Its third-class seats were well-sprung, well-shaped and well-covered. Though without gangways it had complete lavatory access by short side corridors. Its weak point was in the lighting; the enormous pendant lamp in the clerestory

roof, burning compressed oil gas in duplex jets, shed a rather subdued light in the hours of darkness, but the undergraduate and the fruitily-hatted schoolgirl were probably well-used to gas-jets in their own homes. Of course, in the event of bad trouble, that gas could set the carriage on fire (a sadly recurrent Midland misfortune).

Figure 351 shows a London Midland and Scottish corridor third class of 1932, a prototype still followed in the second class of to-day. Folding elbows were just beginning to appear. The electric partition lamps were excellent, and so was the single large window, though the single sliding light at the top was soon found to be too shallow. The enormous floral pattern of the plush was characteristic of the L.M.S. in the '30s. The floor covering was of rubber. The body was of wood with steel outer panels on a steel underframe.

352

353

354

FAMILY AND DINING CARS

In Figure 352 is a Great Central Railway third-class coach, c. 1900, of what once was a very common British sort. It seated 80 passengers in quite reasonable comfort, but they had no lavatory access. Lighting was electric.

In the days of large families and no motors, payment of a sufficient number of fares secured exclusive use of a family saloon, an extremely civilised conveyance which the companies would lay on from any one to any other station in Great Britain. That shown in Figure 353, with its observation end, was built by the Great Western Railway in the late 1890s.

Figures 354 and 355 show Midland Railway dining carriages of 1904—07 (the M.R. used the term 'car' only for Pullmans). They were designed by David Bain, a great believer in passenger comfort as an earner of dividends, and some of their kind lasted, on remoter Scottish lines, into the late 1940s. One is at Clapham Museum. Dining service for all passenger classes was first provided by the Great Eastern Railway in 1891. The other companies rather slowly and reluctantly toed the G.E. line. All these carriages exemplify the clerestory roof, which improved daytime lighting and gave a pretty effect, but was both vulnerable and a dirt collector.

355

DINING ON TRAINS

In spite of their appearance at the beginning of the 1880s dining cars remained for a long time a rarity in Continental Europe. Generally they were adjuncts to the old *trains de luxe*, composed of sleeping cars, and intended to save travelling time by cutting out the long stops for meals. There was usually a platform waiter, too, who swooped on the first-class compartments as soon as the train stopped, and refreshed their leisured occupants.

Constant Cap's picture [356], painted in 1885, catches the mood — the business of hurriedly feeling for loose francs, the waiter's veiled glare, the liberal cups of what in those days would be really good coffee, and the aspect of the 'lavatory-first', as English coach-builders called it. This was a Belgian car.

R. T. Roussel's water colour [357] was one of several, more or less alike, which were commissioned by the London and North Western Railway and used as headings to the dining-car menu-cards, in and about 1905. He varied the figures, but someone was inevitably telling a story. The car shown in this version was a West Coast Joint Stock vehicle on an express between London, Euston, and Glasgow Central (or possibly Edinburgh Princes Street). It is a first-class car; the difference was almost entirely in the arrangement of the seating. The old second-class being moribund, the alternative would be a third-class car, this having off-central gangway with two persons abreast on one side and slightly narrower single seats on the other. Further, it would be a wooden-bodied 12-wheeler, with lighting by electricity and cooking by gas. The running qualities would be excellent — one of the London and North Western company's strong points.

357

DINING CARS

Dining cars, which date back to George M. Pullman's inspiration and early practice in North America, form a fascinating study. Pullman himself called his earliest examples 'hotel cars' and, indeed the first one, on the Great Western Railway of Canada in 1867, was convertible into a sleeper at night.

The conventions of eating on a train have changed from time to time, and varied from one country to another. The first real dining car — that is, a car with its own kitchen as opposed to an ordinary Pullman which served pre-cooked meals — in Great Britain was the *Prince of Wales* on the Great Northern Railway's Leeds-London business service in 1879. This, indeed, had been converted from a Pullman called *Ohio*, one of those which Pullman introduced to certain British railways from 1874 onwards.

The practice of travelling all day in the same car, and having one's meals brought to table in it, persisted for a long time on most British railways. It was particularly favoured by the Midland Railway [Figure 358] and its overstuffed magnificence in this photograph of 1906 encouraged by suggestion the old English custom of sleeping after a heavy meal. To this day one can enjoy a meal without leaving one's place in British Pullman trains, a circumstance often commended by foreign visitors.

England was the first country to admit all passenger-classes to dining arrangements. That was on the Great Eastern Railway's Harwich-York Continental service in 1891. In Western Continental Europe, from a beginning in 1881, the diner has nearly always been a travelling restaurant, for temporary occupation only, and the same convention was soon adopted in both the Americas. Figure 359 shows a spacious British-built diner on the Buenos Aires and Pacific Railway in 1929. The Argentine car took 56 diners at a sitting. One is impressed by its roominess; a fair advantage had been taken of the broad gauge (5 ft. 6 in.). The seats are well-designed, but not meant to encourage post-prandial nodding. The mock-clerestory shape of the inside roof is noteworthy (this was quite a feature of some South American railways) and so are the sliding venetian shutters to the windows, a welcome arrangement on a long journey across sun-scorched pampas. Quaint to European eyes, are the basketed aspidistras in what convention would regard as the hat-racks.

358

360
361

OLD BRITISH PULLMANS

Nine years after George Mortimer Pullman had built the first of his 'palace cars' in the United States in 1865, he introduced them on a slightly smaller scale to England at the invitation of James Allport, General Manager of the Midland Railway. Several companies received them with enthusiasm; others would have nothing to do with them. Pullman, nevertheless, was a new word added to the English language, synonymous with comfort and elegance in travelling.

Until 1908, British Pullman cars were prefabricated in the United States, to be erected here. Figure 360 shows the *Duchess of Norfolk*, built in 1906, on the London, Brighton and South Coast Railway. The old Brighton company and its successors faithfully furthered the worthy cause of Pullman operation.

Some of the early Pullmans lasted for a tremendous time, even after they were out of service and grounded for use as sheds and bungalows. Figure 361 shows one of the original Midland cars of 1874 in use as messroom at Tilbury in 1961. Some pieces had been cut out of both sides to provide intermediate doors, and the annexe at the nearer end was improvised from these and from some odd bits of an old Great Eastern coach. The very substantial timber bodies would last as long as the roof remained watertight.

The sad-looking ruin [362] is that of the *Duchess of Albany*, built for the London and South Western Railway's Bournemouth service in 1890, later on the Brighton line, later still part of a bungalow and lastly, as shown, a tumbledown shed, rich in birds' nests (c. 1960).

362

363

CAR DESIGN, NORTH AMERICA

Three rear-end views of peculiar variety: Frederick U. Adams patented a streamlined train — he called it a 'windsplitter' — and the Baltimore and Ohio Railroad gave it a trial in 1900, when it was photographed on the historic Thomas Viaduct in Maryland [363]. Adams' hopes of incredible speed were not, however, realised. An ordinary small American-type locomotive, without casing except over the top of the tender, did what might have been expected of it, but no more.

In Figure 364 is one of the last examples of the traditional North American observation car with an open balcony at the rear. It is shown on a Canadian Pacific train, northbound beside the Connecticut River from Boston to Montreal in 1949. At the head is a single-unit C.P.R. diesel. The automatic home and distant semaphores have moved to 'danger' with the passage of the train.

Figure 365 shows that other highly traditional feature of American rolling stock, the freight caboose, with its high cupola. In British phraseology the caboose is describable as a goods-brake large enough for several men to live in reasonably comfortably. This one, on the Atchison, Topeka and Santa Fe Railroad, has radio communication with the driver's cab.

364

20TH CENTURY PULLMAN CARS
IN GREAT BRITAIN

These two pictures well illustrate changes in taste and fashion during the first third of the present century. In Figure 366 is the interior of the *Princess Patricia*, one of the last American Pullmans to be built for British service, on the Brighton Pullman Limited of 1906. Decoration was in sumptuous green and gold. The chairs were pivoted. Small tables could be installed at the request of passengers.

In Figure 367 is a corresponding car of the 1930s. The big chairs are movable. The tables are more of fixtures. The clerestory and the baby-doll lamp-shades are gone. But still the style remains classic Pullman. Company fortunes had looked up. Under the autocracy of Lord Dalziel, who bought the undertaking as a going concern, by the 1920s Pullman services extended from the South Coast to Aviemore in the Central Highlands.

367

SPECIALISED INTERIORS

The first dining-car kitchen in Europe belonged to the Pullman *Prince of Wales* in 1879, on the Great Northern Railway. The Great Northern also produced, in 1921, the electric kitchen-car, part of which is shown in Figure 368, and on the same London-Leeds service as the pioneer diner. The perforated object overhead is not a neatly-stowed collander but the casing of an electric fan.

Travelling Post Offices, an entirely British invention (America did not have one until as late as the 1860s on the Hannibal and St.

Joseph Railroad) have remained true to type from the first. Changes have been in the size of the Post Office carriages, and improvements in structure, lighting, ventilation and sanitation.

These views are typical of the middle years. Figure 369 shows a London and North Western sorting carriage of 1900, still gaslit and close in the roof. Figure 370 shows a T.P.O. of 1935 on the London Midland and Scottish Railway. On the left is the lever for working the net to pick up pouches at speed, and the arms for dropping the mails to the lineside net are beyond the heavy curtain. The heavily padded sorting tables have swinging stools.

AUSTRALIAN INTERSTATE TRAINS

It was not until October 25, 1917, that the first booked passenger train started off on the long dry hike between Kalgoorlie, Western Australia and Port Augusta, South Australia. As might have been expected at that time, there was a break of gauge at both ends of the 'Trans', which was laid to the standard 4 ft. 8½ in. gauge of New South Wales and worked by steam locomotives of N.S.W. types.

Figure 371 shows the first of the original Trans-Australian trains, with the necessary extra water-tank wagon, and a staff caboose, between the tender and the highly Pullman-esque carriages.

The first interior view [372] comes from a somewhat similar first-class car built for the Melbourne-Albury and Melbourne-Adelaide interstate expresses during the early 1900s; not quite American, not quite English, but with a wonderful agglomeration of velvet and basketwork, coloured glass and lincrusta-walton, and all that was highly esteemed by the luxury traveller of the period.

In Figure 373 is the first-class recreation room of a present-day train on the 'Trans'. It is air-conditioned; it is spacious; and when one considers the monotonous scenery of the Nullarbor Plain, including 328 miles of dead-straight track, it is clear that the piano is no mere piece of ostentation. On a train as on a ship, let people sing and time will pass more quickly.

371

BUFFET CARS, U.S.A. AND SOUTH AFRICA

The term *buffet car* appears to be exclusively British (the old French term was *wagon-bar*), and we shall continue to use it, though in other countries, especially in the United States, it has all sorts of names. Figure 374 shows an American example ('counter-lounge') on the Pan-American of the Louisville and Nashville Railroad. This train connects Cincinnati and New Orleans, and the car plies as far south as Montgomery, Alabama. Grapes form the theme of the typically American wrought-iron screens, though the only visible beverages seem to be coffee and 'Coke'.

In Figure 375 is a comparable car on the Blue Train between Cape Town and Johannesburg, on the South African Railways. There appears to be more variety in the forms of refreshment. What is not so apparent is the fact that this fine, spacious car is running on the 3 ft. 6 in. gauge, in spite of the body-width of up to 10 ft.

375

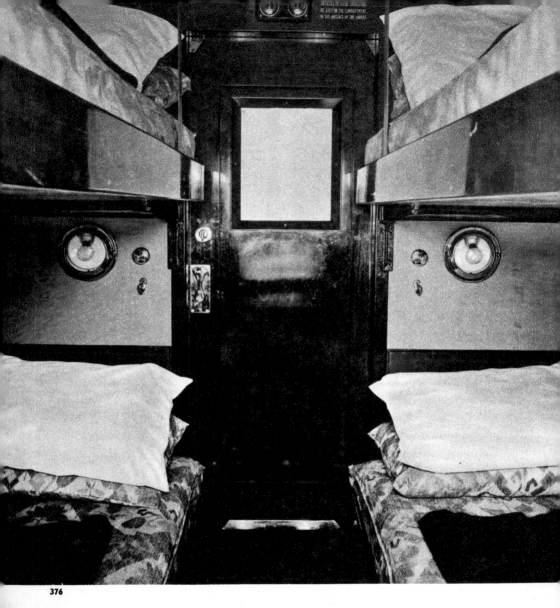

376

BRITISH SLEEPING CARS

Although sleeping cars had first appeared in
Great Britain on the East and West Coast expresses as far back as 1873, it was not until
1928 that we provided them for any but first-
class passengers. The northern lines made
them like ordinary day compartments, with
folding upper berths added. The Great Western Railway furnished real cabins, but without
bed-linen apart from the pillow-cases [376].

First-class single berth compartments appeared on the East Coast expresses in 1894.
They became the standard British form. An
example of the present day is shown in Figure
377, and the companion picture [378] shows
a modern two-berth second-class sleeper. Once
the public had sampled the latter, the old four-
berth convertibles faded away. Compared with
Continental rates, British sleeping cars today
furnish extraordinarily cheap reservations, by
far the best value for money in all Europe.

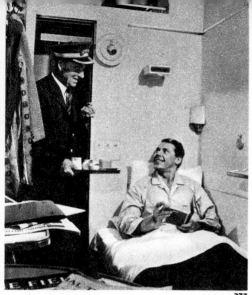

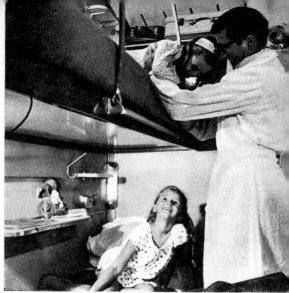

377

378

CONTRASTING INTERIORS IN FRENCH AND SWEDISH SLEEPING-CARS

Both scenes show second-class compartments. Figure 379 shows an admirable peculiarity of Swedish long-distance trains, the 'mothers-and-babies-only' compartment with its super-imposed cots faced by a passenger seat and, just out of the picture to the right, an attached lavatory not accessible from the side corridor.

The Continental six-berth *couchette* sleeper, a French example of which is shown in Figure 380, has had many funny stories told about it, and scarcely compares with the British two-berth second class, but one can get a fairly large family bedded down in it.

379

380

381

MODERN CHINA

In China today one may travel 'hard', in an extremely Spartan day coach over the shorter distances (by Chinese standards), or in a 'soft' one with high-backed wing seats and anti-macassars, or even sitting at a table with a potted palm for company. The interior shown in Figure 381 belongs to the first of these categories. So great has been destruction by war and commotion within recent memory that contemporary rolling stock on important through runs is necessarily of recent design and construction, with many marks of Russian influence (Figure 382, which shows a train waiting at Shilong, near Canton).

Like the American train of long tradition, the principal express between Peking and Tientsin is completed by a library-observation car with the addition of a loudspeaker which utters announcements, political exhortations and what might be called compulsory music. (The last-named abomination, be it admitted, is a western invention.) Figure 383 shows that in this style of car the chairs are reasonably comfortable, but there is no carpet and there are no matches in the neat match-holders of the carriage tables. These things are not necessary. What is necessary, and is being carried out as quickly as possible, is a great expansion of the Chinese railway system, far beyond the narrow bounds that sufficed in the old days.

PENDULUM SUSPENSION

For years, railway mechanical engineers have been trying to produce a successful pendulum suspension for railway carriages whereby the outward sway on curves, peculiar to all land-surface vehicles, should be counteracted in the passenger-carrying body so that the pull of gravity and that of centrifugal force would balance one another to the benefit of passengers. The Americans were about it before the war. The vehicle proper naturally tends to tip over on the outside of a curve, and if the curve is flat it will do so with unhappy results at any appreciable speed, hence the super-elevation of railway curves and the banking of roads, most pronounced in race-tracks. But even on a well-superelevated railway curve, entirely adequate for the vehicle itself, the passengers will still feel themselves being drawn to the outside of the curve. Pendulum-suspension of the body results in the latter tipping inwards to an even greater extent than does the underframe on a calculated angle of superelevation. Disadvantages are the complexity of the vehicle involved and difficulties of intercommunication.

Figure 384 shows a recent French 'pendulum' coach in which the inward inclination of the body comes to 18 degrees relative to the bogies. This is all very well for a trailer coach, but as Figure 385 shows, with a train seen from the rear, application of it to a motor coach would bring the pantograph or collection bow clean off the overhead contact wire. The pantograph visible in the photograph belongs to an orthodox motor vehicle in front of the pendulum car. At the present time, pendulum bogies can be applied to a trailer or a control-trailer car only.

385

OBSERVATION CARS

One of the last of the old, sumptuous private railroad cars in the United States was the *Gold Coast* [386], built for the Central of Georgia in 1906, latterly owned and used by Lucius Beebe and Charles Clegg in Nevada and finally presented by them to the Pacific Coast Chapter of the Railway and Locomotive Historical Society. It exemplifies classic Pullman style during the first quarter of the 20th century, and not least the open, brass-railed observation platform which once was the indispensable tail-tip of every American passenger train esteemed to be of any consequence whatever.

As far as the observation end had a successor, it was in the elevated observation dome, exemplified in the view of the Empire Builder on the Great Northern Railway [387], whose caravan length is distinguished by three semi-dome and, in foreground, one full-dome car. The latter, in Great Northern phraseology, 'seats 75 passengers on the sun deck level.' The idea is old. Something like it appeared, though without lasting consequence, on the Russian railways as far back as 1867, as a sort of solarium situated in the middle of a sleeping car.

386

388

389
390

CHANGING FASHIONS IN CARRIAGE DESIGN

All of them belonging to the present century, these four examples show the impact of changing fashion on the design of railway passenger vehicles. The majestic wooden 'parlor' car in Figure 388 is characteristic of American Pullman practice at the beginning of the century, though in fact it was not owned by the Pullman organisation but by its operating company, the New York, Ontario and Western Railroad. The paired windows under depressed fanlights, the oval lavatory lights, the big clerestory and the equalised six-wheel bogies are all typical of the United States in the Theodore Roosevelt phase.

Equally important-looking, in its high Continental way, is the Italian-built sleeper of the International Sleeping Car Company (*Wagons Lits*), also dating from the early 1900s, in Figure 389. It was of these that the great, solid-block *trains-de-luxe* were composed in pre-flying days. Their kind could be seen from Spain to China, splendid in varnished teak

with polished brass emblem and lettering, full of embossed blue velvet and fine linen, for the conveyance of millionaires, diplomats and international spies according to contemporary romances. They were ubiquitous until their long, blue, steel successors came in the '20s.

The British Isles saw the beginnings in 1874 of what most Europeans mean by the words 'Pullman car', a comfortable vehicle for daytime travel, in which meals are brought to the passenger wherever he sits. France and Italy took them up in the '20s, and so did Germany, though without Pullman or Wagons-Lits ownership, in the original Rheingold Express of 1928 [390]. Plush and antimacassars were still well in.

A modern car is shown in Figure 391, from British Railways' Western Region. It is plainly opulent. It is air-conditioned. It belongs to one of the inter-city diesel Pullman sets which in England correspond to the Trans-Europe Express services abroad. Some jester called them 'expense-account trains', but so far they have successfully competed with other forms of business transport.

391

392

OBSERVATION CARS: ITALY AND GERMANY

European treatment of the 'vista dome': Figure 392 shows an Italian interior of the 1950s, with an upper-level observation room. The chairs in the foreground are possibly an acquired taste. There is something menacing about their great wings. Note the slots in the backs, presumably to receive the vertebrae.

Somewhat later, belonging to the early '60s, is the domed observation car of the Rheingold Express, German Federal Railway, with two jolly barmaids conducting business on the lower level (Figures 393 and 394). Both the Italian and the German domes reveal a preference for much more angular forms than the American style.

393

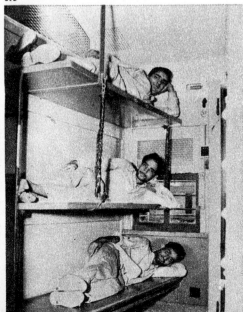

MODERN INDIAN INTERIORS

The recent Indian third-class sleeping car is strangely evocative. There is something of old Russia in it and something of China. The upper berth is fixed, and the intermediate one hinged to allow for daytime use [395].

The diner [396] could belong only to India. From the kitchen compartment two serving hatches open on to the saloon, vegetarian and non-vegetarian respectively. The vertical electric fans are numerous and ideally placed.

The first-class day coach in Figure 397 is a reclining-seat carriage in which, by adjustment, one can achieve a semi-prone position. The official term is 'slumberette'. The carriage is fully air-conditioned and, in this case, is running between New Delhi and Agra.

396

397

MODERN BRITISH INTERIORS

Nowhere, outside the British Isles, would one find a more comfortable ordinary second-class coach than that shown in Figure 398. This is part of a tradition going back to the decision of the Midland Railway in 1875 to provide an upholstered third class, with which other companies had to compete. The seats are deep and well sprung; there are movable tables. The electric lighting however, is less good than in many older coaches.

Figure 399 shows a mock-up (1965) of a ten seat first-class compartment which, in the official description, 'has been designed to give first-class business passengers a standard of comfort in seating and space far above that possible in a private car or aircraft.' As far as

398

399

private cars are concerned in the comparison, the carriage does that, though it is dangerous to put a limit on the possibilities of aircraft. No road vehicle can be as comfortable as a railway carriage at its best.

One cannot, however, say that either of these interiors of the 1960s exemplify an aesthetic triumph. If there is any style at all, it might be described as *Contemporary-Philistine*, the style of burgesses without art trying to be fashionable. The first-class carriage suggests an at-tempt at austere grandeur which only succeeds in being fussy and gadgetty. The lighting is on the whole good. Since the ceiling consists of a false roof, it might have been made symmetrical with coving along both sides instead of suggesting, as it does, a broadened, flattened version of the old clerestory roof as applied to a side-corridor coach. The open-gangway second-class coach, of less self-conscious design, is thus much better, though the octopus-pattern uncut moquette is hardly a triumph.

CONTRASTS IN PASSENGER TRAFFIC

Marxist China still perpetuates the provision of 'hard' and 'soft' coaches. One of the latter is shown in Figure 400, a not very distant relation of the American 'reclining seat' day coach. No concession to ornament is made in the styling of the car body, yet the trimmings are, to western eyes, quite Victorian. Observe the loose covers to the seats (Russia provided these, over half a century ago) and the antimacassars of machine-made lace.

Figure 401 is from present-day America, and shows a tubular day-coach on the Pennsylvania Railroad's train *The Keystone*. Walls, floor and ceiling are welded into one piece; between the bogies there is well construction bringing the floor to within 24 in. of rail level, and the centre of gravity down to 45 in. The car is 85 ft. long.

400

401

TRAIN HOSTESSES

The train hostess is widely regarded as a very new character in railway passenger traffic, borrowed from the air-lines. For all that, she was to be found in both Russia and the United States in the 1930s and Figure 402 shows her in the Irish Republic today.

STEAM LOCOMOTIVES
OF THE 20ᵀᴴ CENTURY

CITY OF TRURO / DUKE OF CONNAUGHT

In the first few years of the present century there was intense competition for American mail and passenger traffic from Plymouth to London, over the two routes owned respectively by the Great Western and the London and the South Western companies. The latter had the advantage of a shorter distance. In Devonshire both lines were extremely hilly. The South Western line climbed round the north side of Dartmoor; the Great Western, though not having to surmount so great a hump, had a long and severe climb from Plympton and along the south side of the Moor. But east of Exeter, the South Western remained the more exacting of the two. Some extremely fast running was made by what were then among the best express engines in Europe; Dean's and Churchward's on the Great Western, and Dugald Drummond's — very

Scotch in design — on the South Western. The trains were fairly light and the drivers entered into the spirit of the thing.

A classic run was made by the Great Western on May 9, 1904 with the Ocean Mail (a purely Post Office train carrying no passengers). Churchward's engine *City of Truro* [403] ran from Plymouth to Bristol in 128 minutes. Average speed to Exeter was 55.71 m.p.h., and thence to Bristol, 70.27 m.p.h. Charles Rous-Marten, who was on the train, recorded a maximum speed slightly in excess of 102 m.p.h. going down Wellington Bank. From Bristol to Swindon one of Dean's 7 ft. 8½ in. bogie single-drivers averaged just over 70 m.p.h., and thence to Paddington, over 77 m.p.h. This engine was the *Duke of Connaught* (the one in Figure 404, on a down West of England express, is the *Iron Duke*).

The four-coupled engine, *City of Truro*, was basically of Dean's design, but with the boiler and the front-end modified by Churchward.

403

404

The Belpaire-fireboxed boiler with the second ring coned, without dome, and the long smokebox supported on a saddle, were typical of Churchward's work. The top feed arrangement with the clacks on each side of the safety-valve mounting, were also his, but a later addition for the photograph shows the engine as she is today, preserved in the Great Western Museum at Swindon after a long and honourable career.

The races of the 1900s, however, ended in tragedy. On July 1, 1906, the Great Western completed, by a short link between Castle Cary and Langport, a new route to the West which gave it a shorter, instead of a longer line than the South Western's. Very early in the morning of the same day, the South Western company's up American boat train, going through the Salisbury curves at most reckless speed, was derailed and smashed to pieces, with heavy loss of life. After this, it was *unlucky* not to stop at Salisbury.

EARLY 20TH CENTURY FRENCH LOCOMOTIVES

Compound expansion in locomotives dated back to the mid 19th century, with Nicholson's experiments at Stratford on the Eastern Counties Railway. But there were no more successful engines of their time than those developed in and after 1886 by de Glehn of the Alsatian Mechanical Construction Company, and du Bousquet, Chief Mechanical Engineer of the Northern Railway of France.

In Figure 405 is a de Glehn-du Bousquet compound 4-4-0 express engine of the series known as 'les Grands Chocolats', built in the late '90s. This, No. 2.175, was one of 20 with 213 lb. boiler pressure. The still more famous de Glehn Atlantics began to appear on the Northern Railway in 1900, and Figure 406 shows one of them heading an English boat express near Etaples. Thirty-five were built, and all carried a working pressure of 227 lb.

407

per sq. in., a very high figure for the period. The older de Glehn engine is also shown near Etaples, with an English mail train. The sixth carriage is a Travelling Post Office with apparatus for mail exchange at Boulogne, which the Calais trains passed without stopping.

Compound locomotives became very common in France, but there were exceptions. The handsome Pacific type express locomotives of the Midi Railway, before its electrification, were of both compound and simple varieties, and one of the latter is shown in Figure 407. They were, further, of very stylish design and, but for the sandboxes before and in rear of the domes, rather suggested British practice in India.

408

HUNGARIAN COMPLEXITIES

Hungarian locomotive design, to other eyes, sometimes bordered on the fantastic. The four-cylinder tandem compound express engine in Figure 408 was nevertheless a very good engine of its day. In the 1890s she would loaf along with the Orient Express. East of Vienna, high speeds were neither encouraged nor expected, and with a much heavier train she could still pull. The arrangement of low-pressure cylinders in front of the high-pressure, with a common piston rod to each pair, did indeed result in a rather substantial movement of reciprocating masses, and to our eyes the engine seems very head-heavy. She provides a late example of the use of Joseph Hall's cranks, with all the 'works' outside frames which were also out-

409
410

side. Right up to the 1930s such engines were still usefully employed on ordinary passenger trains, and in piloting international expresses. A small but characteristic feature of old engines in the Austro-Hungarian Empire was the funnel, just behind the dome, for filling up the boiler when cold. None but a fool left a dead engine full of water on a winter night.

The 2-6-2 passenger engine in Figure 409

FRENCH STEAM LOCOMOTIVE DEVELOPMENT

There has always been something interesting to expect from France, and steam locomotives during the first half of the 20th century have been no exception to the rule. Indeed lasting influence was begun towards the end of the last century in the design of four-cylinder compound engines for fairly heavy, and often very fast passenger trains.

Baudry on the Paris, Lyons and Mediter-

might be described as an untidy version of the Italian type shown on page 293, but it was very useful. The tank engine [410] had a flexible coupled wheelbase on the Lindner system, as well as a trailing bogie, for heavy work over severe curvature. Elegance in design does not seem to have been a major consideration with Hungarian builders; the tank engine is the most nearly shapely of the three.

ranean Railway, too, went in for what might be called, though incorrectly, a form of streamlining. The French terms, however, were honest; his engines were called variously *Locomotives à bec* (Locomotives with beaks) and *Coupe-vent* (Windcutters). One of his second series (*les grosses C*) is shown in Figure 411. There were 120 of them, built during 1899 and 1900.

The splendid compound express engines whose design was worked out on the Northern Railway of France late in the last century by

411
412

290

de Glehn and du Bousquet became exceedingly numerous and were much copied, though it needed a French artist of a driver to show what these great locomotives really could do.

Figure 412 shows one of the superheated four-cylinder simple 4-6-2 (Pacific) type engines of the P.L.M. dating from 1912 and later converted to compound expansion. Last of the class came out in 1925. Of these, 11 were completely rebuilt and modernised in 1940. Figure 413 shows one of these near Vichy with the Thermal Express in the 1960s.

413

414

PRE-1914 EUROPEAN CLASSICS

Three Continental classics of the years before 1914: Danish State Class P No. 907 in Figure 414 exemplified the wide-firebox Atlantic type at its best, the type which in England gave such successful results on both the Great Northern and the London Brighton and South Coast Railways. The Danish engines, however, were four-cylinder compound with the high-pressure cylinders inside, at a higher level so that the connecting rods would clear the leading coupled axle.

A much simpler engine was the Italian State 2-6-2 of class 685, with two cylinders and driving wheels in the middle [415]. The leading coupled axle and the leading carrying one were combined in a Krauss-Helmholtz bogie which, with suitable side-play allowed in the forward side rods, gave the engine the flexibility of an Atlantic with the superior adhesion of a six-coupled. The class was used as a basic

model by the Russians in their Su class, which during the 1920s and '30s became one of the most numerous on the railways of the Soviet Union.

Extraordinarily successful, too, were the four-cylinder 4-6-0 engines first built for the Dutch State Railways by Beyer, Peacock and Company of Manchester in 1913, and subsequently standardised by the Netherlands Railways Company [416]. A later Dutch contribution to the design was the clipper-section tender, giving increased water capacity without disturbing lateral clearances.

Styling of these three engines is worth remark. The Danish and the Italian have austere lines, plus conical fronts and prow-shaped cabs. The Dutch engine largely follows English conventions, with brass-cased boiler-mountings and a copper-capped chimney. The Danish chimney had an outer casing like a ship's funnel, adorned by a band showing the national colours.

415
416

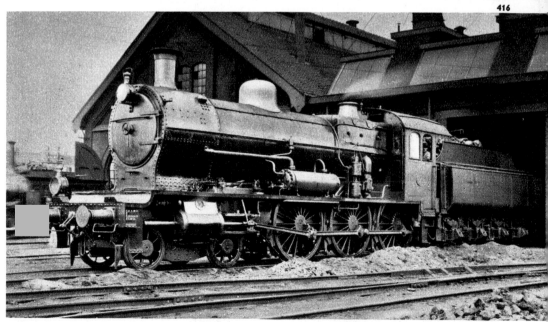

BRITISH VARIETIES, EARLY 20TH CENTURY

During the first quarter of the present century, the immense variety of British steam locomotives was the wonder of many visitors, a circumstance due to the existence of about 120 railway companies until 1922.

Figure 417 shows a Midland Railway goods train hauled by a Kirtley double-framed engine of the 1860s. One of these (M.R. No. 778) was at work from 1869 to 1951. Mainstay of Midland fast passenger service was the Deeley three-cylinder compound, an improved form of Smith's (see page 121). These engines appeared in 1905 [418]; a modified form was still being built by the London Midland and Scottish Railway 20 years after.

Figure 419 shows a very different type, the London, Brighton and South Coast Railway's Atlantic type, which in its turn was closely akin to Ivatt's on the Great Northern. This shows one of the second, superheated variety, waiting to be turned at Brighton in the 1950s.

417

418

SWEDISH LOCOMOTIVES : EARLY 1900s

Swedish railways, especially those owned by companies, but including the State lines, continued in the present century to build steam locomotives with inside cylinders only, while Continental railways had dropped them completely. In this respect, Swedish practice was lined up with British and Irish, though indeed there were many outside-cylinder engines too. Figure 420 shows No. 52 of the Bergslagen Railway, built by Nydqvist and Holm of Trollhättan in 1905. She was one of the earliest Scandinavian locomotives to be equipped with Schmidt's superheater, later employed with one modification or another in locomotives all

421
422

over the world. While the Bergslagen Railway handled heavy iron-ore traffic from Central Sweden to the coast at Gothenburg, passenger trains were relatively light and this, an express engine, was a modest one.

In 1906 the Swedish State Railways began the building of much larger engines for the express passenger trains between Malmö, Gothenburg and the capital. There was a large boiler with superheater, and the unusual combination of the Atlantic type wheel arrangement, bar frames as in America, and inside cylinders [421]. These were the only 4-4-2 engines built by the Swedish State company.

As the use of relatively big locomotives advanced, the 4-6-0 arrangement was most generally adopted, and Figure 422 shows the final version of the Swedish inside-cylindered express locomotive, in No. 17 of the Kalmar Railways, an amalgamation of the Savsjöstrom-Nässjö Railway and the Kalmar-Emmaboda, linking the State Railways Malmö line with the South-east Coast. Observe the equalised bogie suspension and the outside drive to inside valve gear. The engine was built by Motala Works in 1930.

BAVARIAN S. 3/6

In the early 1900s, Anton Hammel, Chief Designer to Maffei's works in Munich, evolved a blending of the best in contemporary European and American locomotive practice, and in July, 1908, the firm delivered to the Royal Bavarian State Railways the first of his classic four-cylinder compound Pacific type locomotives, class S. 3/6. The high-pressure cylinders were inside and inclined, with the low-pressure cylinders horizontal and outside, all driving on to the second coupled axle. Bar frames and a long wide firebox bespoke American influence. There was no more successful design of its time. From 1908 to 1931, 145 examples were built, with but slight variations and detail improvements, most of them by Maffei, though

423
424

the last 18 were built under licence by Henschel of Kassel.

In their day they worked every sort of German passenger train — and not only in Bavaria — from the majestic Rheingold Express to the heavy Sunday excursions between Munich and the mountains. They hauled them quietly and without fuss, climbing the long hill stretches with the same effortless ease as one expected on the great plain west of Munich. Most of them had 6 ft. driving wheels, though

18, built during 1912   13, known to the enginemen as *die Hochbeinigen* ('the Longlegs') had 6 ft. 6 in. One of these has been preserved in the Deutsches Museum, Munich. In form, they were most beautiful examples of the Central European style. One's impression was of a steam locomotive like a work of Mozart transmuted from music to mechanical engineering. The last of them ran until 1965, as shown in Figures 423 and 424. Figure 425 is an official works photograph.

425

NORTH GERMAN LOCOMOTIVES

Oldenburg was a relatively small North German State under the Hohenzollerns' Empire, but it maintained its own railway system quite distinct from the Prussian-Hessian system. The styling of Oldenburg's 4-4-0 express engine No. 210, *Gerda* [426], was indeed Prus-

sian of the early 1900s, to which she belonged, but she was the sort of engine then designed and built for working fast but not unduly heavy passenger trains in fairly flat country. She was a Von Borries two-cylinder compound, and the photograph shows the enormous low-pressure cylinder on the left side. The steam-worked bell in front of the chimney

426

was useful in a land of many road crossings, though not often seen on express engines.

Characteristic of the '20s and '30s is the two-cylinder Pacific shown in Figure 427. Class 01 appeared in 1926 and class 03, which is shown, was very similar apart from slightly lighter axle-loads. The photograph is recent, and shows No. 03.137 based on Minden, with the present Bundesbahn smoke-deflecting shields, chime whistle, and other features.

German State Railway 05.001 [428] was an experimental high speed 4-6-4 locomotive, of which two were built by Borsig of Berlin and underwent trials early in 1935. They were three-cylinder simple, with coupled wheels as large as 7 ft. $6\frac{1}{2}$ in. in diameter and a working pressure of 284 lb. per sq. in. A speed of $125\frac{1}{2}$ m.p.h. was reached with a light test train including a dynamometer car, making a world speed record for steam.

427
428

429

JUNGLE AND DESERT

These two views have not much relationship, but they emphasise the penetration of railway transport into country of widely differing — in fact of almost every conceivable — terrain (excepting the Antarctic Continent which still remains to be conquered by some future pioneer).

The train in Figure 429 is the Golden Blow-

pipe heading southwards from the State of Kelantan to Southern Malaya and Singapore after the line's rehabilitation in 1954. (Ten years later, diesel electrics had replaced the sprightly narrow-gauge Pacifics shown double-heading the train.) Much of the route is through deep jungle. One hears plenty of the jungle animals, but sees little of them, though a monument was once raised to a bull elephant who charged a train in defence of his herd,

430

which was doubtless browsing its way through the overhanging trees. The elephant died, but the offending train was quite spectacularly derailed.

Very different from the Malaysian jungle is the burning-hot centre of Australia. Long ago the Central Australia and the North Australia Railways started out to meet one another, but they have not done so yet. Figure 430 shows a Commonwealth Government train, in steam days, heading north towards Alice Springs. The locomotive is closely akin to the old Queensland C 16 class, but she takes a spare water-tank wagon behind the tender, a practice also adopted on the standard-gauge Trans-Australian Railway before the diesels came. The Central line is on the 3 ft. 6 in. gauge, like up-country lines in South Australia and almost the entire Queensland system, hence the use of 'C 16s'.

LOCOMOTIVES FOR MINOR RAILWAYS

Many firms of locomotive builders have specialised in engines for minor railways, both public and industrial, from the mid-19th century years on, and such construction is well exemplified in the view of Andrew Barclay's erecting shop at Kilmarnock [433]. It is easily dated at 1901 by the new locomotives in later stages of erection and fitting. On the delivery road to the right is the *Lady Margaret*, just completed for the Liskeard and Looe Railway and ready for her long maiden journey to Cornwall. About her are 4-6-0 tank engines Nos. 1 to 4, for the 3 ft. gauge Londonderry and Lough Swilly Railway, over in Ireland.

In Figures 431 and 432 are formal works photographs of two very small engines with ultimate destinations much more remote. The very stylish little 4-4-0 tank engine [431] was built in 1914 by Peckett and Sons of Bristol for the Sarawak Government Railway, which gave her the name *Bulan*. More recent is the 2 ft. 6 in. gauge 2-4-2 tank engine in Figure 432, one of three built during the 1930s by W.G. Bagnall of Stafford for the Mysore State Railways, and having Lentz poppet valves worked by rotary cam gear. The engine has electric headlamps, served by the small steam turbo-generator behind the dome.

431

432

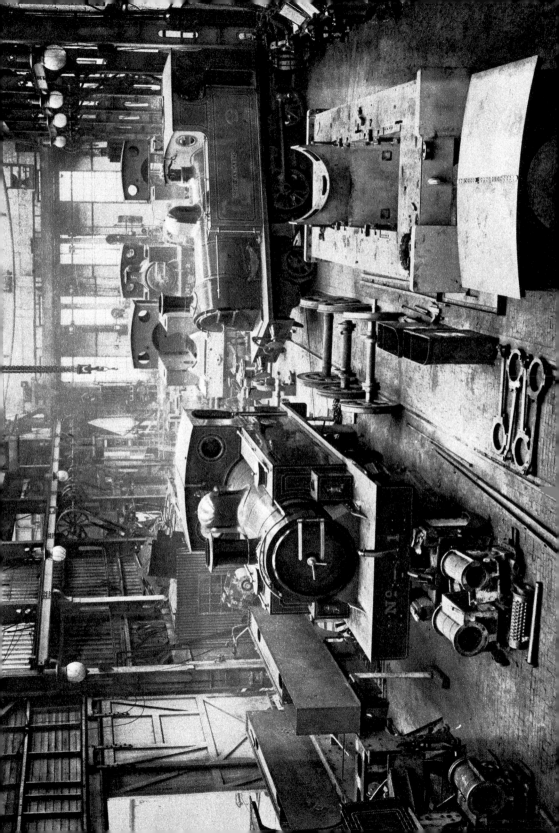

British narrow-gauge railways usually could be relied on to penetrate wild places of singular beauty, and where such lines survive, so will it be found. The Vale of Rheidol Railway from Aberystwyth to Devil's Bridge in Mid-Wales is one of those still with us, sustained by its seasonal tourist value [434]. It is on 1 ft. 11½ in. gauge and was opened on December 22, 1902. Ownership was successively in the hands of the original company, then of the Cambrian Railways, the Great Western Railway, and British Railways Western Region.

Far away in the North Midlands and not, alas, with the Welsh line's longevity, was the beautiful Leek and Manifold Valley Railway in North Staffordshire. Its origins were in local politics. The burghers of Leek wished to divert the custom of the Manifold Valley farmers from Ashbourne to their own town. The railway was built to the 2 ft. 6 in. gauge by E. R. Calthrop, who based his line on Indian light railway practice. Even the locomotives and vehicles were closely akin to those of the Barsi Light Railway in India. The line was opened in the summer of 1904, and a standard gauge connection from the North Staffordshire Railway came in the following year. The N.S.R. maintained and worked the line until it came into the London Midland and Scottish system in 1923. Figure 435 shows one of the first trains with the 2-6-4 tank engine *J. B. Earle* heading a pair of the line's unusually superior coaches, painted in the original canary yellow favoured by Calthrop. This, and the costumes of the period, effectively date the photograph. The line was closed in March, 1934.

435

AUSTRALIAN AND NEW ZEALAND LOCOMOTIVES

Locomotive design in the Southern Hemisphere during the earlier years of this century was very largely British by tradition, but more so in Australia than in New Zealand. A. L. Beattie's class Uc 4-6-0 passenger engine [436] for the New Zealand Government Railways, built in Glasgow by Sharp, Stewart and Company in 1901, anticipated in miniature (on 3 ft. 6 in. gauge) what became general practice on the British railways a couple of decades later. Boiler pressure was 200 lb. per sq. in., and the engines had the final form of Walschaert's valve gear. In the styling however, the bell-mouthed, brass-cased dome recalled much earlier days under the Beattie family, on the London and South Western Railway.

Figure 437: Scottish influence is apparent in the elegant Queensland Government 4-6-2 tank engine, also on 3 ft. 6 in. gauge, built before 1914, and the forerunner of a much more numerous class with a trailing bogie. The slide-valves above the cylinders were a solitary American feature.

There is an appearance of Great Western influence in the New South Wales Government 4-6-0 engines, first built in 1914, and shown by Figure 438 on the Prince of Wales' special train in 1920. The coned third ring of the boiler, in conjunction with a Belpaire firebox, certainly suggested Swindon practice, though not the dome on the second ring. Although in their early days these were rather disappointing engines, front-end modifications greatly improved them. All 35, built between 1914 and 1923, were still in service in the N.S.W.G.R. centenary year, 1955. Latterly they were used in the north of the State, ranging from Newcastle to South Brisbane on the standard-gauge interstate line into Queensland.

436
437

THE MAIL ENGINE

In 1902 India was endowed with a standard Mail Engine, which was to become almost universal and to stay so for a good half century. It was inevitable that government in a country of such diverse peculiarities should love *standards*; human society is like that. The classic Indian mail engine of the 20th century certainly was a very good design, a simple and adequate two-cylinder 4-6-0, an engine more British than the English, and not surprisingly so for its basic design was distinctly Scottish. It came in 1902, and the type was still being built and delivered to the Government of India in 1950, subject to the introduction of superheating and front-end improvements. It was to be found wherever one found inter-city lines of the 5 ft. 6 in. Indian broad gauge, and was initiated by the Bengal-Nagpur Railway's

class G. The B.N.R. *Hercules* is shown in Figure 439.

The 1920s saw a big-engine movement, resulting in the production of new standard mail engines of the Pacific type, in three classes. Figure 440 shows *Lord Minto* of the Eastern Bengal Railway class XB, heading the Darjeeling Mail. The new giants were suspected of unsteadiness, after several accidents of increasing severity, culminating with a terrible derailment near Patna in July, 1937. A special Pacific Locomotive Committee was appointed under Government and prepared a massive report in 1939, which most people soon forgot owing to the outbreak of war. But the life of the old, tried Mail Engines was doubtless prolonged by the alleged misdeeds of the new ones. Figure 441 shows a heavy metre-gauge passenger and mail engine of the Bombay, Baroda and Central India Railway.

440

441

LAST DAYS OF FRENCH STEAM

In some countries, the steam locomotive has departed like a worn-out old horse. In France she has retreated like a lion. The French have long had a way with steam, as they have now with electric traction. These shots from the latter days of French steam convey something of its majesty and dignity to the end. In Figure 442 a Chapelon Pacific, formerly of the Paris-Orleans system, with a Calais-Paris express, roars past Kilometre-post 231 near Etaples. Andre Chapelon's improvements to the front-end and exhaust arrangements would alone entitle him to the High Table in the Hall of Fame.

Figure 443 shows one of the last designs in French steam history, a class S 4-6-4 near Creil with up train No. 175, conveying a through sleeper from Stockholm to Paris. Streamlining is internal, in the design of steam passages, as

442
443

well as being apparent in the outer casing.

Largest of the French steam express locomotives were the 4-8-2 (*La Mountain*,) the oldest examples of which appeared on the old Eastern Railway in the middle 1920s. Figure 444 shows a later version, incorporating both Paris-Lyons-Mediterranean features and the mark of Chapelon from the Orleans. She is leaving Vichy with up express No. 1110 from Clermont-Ferrand. All three photographs date from the early 1960s. It was, indeed, a proud retreat.

444

NEW ZEALAND STEAM

These three illustrations cover a considerable time, but all are characteristic of New Zealand motive power as many have known it. In Figure 445 is one of the special tank engines (class H) for working the old Rimutaka Incline on the Fell system which, in addition to the orthodox drive, had cylinders driving horizontal grip wheels engaged with the raised centre rail on the steep grade sections (1 in 15). No. 201 was one of four built by the Avonside Engine Company, Bristol, in 1875. Two more were built by Neilson of Glasgow in 1886. For years, freight shunting in New Zealand was done by old engines of one sort or another.

In 1930, however, came the class C 2-6-2 engines shown in Figure 446, which were strangely like a miniature version of the Russian class Su passenger engines. Equally capable of handling local goods, they were a first-rate investment. Observe the headlamps at both ends, and the sloping back to the tender, giving good visibility during marshalling operations.

For many years long-distance passenger traffic in New Zealand was handled by Pacific type (4-6-2) engines, of which class AB were the most famous. The 1930s, however, saw the advent of much larger eight-coupled express locomotives (class K), and we now exemplify in Figure 447 one of 16 oil-fired 4-8-2 express engines (class Ja) built by the North British Locomotive Company in 1951. Both British and American influence is apparent in the design. With a working-order weight of 110 tons, and limited axle loads on the 3 ft. 6 in. gauge, class Ja could sustain 50 m.p.h. with a 400-ton train, and the rated maximum load was 900 tons.

445

446
447

448

INFLUENCES IN SPAIN

Spain has ever been the land of contrasts, in her railways as in many other things. Her broad gauge of 5 ft. 6 in. has allowed for generous construction in early as well as recent times. In the 1960s one still can see locomotives over a century old shunting in the yards or heading local goods.

Much French capital went into the old Spanish railway companies, and locomotive design developed along strongly French lines.

The long-boiler outside-cylinder 0-6-0 goods at Cadiz [448] is a typical French Bourbonnais apart from the broad gauge, and beyond her — contrast again — is a modern and doubtless luxurious *Wagons-Lits*.

Owing to 19th century friction between British and Spanish governments far less British capital went into Spanish Railways than into those of South America. The Great Southern of Spain Railway was, however, a British undertaking, mainly an iron ore carrier, and dated from the 1880s. Figure 449, taken

449

in 1962, shows one of the original British loco-motives, a 2-6-0 named *Pulfi* built by Neilson and Company of Glasgow, heading a mixed train from Aguilas at Almendricos. Apart from her Spanish National (RENFE) numbering, and the loss of her original brass dome-casing, she has changed little in her 70-odd years.

Far different yet equally typical of Spain as the ancients is the enormous 4-8-2 in Figure 450, leaving Cordoba with a combined mail and express train from Madrid to Malaga and Algeçiras. The style is still French.

NARROW GAUGE IN SPAIN

While the main-line companies of Spain, which were ultimately amalgamated into RENFE (Red Naçional de los Ferrocarriles Españoles), adopted the broad gauge, many local and mountain lines were built to narrow gauges, particularly in the North. The Santander and Bilbao Railway, taken over by the State in 1962, but still distinct from the National system, has 91 miles of route on metre gauge.

In earlier days British influence was strong,

and Figure 451 shows a train which might, apart from the second carriage, have come straight out of Western Ireland. The 4-4-0 tank engine *Udalla* was built by Dübs and Company of Glasgow. Observe, at the far end of the train, the ticket collector beginning his door-to-door visits along the outside of the train.

In Figure 452 is a larger and more recent engine, of obvious German design, on the metre-gauge Cantabrian Railway, also based on Santander. The articulation of engine and tender is closely akin to that of the ancient Austrian Engerth type illustrated on page 57.

The Malaga Suburban Railways have one of the rarer metre-gauge systems in the South, and Figure 453 shows a train at Malaga. The engine suggests France and the coaches recall the vanished narrow-gauge lines of New England. We have a certain sentimental regard here; one of these was the first train we saw after our ship had had an anxious encounter with an enemy submarine in June, 1940. The engine's majestic whistle was as music after the ship's alarm klaxon!

452

453

ARTICULATED STEAM LOCOMOTIVES

Anatole Mallet's articulated locomotives had their beginnings in France, following his experiments with very small compound tank engines on the Bayonne and Biarritz Railway in 1876. The classic Mallet engine had two sets of coupled wheels, the after group in rigid frames and driven by high-pressure steam, and the forward set in a great bogie with low-

456

pressure cylinders fed through a flexible connection from those in the rear. In Figure 454
is a Mallet tank engine built by Maffei of
Munich for the Swiss Central Railway in 1893,
and now in the Verkehrshaus at Lucerne. The
Spanish broad-gauge (5 ft. 6 in.) engine is one

of a series built by Henschel of Kassel for the
Central Aragon Railway from 1912 onwards
[455]. Giant Mallets appeared in the U.S.A.
from 1902 onwards. That shown in Figure 456
is shown hauling coal on the Nicholas, Fayette
and Greenbriar short line in 1953.

SCANDINAVIAN VARIETY

Iron-ore traffic is the lifeblood of several Swedish railways, and this is certainly the case with the Grängesberg Oxelösund Railway, which is sufficiently tied up with the iron industry to have escaped nationalisation. In its days of steam haulage, it was said that the Locomotive Superintendent, Harry Johnson, was nearly at his wits' end to muster some passenger engines which the Traffic Department would not press into ore haulage. Hence the high-wheeled 2-4-4 tank engine shown in Figure 457. The design was a late development of one produced by Krauss and Company of Munich at the end of last century, and had a Helmholtz bogie containing the leading carrying wheels and leading coupled wheels,

457
458

with an ordinary Adams bogie at the rear. Only the middle axle was rigid. With fairly light passenger trains, the engines did well, while nobody in his senses would have put one on an ore train.

Three-cylinder locomotives were rare abroad, though much used in Great Britain. Figure 458 shows, however, a three-cylinder express engine built by Nydqvist and Holm for the Bergslagen Railway in 1927. The class was on the Swedish-Norwegian international trains between Gothenburg and Mellerud until the line was electrified in 1939.

2-8-4 express engines have been rare. Austria produced the first, then in 1935 the Norwegian State Railways adopted them, with four-cylinder compound expansion, for the Dovre line from Dombos to Trondhjem. One of the second of three series, with double blast-pipe and chimney, is shown in Figure 459. The original engine was named *Dovregubben* (The Dovre Giant).

459

MIDLAND RAILWAY

The Midland in the hills: for more than a century, steam hoisted the Bristol-Gloucester-Birmingham traffic up the 1 in 37.7 incline from Bromsgrove to Blackwell in the Lickey Hills, opened in 1840. For many years it was an ordinary experience to see a train going up with four locomotives; two express engines in front and two tank engines behind.

The Midland company in its latter years was regarded as a 'small-engine railway', and indeed its solitary giant — by contemporary British standards — was the four-cylinder 10-coupled banking engine built for the Lickey Incline in 1919. Known to many as 'Big Emma', she worked until she was worn out, ust before the coming of diesels. Two aspects of her massive front are shown in Figures 460 and 461, both taken on a chill winter evening at Bromsgrove when she was new. Her imposing, almost American, headlamp was also unique in British practice, and was intended to save her from getting into mischief when she came up the bank on a moonless and dirty night.

As a Midland contrast, one of R. M. Deeley's celebrated three-cylinder compound express engines is shown, in London Midland and Scottish days, heading a Manchester to London express near Chee Tor amongst the Derbyshire limestone [462]. The engine is unaltered from her Midland state, but most of the coaches are of later design. A solitary Midland Railway clerestoried brake-third brings up the rear.

460

461
462

FEEDWATER HEATERS

Steam locomotive feedwater heaters and their necessary pumps are over a century old — Joseph Beattie made uncommonly effective ones on the London and South Western — but their universal application never came about. During the 1920s and '30s, however, their use was to become widespread both in Continental Europe and in North America. English designers seemed to be at a loss as to where to put them. America and Austria, among many others, found it quite easy. Figure 463 shows a Central Vermont 2-10-4 at St. Albans, Vt., in 1946, and Figure 464 an Austrian Federal 4-8-0 at Graz, Styria, in 1963. There have ever been a Golden Rule and an Inflexible Condition. The feedwater must not come in contact with the exhaust steam that warms it, or it will absorb impurities. Secondly, there *must* be a pump, for an ordinary injector will not work with hot feedwater.

463

465
466

AMERICANS ABROAD

In the great days of steam traction, British, German and American locomotive builders jostled one another in the supply of motive power to non-industrial countries, and the American lure was a good, cheap engine that could be bought, as someone said, 'off the peg'. All the same, the mighty Pennsylvania Rail-road itself might not have produced a more stately and patrician-looking American pre-1914 Pacific than that shown in Figure 465. She belonged to the Japanese-owned South Manchuria Railway which, on standard gauge, linked the broad-gauge, Russian-owned Chinese Eastern Railway with the railways of China proper. The C.E.R./S.M.R. break-of-gauge was at Changchun.

467

Far away and far otherwise is the subject of Figure 466. Scarcely known to the rest of the world is the little, dark, fear-stalked republic of Haiti, but the Americans found a market for locomotives there. This one is a little 2-6-0 on the 3 ft. 6 in. gauge National Railways of Haiti. Observe the outside frames and balance cranks.

This is not Haiti's only railway system.

There is a 2 ft. 6 in. gauge outfit with the almost incredible title *Chemins de fer de la Plaine du Cul-de-Sac*. Both systems have headquarters at Port au Prince. By comparison, Figure 467 is of almost stodgy orthodoxy. There is fairly obvious German parentage in the sloped-tank dock shunter of the Mozambique Railways below the cranes of Lourenço Marques.

BRITISH LOCOMOTIVES FOR EXPORT

From the time of the Stephensons, steam locomotives have been one of Great Britain's major exports, and Vulcan Foundry of Newton-le-Willows began in the 1830s under the Tayleur family, with Stephenson sponsorship. In Figure 468 is a standard-gauge 4-8-4 passenger engine built by this firm for the Chinese National Railways in 1935, a remarkable example of a really big engine with relatively light axle-loads, simple in design, suited to the rather decrepit permanent way of a country already torn by war. The 4-8-2 engine in Figure 469, five years older, was built for the Nigerian Railways, and exemplified what could be done for a 3 ft. 6 in. gauge line fairly lightly laid.

Coming forward to 1946, when much of Europe, and particularly Europe's railways, lay in wreckage, we see the first of the British 'Liberation' engines, not yet fully assembled though nearly so, under steam in the Vulcan Foundry yard [470]. This one, we believe, went to Jugoslavia. There were to be many hundreds of them in Eastern Europe, where at that time a locomotive in working order was a treasure above price. Unassumingly stands the Egyptian suburban tank engine in Figure 471. In pre-diesel days, her kind worked the local services of Lower Egypt, and not only from British works. Some were built by Breda of Milan.

468
469

ERECTING SHOPS

Erection of steam locomotives — their assembly from parts made in other shops — always followed the same pattern. In Figure 472, showing part of the great and famous erecting shops at Swindon in the 1950s, two machines are drilling holes in the assembled main frames and smokebox saddle of a Class 3 2-6-2 tank engine (1952). On the right, a frame lies on its side with the horn-blocks attached. Wheels and axles already finished wait for the nearly final stage when the engine will be lifted on to them. Above the right-hand drilling machine are two fully assembled radial trucks, but boiler, cylinders and motion are as yet elsewhere.

In Figure 473, a British Railways Class 6 Pacific-type passenger engine is approaching the stage at which it will be lifted bodily by the overhead gantry cranes, to be lowered on to its wheels on another of the shop roads. Cylinders, part of the valve gear, and the injectors are already mounted. Observe the forward and after coupling rod, which must wait for the wheels, neatly laid on the wood-block floor. This scene was taken in the erecting shop at Crewe, also in the early '50s.

473

STEAM TURBINE LOCOMOTIVES

Almost as soon as the electric locomotive had been proved practical in service, there were attempts to produce one which could carry its own power-station on its back (the principle of the modern large diesel-electric engine). Heilmann produced such a thing in France (with a reciprocating steam engine) at the end of the last century, and Ramsay did the same with a steam turbine in Scotland a decade later.

Both were terribly cumbersome machines, though with the virtue of originality. The remains of the first Ramsay engine were incorporated in a straight steam turbine locomotive, the Reid-MacLeod engine, early in the 1920s. R. B. Haddon's extremely rare photograph [474] shows this on a trial run between Glasgow and Edinburgh in April, 1927. It had been exhibited at the British Empire Exhibi-

474
475

328

tion in 1924. In the picture, the condenser end is leading, as it was intended to do, and the very inadequate boiler (a legacy of the first Ramsay engine, like the motor bogies) is vehemently blowing off in rear. The idea that a turbine locomotive must condense, like a marine engine, was hard to discard; at the same time MacLeod, a marine engineer, had little idea of the enormous demands made by any railway locomotive on its boiler.

Ljüngström in Sweden made further experiments with the condensing turbine locomotive, with sufficiently good results for Beyer, Peacock and Company to build a large version which underwent trials on the London Midland and Scottish Railway in 1930. The boiler, as well as bunker and tanks, was on the tender. Figure 475 shows the general arrangement; Figure 476 shows the engine, from the condenser end, leaving St. Pancras, London.

476

477

478

NON-CONDENSING TURBINE LOCOMOTIVES

Though admirable in theory, and essential for steam navigation, the condenser was an almost unmitigated nuisance in land transport. The Russians used it to a limited extent in waterless country, with ordinary reciprocating locomotives, and the Germans did likewise when invading Eastern European territory where the water-supply had been disrupted. Ere that, Ljüngström in Sweden produced non-condensing turbine locomotives with much happier results, though national policy was already committed to general electrification. Figure 477, from a photograph taken at Eskilstuna in 1936, shows three non-condensing turbine locomotives which satisfactorily worked the heavy iron-ore trains of the Grängesberg-Oxelösund railway from the Bergslag to the Baltic Coast before the line's ultimate electrification. The first of them appeared in 1932,

and could shift 1,831 tons up a gradient of 1 in 100, though it was not a really big engine. Compared with the orthodox type, of closely comparable dimensions, fuel saving was reckoned at 10 per cent. per h.p. hr. As will be seen, the turbines were mounted forward, with the gears and jackshaft drive.

In the early 1930s the London Midland and Scottish Railway applied the principle, as in Sweden, to a standard basic design, the first of Sir William Stanier's Pacifics [478]. The engine worked successfully for many years. At last, under the dead hands of war, aftermath and change, she was reduced in the interests of standardisation to the reciprocating form of her half-sisters, and in 1952 had a tragic end in the Harrow collision. Figure 479 shows the non-condensing turbine locomotive expanded to maximum dimensions by the Pennsylvania Railroad, a courageous essay, though steam was already dying in the United States. Observe the roller bearings to the side rods.

L. M. S. PACIFICS

On the London Midland and Scottish Railway during the 1930s Sir William Stanier brought off one of those locomotive revolutions which periodically distinguished the history of railways. Previously, under Sir Henry Fowler (a Midland man who had become Chief Mechanical Engineer by right of seniority) the railway had never quite succeeded in getting away from the traditions of its predecessor companies. There was still intense jealousy between Crewe (London and North Western) and Derby (Midland) with Horwich (Lancashire and Yorkshire) in between and liking neither.

Stanier came from the Great Western, and brought some of the ways of Swindon, as well as his own way, which was considerable. He brought Great Western ideas on boiler design and front-end arrangement, with most profitable results. At the same time he was prepared to allow a high degree of superheating, whereas the Churchward school in which he had been brought up at Swindon stuck tenaciously to relatively slight superheating surface.

The results were famous. The first Stanier four-cylinder Pacifics began with *Princess Royal* in 1933; later development included most importantly the provision of a still larger boiler. Drive was divided between the first and second coupled axles in both cases, but the larger engines had the outside cylinders over the bogie instead of in rear of it. Stanier's streamlined version of his Pacific is illustrated on page 352. Of the large, non-streamlined variety, the *City of Lichfield* is shown in Figure 480, heading the northbound Royal Scot near Harthope on the climb from Beattock to the summit of the West Coast Route in the Southern Uplands of Scotland. The time of the picture is of British Railways. All through the war the engines had been performing prodigies with the immense, crowded trains which service journeys, added to restrictions on ordinary facilities, had inevitably entailed.

H. G. Ivatt, son of H. A. Ivatt of the Great Northern, succeeded Stanier as Chief Mechanical Engineer of the London Midland and Scottish. One of his slightly modified versions of the Stanier Pacifics, *City of Stoke on Trent*, is shown in Figure 481. These beautiful engines were the most powerful steam express locomotives ever used in Britain.

481

THE BEYER-GARRATT IN AFRICA

Through the latter days of steam, South and East Africa have been the land of the Beyer-Garratt locomotive. Figure 482 shows one at the summit of the Kenya and Uganda main line, 9,136 ft. above sea level. The open downland scarcely suggests that this point is just two miles north of the Equator.

482

483

BEYER–GARRATT LOCOMOTIVES

The Beyer-Garratt locomotive takes its name from Herbert W. Garratt, the original patentee, and the famous firm of Beyer, Peacock and Company, which acquired the rights. Each locomotive unit consists of two distinct engines, practically identical in arrangement and weight, supporting through pivots a heavy girder frame which carries the boiler. The latter can consequently be made very large indeed, and the whole comprises a locomotive of great flexibility coupled with light axle loads and tremendous haulage capacity. The earliest examples, however, were small engines. First of all was a little double 0-4-0 for a light 2 ft. gauge line out of Zeehan on the Tasmanian Government Railways in 1909, and in 1911 a slightly more powerful one was built for the Darjeeling-Himalayan Railway in northern India.

The great days of the type, when the giant Beyer-Garratt arrived, were from the 1920s to the late '50s. They were built for lines over much of the world, excepting North America which clung steadfastly to the Mallet articulated locomotive. Russia invested in a solitary, very large sample engine in 1933 but thereafter stuck to orthodox types.

The greatest field of the Beyer-Garratt was in Africa, above all in the Union of South Africa and in the East African countries. Examples occur again and again in our pages, and they have been used on all sorts of heavy traffic, passenger and goods. Figure 483 shows the boiler unit of the *Mount Meru*, one of the numerous examples on the East African Railways, lifted clear of the engine units in the shops at Nairobi. Clearly visible is the front pivot. The weight of the boiler unit, when in position, is balanced, giving even distribution of weight, by the tanks and bunkers.

484

ENGINES OF ALL WORK

Sir William Stanier's 6 ft. mixed traffic 4-6-0 locomotives for the London Midland and Scottish Railway, dating from the middle 1930s, were what modern commercial jargon might have described as a good buy. They had much in common, but with improvements, with the Great Western 'Hall' class of about a decade earlier, on which Stanier, then on the G.W.R., had worked under C.B. Collett.

Right through the war years one could find them anywhere from Caithness to Dorset, and in the last years of steam's retreat, which were the middle '60s, they were holding a substantial part of the last *redoubt* north of the Thames. In Figure 484 one of them is heading a Glasgow-Inverness express in September, 1950, north of Carr Bridge. The girder culvert below the engine stands in the place of an arch, over the Baddengorm Burn, which was swept away by mountain floods while a train was crossing it on June 5, 1914, killing five passengers. In a country of flood and falling rock, this was the Highland Railway's worst accident.

Figure 485 shows the arrival of the Irish Mail from Holyhead at Euston in May, 1948. Figure 486 shows the arrival of the English Mail at Manorhamilton, Co. Leitrim, in the summer of 1947. Both such scenes have vanished. The old Euston station is down, and the Sligo, Leitrim and Northern Counties Railway is no more. The engines at Euston are L.M.S. Royal Scots as rebuilt by Sir William Stanier with taper boilers and double blastpipes and chimneys. That at Manorhamilton is the old Beyer, Peacock 0-6-4 tank engine *Hazlewood*, which, dating from the 1890s, had long survived a spectacular wrecking during the Irish Troubles.

PLATE XXVI Diesels over Africa.

485

486

PLATE XXVII Canadian Pacific diesel;
the tail end.

337

ZENITH OF AMERICAN STEAM

In 1929, with depression ahead but unsuspected, we see the American train of tradition at its zenith. The Great Northern Railway's Empire Builder stands in the Union Station at St. Paul, behind a spanking new 4-8-4 two-cylinder simple engine [487]. For all her great size she is the classic American locomotive, bar-framed and without needless complexities, though with her working parts made as accessible as possible.

Her enormous firebox is now supported on four wheels, where once two, and before that the trailing coupled axle, had been sufficient. Her sandbox is now much bigger than the dome, but the two still occupy the same relative positions. The tender is of a sort which gained favour in the Western States particu-larly, during the 1900s, with a cylindrical tank and the coal-bunker above and ahead of this, but it is fully in proportion with the engine, and carried on two six-wheeled bogies. The cars behind the tender, massive in steel down to the furniture, still exemplify the Pullmanesque, clerestoried form evolved by Pullman and Sessions in the latter part of last century, and on the third can be seen the cistern and chimney of the Baker heater, first real successor, in North America, of the old pot-bellied car-stove.

From the twilight of steam in the States [488] comes the shot of a Northern Pacific 2-8-2, class W 3, patiently standing with a freight at Marshall, Washington, while the semaphore holds her against an eastbound passenger train still on the single-track section ahead. The year is 1950.

487

CANADIAN PACIFIC: FIELD HILL

Field Hill is the deceptively gentle name of the eastbound incline of the Canadian Pacific Railway over the Kicking Horse Pass between Field, British Columbia, and Stephen, on the Divide between British Columbia and Alberta. The respective heights of these places above sea level are 4,076 ft. and 5,332 ft. The distance by road is 10 miles, and that road is mainly on the formation of the original C.P.R. line, which had a ruling gradient of 1 in 23. In the present century this was cut out by a three-level approach with lower and upper spiral tunnels on the northern and southern sides of the Yoho Valley respectively. The ruling gradient is 1 in 50, and the spiralling has cut out the primitive and troublesome switchbacking (running in and out of dead ends) of early days here as in other parts of North America. The present rail distance from Field to Stephen is thus increased by three miles.

Figure 489 shows an eastbound freight train, headed by a 5,800 class 2-10-2 steam locomotive, probably in the late 1920s. The train has just emerged from the upper portal of the upper spiral tunnel. Above it are mingled timber and screes from Cathedral Crags (10,081 ft., forming the northern bastion of Cathedral Mountain) while beyond and above is the mass of Mount Stephen (10,495 ft.).

Steam traction has vanished from the Canadian Pacific Railway, indeed from all Canada now, but the splendour of steam, above all on Field Hill, will be long remembered. In Figure 490 is one of the T.I.a. class 2-10-4 locomotives formerly used on the mountain section between Calgary and Revelstoke, which has Field Hill roughly midway. The trailing bogie included a booster engine for assistance on starting, and with this the locomotive had a tractive effort of 89,200 lb. Oil was the fuel. Observe also the totally enclosed cab and the hood to the stack for tunnel working.

490

491
492

CANADA: FROM STEAM TO DIESEL

These three views taken by Dr. Philip Hastings quite poignantly evoke the latter days of steam in Eastern Canada, just after the war, when industry, hitherto committed to military supplies, was ready to complete the diesel revolution in North America. Figure 491 shows a train approaching Montreal from the United States, headed by one of the Delaware and Hudson 'elephant-eared' Pacifics, No. 607. The train consists of an express car and a baggage car, two coaches and an air-conditioned Pullman of rather early vintage, and it is crossing the St. Lawrence River near La Salle, Quebec province.

On a grander scale [492] is the passing of a Canadian National express from Quebec to

493

Montreal, with 4-8-4 locomotive No. 6175, and an eastbound freight train behind No. 6202 just east of Rosalie Junction, Quebec. This is not double track with left-hand running, so characteristic of Great Britain and France. The freight train is on a passing siding, and has just got on the move as the passenger train roars west.

Figure 493 is a nostalgic, now vanished, Canadian winter scene. It shows the Farnham branch train, behind an old 4-6-0, leaving Stanbridge, Quebec. The make-up ('consist' is the North American word) is simple: one freight car, one baggage-and-express, and one gaslit wooden coach whose clerestory lights are visible through the vestibule over the conductor's head. This and the bridge scene were taken in 1948; the 'meet' in 1946.

494

GÖLSDORF'S COMPOUND LOCOMOTIVES

Carl Gölsdorf of Austria, who first became famous at the end of last century, was one of the great designers for steam, of the same calibre as Churchward in England, du Bousquet in France and Hammel in South Germany, all contemporaries. His compound locomotives, which made him famous, were free of several bothersome complexities which so often distinguished the application of compound expansion. They started steaming 'simple', i.e. with high-pressure steam in both, or all four cylinders, by admission through a receiver between the high- and low-pressure sides, and then *went over automatically* to compound expansion as the engine accelerated, Figure 494 shows one of the later, four-cylinder arrangements of Gölsdorf's compounding on a 2-10-0 express engine designed for mountain sections.

In use of the taper boiler, Gölsdorf is known to have been influenced by the work of his friend and colleague, Churchward of the Great Western in England. Figure 495 belongs to the 1930s, and shows an Austrian 2-8-4 express engine leaving the international bridge at Passau (observe both Austrian, nearest, and German semaphores). Like the 2-6-4 express engines of Gölsdorf's time, it has an Adams bogie under the firebox, while the leading wheels and first pair of coupled wheels are combined in a Krauss-Helmholtz bogie.

Figure 496, while it shows a 4-6-4 Austrian tank engine of the same period, is the more interesting in that it shows the long, depressed exhaust ejector, in place of the orthodox chimney, which was the outward mark of Dr. Giesl-Gieslingen's longitudinal arrangement of the blast, greatly improving boiler efficiency.

CHURCHWARD AND COLLETT

There were no more successful locomotives of their period than those built by, and according to the principles of, George Jackson Churchward on the Great Western Railway. His most famous were the four-cylinder simple express engines with divided drive, originating in 1906. He believed in liberal boilers with adequate working pressures — 225 lb. per sq. in. was his standard — with long valve travel and plenty of freedom in the steam passages. He adapted the deep, narrow piston ring from motor engineering. Churchward's *Shooting Star* [497] was one of a famous class which easily exceeded 100 m.p.h. on trials.

C. B. Collett continued Churchward's practice after 1921; the old man, though officially

497

498

retired, continued to live opposite Swindon Works until he was killed by a train in 1933. Ten years before that, under Collett, the celebrated Castle class had appeared, and in their time these were to haul, for a spell, the fastest regular train in the world. *Restormel Castle* is shown in Figure 498, and the original engine, *Caerphilly Castle*, is now in the Science Museum, South Kensington.

Largest of what might have been called the Star Family — in size, that is — were Collett's King class of 1927. *King Charles I* is the second engine in Figure 499. Double-heading was extremely rare on the Great Western Railway, but was tolerated on the severe gradients of the South Devon main line between Newton Abbot and Plymouth. The leading engine shown was one of Collett's Grange class.

499

500

CLASSIC GREAT WESTERN

In locomotive styling, as in many other things, the Great Western Railway was a law unto itself. For more than a century, G.W.R. locomotives were not only unlike anything else in Europe; they were unlike anything else in Great Britain and Ireland. To the last the styling was what we would call *Victorian* — with exuberant curves and plenty of highly polished brass and copper. Once, in a broadcast discussion, we asked Sir William Stanier whether there was a convention that Great Western engines, however recent, should look

Victorian; that they should look like William Dean's work in the late Victorian Era. '*Dean*?' he barked. 'Gooch! It was traditional!' And we, because we loved the Great Western engines, heard that splendid bark gladly.

More than 30 years divide the time of these views, and the older photograph of the two [500] shows the more recent design, that of *King George V*, splendidly posed — for so it was — in a portal of Middle Hill Tunnel. (Lord! If only all British railways had been conceived and brought forth on those spacious lines!) In its latter days the portal looks a little threadbare, with bricks showing through the

348

rendering. There was no trouble about the decoration of *fasces* on each side of the great arch. The long unborn Mussolini had not given them a political significance, and nobody had ever heard of a *fascist*. Those *fasces* were an ancient emblem of orderly policing, which everybody expected on a railway, and they looked nice on a tunnel portal. Anyway, they made a picturesque change from the Walter Scott Gothic and North Western Italianate on other lines.

Figure 501 is from a photograph taken in May, 1958, though the design of the Castle class locomotive dated back to 1923. The British Railways lion on the tender alone suggests that this was no longer a Great Western locomotive. She was still painted in the traditional style. The carriages too, though recent, were likewise in the old G.W.R. 'tea-brown and cream'. The train was the Torbay Express, and the scene was the famous sea-wall between Dawlish (in background) and Teignmouth. The line had been made originally for broad-gauge single track. Apart from the enlargement of the tunnels, it was not so difficult, in the early years of the present century, to enlarge it to take two standard-gauge tracks. The Great Western was a majestic railway.

BOSTON AND MAINE RAILROAD

Both these views were taken in New England during the summer of 1949. The passenger train [502] below Cherry Mountain, New Hampshire, was a local of the Boston and Maine Railroad, headed by a light Pacific of the Canadian Pacific Railway. Such often helped out the Boston and Maine on local runs south of the Canadian border, and another C.P.R. engine, 2-8-0 No. 3518, is shown in Figure 503, this time indeed helping an Alco diesel of the Boston and Maine company with a train of frozen beef from Montreal to Boston.

The view shown is near Newport, Vermont.

Even in our youth, the Boston and Maine Railroad had a name for waywardness and ancientry — a sort of American South Eastern and Chatham, it seemed to be — and in much more recent times it earned a particular reputation for intentionally scaring off unwanted passenger traffic by the provision of shabby cars with unusually insolent conductors. But not even the diesel train could save the rags of passenger service on most of the northern New England lines. The automobile and the fast bus inherited what they had not already taken.

502

BRITISH STREAMLINERS, 1930 s

In the middle 1930s the London and North Eastern Railway was contemplating a special high-speed service between London and the Tyneside, using trains on the lines of the Flying Hamburger, a light two-car diesel unit, in Germany. Heavy user on the East Coast Route demanded something more substantial, and Sir Nigel Gresley gave the road to steam after all. Oliver Bulleid, later of the Southern Railway, had much to do with it, including the use of the aerofoil shape in streamlining externally the basic steam locomotive.

On a trial run of the Silver Jubilee train, September 27, 1935, the engine *Silver Link* maintained an average of 100 m.p.h. for 43 miles, with maximum speeds of 112.5 m.p.h., twice. The train began a special fast service between London and Newcastle on September 30. In 1937 such fast steam services were begun between London and Glasgow with the Coronation Scot train, and London and Edin-burgh with the Coronation, West Coast and East Coast Routes respectively. For the former, Sir William Stanier had designed the largest and most powerful passenger locomotives yet seen in Great Britain, of the Pacific type like Gresley's. The streamlining was the result of wind-tunnel experiments.

On June 29, 1937 a maximum speed of 114 m.p.h. was attained on trial by the Coronation Scot. Figure 504 shows the train running south on Dillicar Troughs in 1939. (Compare with *Greater Britain*, Plate XII, facing p. 96.) The *Silver Fox*, one of Gresley's engines on the London and North Eastern, is shown in Figure 505 with the Flying Scotsman near Hatfield in 1935, the year of her building. A later example of the class, the *Mallard*, showed 126 m.p.h. briefly on the dynamometer chart, on a brake-test run on July 3, 1938. Speeds in the 120s represent the maxima obtainable, or likely to be obtained, with the orthodox reciprocating steam locomotive. The *Mallard* is now preserved at Clapham Museum.

504

PLATE XXIX *City of Los Angeles* passing through Echo Canyon, Utah.

505

ELECTRICITY AND DIESEL TAKE OVER

Throughout North America, the oil engine is almost omnipotent today, with electric traction allowed existence in limited areas. This has held its own on the eastern lines of the mighty Pennsylvania Railroad, whose superb Broadway Limited is shown [506] on the first lap, through New Jersey, of its run from New York to Chicago, headed by a 4,800 h.p. GG-1 locomotive. The Pennsylvania has 661 miles of route electrified in the East, mostly on the 11,000 Volt single-phase system at 25 cycles, though 650 Volt d.c. with third-rail contact is used on city lines.

Figure 507 is from a photograph taken in 1948, before the disappearance of steam, and showing an old Canadian National Pacific running off her train on a reversing triangle while, on the right, a Bo-Bo electric locomotive moves in to take the train on the last five miles to Montreal Central Station, passing through

506

PLATE XXX Louisville & Nashville diesel freight locomotive.

Mount Royal Tunnel on its brief journey.

Lastly [508] is a posed photograph of three phases in locomotive practice on the Great Northern Railway, U.S.A. On the right is a 2-8-8-2 oil-burning Mallet steam locomotive; on the left is a 5,000 h.p. single-unit electric locomotive, formerly used through the Cas-cade Tunnel. Between them is a four-unit diesel-electric (5,400 combined horsepower), successor to both the electric and the steam engine. The electric locomotive's pantographs reach for vanished contact wires, but the great water-towers, landmarks of the steam era, still stand defiantly beyond the engines.

507

508

FROM STEAM TO DIESEL
ON THE UNION PACIFIC I

Though fast diesel-hauled passenger trains had been running in the United States since the early '30s, it was after the war that the great transformation took place, culminating in the early '60s with the disappearance of the mighty steam locomotives which, not only to Americans, but to much of the world, were even more a part of America than the Manhattan skyline.

The double-headed train in Figure 509 was photographed on the Union Pacific Railroad

510

in June, 1948. Figure 510 shows the *Grand Canyon*, still steam-hauled in 1952, and still with an open-platform observation car. The cars still follow classic Pullman tradition. Air-conditioning ducts have been housed in the angles of the clerestories, a clever artifice of the '30s, when, having tasted air-conditioning, the American public immediately demanded it, and existing Pullmans adapted as quickly as possible.

In Plate XXIX, facing page 352, is one of the dieselled heirs of that No. 119 which met *Jupiter* at Promontory Point in 1869. Steam has gone, and so have the traditional clerestoried cars. But the logical conclusion of the latter, the 'dome car', has arrived, in a 15-car train headed by a three-unit diesel-electric locomotive. The train is the *City of Los Angeles*, and the place is Echo Canyon, east of Ogden, Utah.

356

FROM STEAM TO DIESEL
ON THE UNION PACIFIC II

On the Union Pacific Railroad, as on several other North American systems, such as the Norfolk and Western, steam died hard. Use of mechanical stokers made possible the operation of very large steam locomotives, akin to the originally French semi-articulated Mallet design with the forward group of wheels pivoted, but with a simple expansion only, all cylinders receiving high-pressure steam from the enormous boiler rigidly mounted on the after frames.

The Challenger class, 4-6-6-4, shown in Figure 511, appeared in 1936, was used for both freight and heavy passenger haulage. The 'Big Boys' of 1941, 4-8-8-4, were among the very largest steam locomotives ever built, and were for long-distance freight haulage [512]. Observe the turnout of the front end, with the first set of wheels, in relation to the boiler and the rear set while standing on a sharp curve. It is demonstrated further by the marker flags.

511

512

Even on the Union Pacific, steam retreated soon after the proving of these magnificent engines. Yet the railway still showed its individuality; while elsewhere the diesel was all conquering, the U.P. has become the first railroad in the world to use gas-turbine locomotives in regular, ordinary service.

An earlier development was that gas turbines were shown to be a practical proposition, for certain power purposes, during the war years of 1939—45, and Figure 513 shows a heavy freight train in the West, headed by a double-unit machine. The third component is, surprisingly to some, a tender.

513

EVENING STAR

When, at the beginning of the 1950s, people admired the new standard steam locomotives of British Railways, both out on the road and proudly displayed at the Festival of Britain in 1952, many indignantly denied that these provided the theme of steam's swan-song in Great Britain. The new locomotives were the result of comparative trials between those of the former railway companies, conducted all over

the country, and their design was claimed to be a symposium of the best that had gone before.

Yet in 1960 British Railways built their last steam locomotive, a standard 10-coupled heavy goods [514]. It was fitting that Swindon Works, the classic Great Western establishment founded by Gooch and Brunel, should have done the job. The name, *Evening Star*, was doubly appropriate. It was the same as that of one of the first Great Western locomotives, the Stephenson 'Stars', and it conveyed all too

358

plainly the twilight of steam. In the first half of 1965, *Evening Star* was condemned. Though she had been the last steam locomotive to be built for our lines, she was not destined to be the last in service. This was a good, simple, straightforward yet powerful design, and one feels that it was an economic blunder that, if they were thus soon doomed, such engines should have been built at all. There were, already, enough good steam engines.

By way of contrast, Figure 515 shows the New Face on the old Great Western line — that of a diesel-hydraulic locomotive heading the down Bristolian just west of Box Tunnel.

514

515

WOOD, COAL AND OIL IN FINLAND

Finland's State Railway system dates from the days when the country was a Russian Grand-Duchy, having been before that a relic of Charles XII's Swedish Empire. Railway development was consequently on the Russian 5 ft. broad gauge, but even in the days of the Tsars technical practice was Scandinavian rather than Russian.

In recent times we have had an example of a railway system which, unlike those of Scandinavia proper, has made no use of electric traction. In the early 1960s it was still possible to see wood-fired steam locomotives and diesels on adjacent tracks. Figure 516 shows a woodburning passenger locomotive of class Hk2 with her pleasantly aromatic fuel piled high on the short tender. The general design dates back to the latter years of Tsarist Russia, though in those days the class were coal-burners, and used on the rather leisurely expresses between Helsinki and the Baltic ports.

In Figure 517 is a Pacific-type coal-burning express engine, as used on the heaviest passenger service until the coming of both diesels and diesel motor- and trailer-coach trains [518]. Noteworthy in the larger steam locomotive is the use of roller bearings to the cranks and side rods. The general aspect is markedly Swedish.

516

517

THE TRANSITIONAL PHASE IN AMERICA

When, in 1932 the Union Pacific Railroad put on the *City of Salina* as a special fast train, one of the first diesel expresses in the world, many people regarded it somewhat as a stunt, as a much elongated, unusually comfortable, articulated bus on rails. The Burlington Route's Zephyrs and the Rock Island Rockets, which followed on neighbour lines, really began to attract attention and so, still more, did the Illinois Central Company's Green Diamond, which made its inaugural run from Chicago to St. Louis on May 17, 1936 [519].

But during the infancy of diesels, including the war years, the enormous steam locomotive remained a characteristic feature of American life and landscape. Of Dr. Philip Hastings'

two views, Figure 520 conjures the face of the American Mallet — the genuine Mallet in this case, having the leading set of coupled wheels driven by low-pressure cylinders with slide valves on top — classic American. The formidable array of Westinghouse pumps on the front of the smokebox reminds us that America was the pioneer of air brakes, beginning about 1869. This was a Chesapeake and Ohio engine shown running in West Virginia in 1953.

Figure 521 shows the front end of a Delaware and Hudson Pacific near Fort Ticonderoga, N.Y., in 1950. The design was pure American, but the flared stack was markedly English (Great Central) and the smoke-deflecting shields were of German origin.

AMERICAN RIGHT-OF-WAY

More from the American present and not-too-distant past. Figure 522 shows the Empire Builder on the Great Northern Railway crossing the Rockies in Montana with a three-unit diesel. From the days of steam comes Figure 523, showing a Baltimore and Ohio coal train, headed and banked by Mallets in the 1920s, and in Figure 524 a Milwaukee extra-freight, headed by an old Pacific, crossing the Union Pacific viaduct over the Spokane River in 1951.

522
523

PLATFORM-SIDE VIEWS

There is a certain charm in the odd snapshot, taken on the spur of the moment at some strange station, possibly with a very old hand-camera. It may be taken by the chance traveller, and its kind is taken all over the world, sometimes to the indignation of a station policeman and the possible embarrassment of the operator.

Your author took the Belgian view [525] at Liège in 1930, lured on by the sudden appearance of a de Glehn compound Atlantic, and critically regarded by the *sous-chef* in the right background. One wonders whether the official was sensitive about the quite deplorable third-class carriages — then a common sight — in the left background. A long and cordial conversation with the driver of the Atlantic, however, apparently reassured the man in the imposing headgear, who then left us to it.

Figure 526 was taken under similar circumstances from the off-side of an Austrian train at Spielfeld-Strass, of a German-built Jugoslav State Railways 2-8-2 heading a modest local train of one coach. Neither inspector nor policeman were around to ask questions. The Jugoslav enginemen simply grinned and waved.

525

366

HARRY A. IVATT AND SIR NIGEL GRESLEY

In 1898, Harry A. Ivatt, who came from Ireland and succeeded Patrick Stirling, designed for the Great Northern Railway the first British Atlantic type (4-4-2) locomotives, beginning with No. 990, *Henry Oakley*. Figure 527 shows this beautiful engine at York Museum, her present resting place, though she can still be steamed. (In the right background is a North Eastern 'Tennant' 2-4-0,

and in the foreground a choice open-top third-class wagon from the Bodmin and Wadebridge Railway.)

While the G.N.R. 990 class were more powerful than any previous Great Northern express engines, a still bigger boiler was yet indicated, and this need was satisfied by Ivatt in 1902. G.N.R. No. 251 was the first of many large-boilered Atlantics which, later equipped with superheaters, handled all the heavy East Coast expresses for the next 20 years [528]. As well as the larger boiler capacity, the wide

527

firebox contributed greatly to their phenomenal success. Therein was one of the virtues of the Atlantic type. A 4-6-0 engine, then considered the only alternative, could not have accommodated that wide grate. No. 251, most happily, has also been preserved.

In 1922, Ivatt's successor (Sir) Nigel Gresley brought out the first of his famous Pacific type express engines, worthy successors to the Ivatt Atlantics and the Stirling eight-foot single drivers which had gone before. He used three cylinders with a conjugated valve-gear, the Walschaert radial gear on both also working the valves of the inside cylinder through levers, just visible over the leading wheel in Figure 529. This illustrates *Papyrus*, built in 1929, one of the later Gresley Pacifics with a much increased boiler pressure. On March 5, 1935, when experiments were being made prior to the running of very fast regular trains, *Papyrus* attained 108 m.p.h. with a southbound special train near Little Bytham. Gresley's streamlined Pacifics followed the same year, and gained Gresley a knighthood.

528
529

369

HARRY IVATT'S ATLANTICS

Elsewhere we give a formal view of one of Harry Ivatt's celebrated large type locomotives on the Great Northern Railway, but the class deserves an action picture. Figure 530 shows No. 1447 northbound on an East Coast express near Hadley Wood, to the north of London, in what we may call the middle years. The elder Ivatt was one of the great figures of pre-1914 locomotive practice. He had come from Inchicore on the Great Southern and Western Railway in Ireland, whence came other great locomotive engineers in Great Britain, and whither went, in his latter years, his son-in-law Oliver Bulleid, last of the grand-original C.M.E.s of steam days. This view, in sharper perspective than the other, emphasises not only the relative width of the grate and firebox casing, overlapping the frames, but the

530

531

less definable *presence* of the Ivatt Atlantic.

Figure 531 shows a different conception of the Atlantic type. No. 510 *The Lord Provost* was built in 1920 and used on the North British Railway. Its design was influenced by J. G. Robinson's practice on the Great Central Railway, and was worked out between William Paton Reid of the N.B.R. and the North British Locomotive Company. The long, narrow Belpaire firebox also recalled Church-ward's practice on Great Western engines.

Sir Vincent Raven's Pacifics for the North Eastern Railway, like Gresley's for the Great Northern, came just before the British railway companies' great amalgamation of 1923. They were the largest engines to follow the old, traditional British style with relatively low platforms and all the valve gear inside. Figure 532 shows one leaving Edinburgh Waverley with the Queen of Scots Pullman, about 1930.

532

AMERICAN TOUR OF THE ROYAL SCOT

In the middle 1920s there was a motive-power crisis on the London Midland and Scottish Railway. The company was a fusion of several large and small railway undertakings, whose locomotive departments had been laws unto themselves. The London and North Western at Crewe knew not the Midland at Derby; further, the first Chief Mechanical Engineer of the combined system came from the Lancashire and Yorkshire Railway, but was to be succeeded by the Midland man when he retired.

Hundreds of relatively old-fashioned, and certainly undersized, Midland locomotives continued to be built, while what the L.M.S. needed — and quickly at that — was a much larger and more powerful engine for the ex-

presses to and from Scotland and the North West. By that time, there were not only Gresley's three-cylinder Pacific type engines on the London and North Eastern Railway, there were two very powerful four-cylinder 4-6-0 classes elsewhere, the Lord Nelson class on the Southern Railway and the slightly more recent King class on the Great Western.

The ex-Midland Chief Mechanical Engineer, Sir Henry Fowler, in no form to produce an original design, seems to have sent out an S.O.S. Design of the new engines, while officially his own, was worked out in the drawing office of the North British Locomotive Company in Glasgow. Richard Maunsell of the Southern Railway kindly lent a set of 'Lord Nelson' drawings. The resulting L.M.S. engine, first of the Royal Scot class, had strong

533
534

affinities with the Southern's 'Nelsons', but had three-cylinders instead of four, like the Pacifics on the L.N.E.R. At the same time, Gresley's conjugated valve motion was not used; there were three sets of Walschaert valve gear.

It was a very successful design, as it needed to be, and 50 engines were built straight off. Figure 533 shows *Royal Scot* at Crewe, just before a goodwill tour of many thousands of miles, with a train of representative L.M.S. coaches and sleepers, across the United States and back via the Canadian Pacific in 1933. The rather makeshift headlamp on the smokebox door was installed to fulfil American and Canadian requirements, and the engine also acquired a bell. The latter is shown in Figure 534, in which the train is visiting Montreal. Everywhere it went, people flocked to see it; American- and Canadian- born citizens out of curiosity, settlers out of nostalgia. 'I have seen the Royal Scot!' wrote one, as a Victorian might have recorded for his grandchildren: 'I saw Donati's Comet.'

THE BULLEID PACIFIC

Last of the great men of British steam, Oliver Bulleid, born in New Zealand of English West Country stock, was successively under two most eminent men of the Great Northern Railway, Harry Ivatt and Sir Nigel Gresley. After he had gone as Chief Mechanical Engineer to the Southern Railway, it became known after a while that something rather revolutionary in steam locomotives was on the way.

The first of the Bulleid Pacific-type express engines, of the Merchant Navy class, appeared in February, 1941, and occasioned the liveliest interest on the part of railwaymen and engineers, while howls of horror at its appearance went up from amateur traditionalists. From the point of view of the first-mentioned, use of a pressure as high as 280 lb. per sq. in. was a thing to watch (and for other people to hear if the safety-valves blew off!). But the grand mystery was in the valve gear. Bulleid had designed a radial valve-gear, driven by endless chains and enclosed, with the inside connecting rod and crank, in a sealed oil-bath. After the occasional infantile troubles which beset any radically new design, the Bulleid Pacifics did wonderful work for many years, so long as they were well maintained and intelligently driven. French enginemen would have loved

536

them, and so did the best of the men on the Southern Railway.

A lighter form — the West Country and Battle of Britain classes, followed the Merchant Navies. Bulleid believed that he could handle all the traffic of the Southern Railway's unelectrified lines with but four locomotive classes, with the best possible results and very great savings. So indeed it might have been, had he come earlier on the scene. But he had no faith in, or patience with, State ownership. When it came in 1948, nationalisation would have relegated him to a secondary position. It was considered that the newly constituted British Railways could have but one Chief Mechanical Engineer, and the office went by seniority. So Bulleid went to Ireland, and one of the most exciting phases in British steam locomotive history came to a perhaps untimely close.

Figure 535 shows one of the Merchant Navy class on the Southern Railway, No. 21C 6, *Peninsular and Oriental*, climbing to Honiton, East Devon, with the Atlantic Coast Express. Figure 536 shows *Holland America Line*, by then B.R. No. 35022, on the locomotive testing plant at Rugby on September 5, 1952. By then, British Railways were already committed to new standard designs, of sound but conventional sort.

END OF AMERICAN STEAM

The sunset of steam in North America began in the 1940s. It was a grand sunset. On Pearl Harbour Day, in 1941, the stainless steel, streamlined, steam-hauled version of the New York Central's old established Empire State Express went into service between New York, Cleveland and Detroit. The engine was a Hudson (4-6-4) type, finished and styled to match the cars [537]. Observe also the 'Bok-spok' solid coupled wheels, the monitor-shaped casing behind the stack and the headlamp recessed in the bullet-nosed smokebox.

For years the Southern Pacific Railroad, far on the other side of the Continent, had been working its heavy freight with enormous Mallet locomotives [538]. Use of oil fuel made possible the mounting of the cab in front, with the smokebox at the rear, giving the enginemen the same clear view as on an electric or diesel locomotive. H. Sullivan's shot was made on the Newhall incline, California, in the 1950s, before diesels took over.

Figure 539 is included as a compliment to generations of American steam locomotive engineers (they never were 'drivers' in America). Dr. Philip Hastings caught him on the Norfolk and Western. The cigar bespeaks the dignity and pride of his calling.

537

538

539

TRACKS, BRIDGES AND VIADUCTS

BRIDGES ON THE BALTIC

Western approaches to the Baltic, and the sounds dividing the isles of Denmark, have long formed serious obstacles to all land transport in the area. One of the first gaps to be closed was the Little Belt, dividing Jutland from Fyn, on the main route from Esbjerg to Copenhagen. The Little Belt Bridge [540] was opened between Snoghø and Middelfart in May, 1935. In September, 1937, followed the famous Storstrøm Bridge, 10,537 ft. long, carrying railway, road and cycle track between Zealand and the isle of Falster [541].

Latest of the Baltic bridges is that across the Fehmarn Sound, North Germany, opened on April 30, 1963. The principle adopted here is that of the strengthened steel span suspended from a great steel arch [542]. Once again a substantial cut has been made in distance and travelling time between Central and Northern Europe.

540

543

544

G.W.R. END OF THE BROAD GAUGE I

A major tragedy of railway mechanical history was that Brunel's splendid 7 ft. gauge, coming as it did in the late 1830s was too late to become a national — and perhaps international — standard. Break of gauge has ever been an unmitigated nuisance, as Australia was to find — and still finds — in our own time.

Little by little, the broad gauge mileage of the Great Western Railway and its allied companies in the West of England and in South Wales shrank as one section after another was converted to the 4 ft. 8½ in. standard. In some places this began quite early, but it was a long and expensive task. Nearly all broad gauge lines were built on Brunel's plan, with flat-bottom or bridge rails on heavy longitudinal baulks, held together by cross-transomes at

much longer intervals than the cross sleepers of the ordinary road.

The method of conversion was to cut these transomes down to standard-gauge width, on the off side, and then move the outer baulks and rails inwards. Early conversion was in the Severn Valley and in South Wales. Figure 543 shows the conversion of the Hereford, Ross and Gloucester line in 1869. In the foreground are broad-gauge tracks and beyond these the line has been converted. The occasion is the gang's pay-day. Under the bridge stands the standard-gauge staff train, headed by an E. B. Wilson 0-6-0 engine, probably from the West Midland Railway. Already gone were the days when the Great Western had hoped for a broad-gauge invasion of the North.

Figure 544 shows a standard-gauge train on the Dowles bridge across the Severn, on the line from Stourport to Bewdley.

378

545
546

END OF THE BROAD GAUGE II

By 1892 much of the Great Western Railway which had not been fully converted to standard gauge had mixed-gauge tracks, with two rails on the off side. It made points and crossings complicated, but through working to and from other lines was possible everywhere east of Exeter. Thence to Plymouth, Truro and Falmouth there was still broad gauge only, except for mixed gauge where the London and South Western Railway ran into Plymouth. Figure 545 shows the down Cornishman on mixed gauge. The engine is still of the basic Gooch type. The carriages are convertibles, with narrow bodies on broad-gauge bogies; observe the wide footboards and the extension to the guard's ducket on the leading van. This is a very early example of speed photography.

Shortly before his death in 1889, the vener-able Sir Daniel Gooch, by then Chairman of the Great Western, sadly told his last annual general meeting that the death of the broad gauge could not be long delayed. It was decided upon in March, 1892, execution to be almost immediate. On May 20, the last broad-gauge trains left Paddington for the West. Figure 546 shows the 10.15 a.m. Cornishman at Paddington on that fateful day. The train had been drawn slowly forward, clear of Paddington's cavernous roof, for the photograph. Its final departure was accompanied by a salvo of fogsignals. The last broad-gauge public train up was the night mail from Plymouth, arriving at Paddington early in the following morning. All broad-gauge engines and vehicles were cleared out of South Devon and Cornwall, and the Cornishman, on its return from Penzance, acted as a clearing train. When it had gone, the broad gauge was dead.

379

END OF THE BROAD GAUGE III

West of Exeter, the conversion gangs moved in immediately after the clearing train had passed eastwards on its way from Penzance to Exeter. There were about 3,400 men on the job, navvies recruited from far and wide over England, and their work began at dawn on Saturday, May 21. It lasted through the weekend, and on the Monday morning it was done. Figure 547 shows the work nearing completion on the Kingswear branch, opposite Dartmouth. The nearer rail on its baulks has been moved in; lying along the cess are the severed ends of the cross-transomes; the gang is packing the ballast.

At Swindon Works, far away in northern Wiltshire, all the broad-gauge equipment had been concentrated on 13 miles of specially laid sidings, to await breaking up or, where possible, conversion to standard gauge. During the previous decade many locomotives and vehicles had been specially built with this in mind, but the old stagers were doomed. They can be identified in Figure 548, for the most part, by their domeless boilers. The brass-cased domes in the further rows generally denote convertible engines, built fairly recently to William Dean's designs. Between the engine sidings and the workshops can be seen the tops of broad-gauge carriages similarly assembled. Some of these were then of quite recent design, and fully convertible, but some resembled nothing else on wheels except, perhaps, the choicer antiques of France and Spain, where age meant nothing.

549
550

ELECTRICALLY OPERATED POINTS

Manually operated points and signals are still quite common, though the days when a 'pointsman' stood in the rain beside a lever, stared at a distant semaphore without any interlocking, and scratched his perplexed head as he saw the smoke of a distantly approaching train, are fortunately long past. Figure 549 shows electrically operated points, on a single turnout. The track is of the time-honoured but now far obsolescent bullhead rail, wooden-keyed into cast-iron chairs. Observe the bonding for track circuits at the rail-joint left of the frog. Figure 550 shows an electrically operated point layout, with immunised d.c. point controllers for 25 kV, 50 cycle electric traction. Both examples are from British Railways' Eastern Region.

SMOOTH RUNNING ON POINTS AND RAIL-JOINTS

In very early days, the end-on connection of rails was achieved simply by chairing and spiking them together on one sleeper. William Bridges Adams, inventor of many things, none of which made him a millionaire like Robert Stephenson, produced the bolted pair of fish-plates — the 'fish joint' — over a century ago. It was a tremendous contribution to the stability of the permanent way. In recent times, increasing use has been made of welded rails in great lengths, with expansion joints at intervals.

Figure 551 shows, at the Motherwell long welded rail depot in British Railways' Scottish Region, a 420 ft. length of long-welded rail being lowered, ready to be collected for track-laying. Each gantry crane, of which there are 10 in the view, is capable of lifting one ton. Elimination of running shocks now extends to points as well as rail-joints. Figure 552 shows a diamond crossing at Nicklefield in British Railways' North Eastern Region. There are still the open frogs at the extremities of the diamond, but in the middle of it, passage is continuous, for one road or the other, through the control of electric point machines. With the increase of train speeds, such improvements become essential to easy running.

551

553

RAIL-LAYING IN AMERICA AND RUSSIA

In the old days of both America and Russia, railway track standards long lagged behind those of the more advanced countries in Western Europe. There were exceptions of course; both the eastern lines of the Pennsylvania Railroad and, in Russia, the Nicolai Railway — later the October Railway between Leningrad and Moscow — cherished their roadbeds.

In Figure 553 a train of the Illinois Central Railroad, carries steel rail for relaying in quarter-mile lengths, part of a programme which brought the company's track mileage of

continuous welded rail to 409 miles by the end of 1965. The old rails were in 39 ft. lengths, which was short by British and French standards. The familiar rhythm of the train is lost, to the content of many and the regret of some. In American phraseology: 'Railroading loses its *clickety-click*'.

Figure 554 shows a track-laying machine on the October Railway in the Soviet Union today. The 12.5 metre lengths are being run forward, fully sleepered in concrete (not the steel-tied concrete blocks now favoured in France). French pattern double elastic steel clips secure the rails to the sleepers.

CONCRETE SLEEPERS IN FRANCE AND LEBANON

One of the oldest forms of railway permanent way, which was perpetuated on parts of the London and Birmingham Railway in the late 1830s, involved the chairing of the rails on separate lines of stone sleepers. The mid-20th century has seen widespread use of what is in principle the same thing, but with concrete blocks united by steel tiebars, and of course heavy welded steel rails. Even this form is in itself old; it was not infrequent in India, especially in the 1920s, though the rails continued to be in short lengths and were keyed into the old cast-iron chairs.

In Figure 555 is a fine stretch of modern road on one of the gentle curves of French National Railways' South Western Region, on the main line between Bordeaux and the Spanish frontier (Hendaye-Irun). The rails are welded into very long stretches. The distinctive form of the overhead contact-line supports originated with the former Midi Railway Company, which embarked on general electrification back in the '20s. How very French-traditional are both the A-shaped telegraph poles and the little jericho set so that the master of the house may tranquilly survey his cabbages of a morning!

Like British influence in Ghana (for example) French influence persists on the Lebanon State Railway, and in Figure 556 is seen a characteristic stretch of modern track on the Beirut-Tripoli line, with a Dietrich diesel rail-car running from Beirut to Aleppo.

555

CARE OF THE TRACK: ENGLAND

Laying preassembled concrete-sleepered track off-side by machine [557] on the London and North Western main line of British Railways, London Midland Region (London-Crewe-Manchester and Liverpool). Offside laying means occupancy of two roads, but with a four-road main line it can be carried out, subject to schedules, with relatively little inconvenience. A locomotive moves the tracklayer back and forth from its loading position alongside the train carrying the new sections. In Figure 558 a mechanical trencher is at work along the cess on the North Eastern main line. Good drainage is essential for a good road. For years, the blocking and freezing of points mechanism in severe weather has been a major nuisance for both operator and user on British and other railways. Figure 559 shows a single turnout equipped with an infra-red propane switch-heater.

557

558
559

CARE OF THE TRACK: FRANCE

In Figure 560 is the receiving end of a French mechanical tracklayer. Its rate of delivery is 380 metres an hour, end-on. In Figure 561 is a Matisa power wrench which automatically gives the right degree of tightening to the sleeper bolts. Long welded rails are being used on concrete sleepers with steel tiebars, spring clips on both sides of the rail foot and chevron rubber solepads. The flat-footed rail is universal in modern permanent way design, though for many years bull-head rail keyed into chairs was almost invariably used in Great Britain, and extensively in France. In Figure 562, an up English boat express from Dieppe skims over long-welded rails near Juziers.

560

561
562

563

TRACK-LAYING IN SPAIN

In Spain French influence was strong from early days, and continued in spite of Government insistence, later, on the use of home fuel and Spanish-built machinery. Recent years have seen the introduction of modern French methods in the design and construction of the permanent way. In Figure 563, lengths of concrete-sleepered, steel-transomed track are being taken forward for laying by a road-type motor truck, mounted on steel-flanged pneumatic-tyred wheels set for the 5 ft. 6 in. gauge. In Figure 564 the line, laid and roughly ballasted, is being welded into lengths of 1,000 and 1,200 metres. Figure 565 shows a Fiat three-car diesel unit on the completed road.

564

565

PLANNING AND PREPAREDNESS
IN SWITZERLAND

Swiss contrast. Zürich Main Station, concentration point for traffic between Central
and Southern Europe, and also for east-west
traffic, possesses a layout which many cities
with a higher traffic density still may well envy
[566]. One may compare the station approach
roads, for instance, with those of Liverpool
Street in London, with its six-road bottleneck
leading to 18 passenger platforms. To its
credit, the wonder is that Liverpool Street
manages so well. Even before electrification,
it received and dispatched suburban trains on
a 2½-minute headway over one up road and
one down (Enfield and Chingford lines).

But the splendid layout of Zürich reflects
the more enlightened attitude of the Swiss
Federal Government to the importance of railway transport, compared with those of certain
English-speaking nations. Not without reason,
of course! In a high Alpine country, under
winter conditions often most severe, the railway is the only conveyance that never ceases.
Preparedness is the same, whether in the
industrial north-east or in remote mountain
places. Figure 567 shows how the Rhaetian
Railway, on metre-gauge single track, deals
with snow (Chur-Arosa line).

567

568
569

SNOW

Snow can stop every vehicle that goes on land, but the last thing to be stopped anywhere, when motors are stranded with their occupants in the high hills, and heavy aircraft are grounded, is the train. These three photographs were taken in British Railways' Eastern Region during the great freeze-up of 1961—62. In Figure 568 a Brush diesel-electric locomotive brings an up Cambridge train through Roydon station on the Great Eastern line, on time, like little else. On the right the colourlight signals, deeply hooded against just this eventuality, faithfully carry out their safeguarding function. Figure 569 shows a window on a Pullman car of the Queen of Scots at Kings Cross. The beautiful study in Figure 570 was taken, straight into the sun, on the same day. It shows an East Coast express on the Great Northern line near Hatfield.

THE TAY BRIDGE DISASTER

The first great railway tragedy — apart from many more or less gory accidents to trains — was that of the first Tay Bridge. The two-mile width of the Tay at Dundee had long been a serious break in the East Coast route to Aberdeen, and all through traffic had to be routed either through Perth or by the Forth and Tay ferries. Thomas Bouch designed a giant single track bridge. It was opened for passenger traffic on June 1, 1878. Queen Victoria rode over it a year later and knighted Bouch.

In the great gale of December 28, 1879, the high girders forming the middle of the bridge fell, taking with them the northbound mail train with about 78 persons. There were no survivors. Figures 571 and 572 show a view of the broken bridge from the north end, and a crowd studying the wreck from the sea wall. Long inquiry showed that Bouch's calculations of the lateral pressures exerted by high wind were hopelessly inadequate. But further, the contractor, Hopkins, Gilkes and Company, had been guilty of extremely bad work and the quality of the cast-iron columns was deplorable. Sir Thomas Bouch, mentally and physically broken, met his end in retirement late in 1880.

Thanks largely to the courage of Stirling of Kippendavie, the North British Railway Chairman, the replacement of this disastrous bridge was undertaken as quickly as possible, with W. H. Barlow and his son Crawford Barlow as engineers. An admirably solid structure, carrying two tracks, it was authorised in 1881, completed in 1887, and has stood fast ever since [573].

571

FORTH BRIDGE

Queen of Britain's railway bridges, indeed after 70 years still queen of all main-line railway bridges, the Forth Bridge [574 and 575] stands changelessly across the great estuary which once separated Celtic from Saxon Scotland. Longer spans have been built since 1890, and ere that the unfortunate first Tay Bridge and its successor were both longer structures.

The greatest spans are those of suspension bridges. But in comparison with other steel cantilever bridges the Forth Bridge's two spans of 1,710 ft. each may be compared with the single 1,800 ft. clear span of the Quebec Bridge on Canadian National Railways, the 1,400 ft. main East Bay span of the San Francisco-Oakland Bay Bridge in California and the two 1,182 ft. main spans of the Queensborough Bridge, New York. Each of the Forth

Bridge main spans exceeds the single steel-arch span of Sydney Harbour Bridge (1,650 ft.).

The Forth Bridge was built to the design of Sir John Fowler and Sir Benjamin Baker, with Sir William Arrol as contractor. It allows a clear headway of 157 ft. below the intermediate spans and was opened by the Prince of Wales, afterwards King Edward VII, on March 4, 1890. Its total length between abutments is 8,298 ft. Projects to bridge the Firth of Forth went back to early in the century, before the coming of railways, but in the late 1870s the contract was already signed, and construction had begun, for a suspension bridge to the designs of Thomas Bouch (upper drawing in Figure 576). On December 28, 1879, Bouch's Tay Bridge was blown down in the great storm of that day, taking with it the evening mail train to Dundee (see previous page). The contract for his bridge was cancelled.

575
576

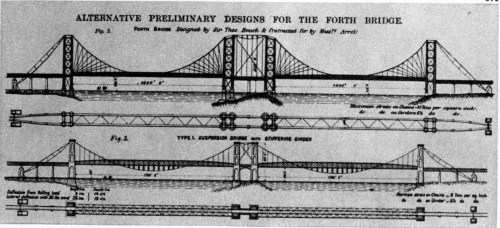

ALTERNATIVE PRELIMINARY DESIGNS FOR THE FORTH BRIDGE.

BRITANNIA TUBULAR BRIDGE

The Britannia Tubular Bridge across the Menai Straits, some way south of Telford's original Menai Bridge on the Holyhead road, is interesting architecturally as well as by virtue of its engineering [577]. Although the work of Robert Stephenson, and dating back to 1850, there was no aping of classical or Gothic styles, which were such a feature of 19th century railway structures. Clearly neither of these could possibly belong with rectangular iron tubes containing separate up and down roads. So the bridge came to exemplify a style of its own, and in an era of ornateness its sole concession to emebellishment was in the mounting of highly stylized stone lions, each side of the line at the abutments.

Original authorship of the bridge, and its principles of construction, was bitterly argued. Nominally it was the work of Robert Stephenson, as remarked. But William Fairbairn claimed it, with some strength to his case, and while the works were still in progress ended his partnership in anger and frustration. Sir George Grove, as a young man, had something to do with it; Stephenson originally proposed cast-iron arches of 350 ft. span which, one feels, might have brought discredit and disaster.

Most fortunately in this case, Admiralty objections, including refusal to allow blockage of the fairway for even a single day, caused this scheme to be abandoned. The iron tubes which were employed instead were floated out, one by one on pontoons, to be raised into position on the stone piers. No scaffolding was employed.

577

578

HELL GATE AND SYDNEY HARBOUR BRIDGES

Long steel arches with suspended spans became a feature of railway, and other, bridge-building during the first half of the 20th century, though they had a forerunner in Brunel's tubular spans, e.g. at Saltash (Figure 591, page 411). Hell Gate Bridge and its approach viaducts [578] exemplifies the type. Belonging to the Pennsylvania Railroad and opened on April 1, 1917, it gives across the East River a direct connection between the New England states and the rest of the Union. The main

579
580

span is 1,017 ft. and at the time of construction was claimed to be the longest steel arch in the world.

In size it was greatly surpassed by the Sydney Harbour Bridge in New South Wales, opened on March 19, 1932. Figure 579 shows this under test. During the test all four railway tracks were subjected to the weight of long lines of dead locomotives, which had been awaiting general overhaul or, in some cases, scrapping, at Eveleigh Locomotive Works. For the electric suburban trains it provides an invaluable link between the two parts of the Sydney metropolitan area [580]. The main span is 1,650 ft. long, and with approaches the total length is 3,770 ft. It allows a clear headway of 170 ft. and the largest ships pass under it with ease.

BRITISH BRIDGES

Quite apart from the giants, the British railway system is particularly distinguished by its thousands of bridges and viaducts, many of them dating back to early Victorian years. To the early railway constructors deviations to suit the land contours, and save money thus, were anathema. Robert Stephenson liked to build straight through, as he did through the Kilsby Ridge on the London and Birmingham line; Joseph Locke liked to build up and over. But both liked to build as straight as possible. Figure 581 shows a fine old iron skew arch across the Grand Union Canal on the main line from London (Euston) to the North. The view was taken at the end of the 1940s, just after the formation of British Railways. The

'Black Five' 4-6-0 engine still retains the old initials of the London Midland and Scottish Railway.

Figure 582 is from a photograph taken about half a century ago, showing a Great Central local train crossing Dinting Viaduct on the Manchester-Sheffield main line over the Pennines (it also goes for more than three miles through them between Woodhead and Dunford Bridge).

By contrast, and offering some of that graceful splendour characteristic of the beautiful granite viaducts on the Midland line along the Pennines, is that of Arlen Gill [583]. Though not the longest of them, it sweeps across the dale most handsomely.

582
583

ENGLISH VIADUCTS

Across the valleys of the English North Country stood the great stone railway viaducts of the early Victorian engineers, and there they still stand where there is traffic for them to carry. Many are in beautiful places, but in others the factory stacks and the terraced workers' houses of the 19th century line the bottoms that once were so green. Kenneth Field's two photographs show the viaduct at Durham [584] with a Newcastle local train crossing, and that at Longwood on the Manchester and Leeds line [585], with a Newcastle-Liverpool express — a Midland class 2 piloting a Stanier class 5 — crossing the spans that were completed in 1847.

Those viaducts stood like rocks. But sub-

584

585

sidence could upset them, very, *very* rarely. This happened at Penistone on the Lancashire and Yorkshire Railway, on February 2, 1916, and the fallen arches took an L. and Y. 2-4-2 tank engine with them [586]. The fall was slow enough to give the enginemen warning, and they escaped from that mighty cropper in time. The viaduct was repaired and the L. and Y. resumed its connection with the Great Central at Penistone.

586

BRIDGES OF NORTH-EAST ENGLAND

North-eastern England is big-bridge country, as befits an area which saw the first real railway bridge — the Causey Arch — in the 18th century (see page 12). The railway bridging of the Tyne at Newcastle goes back to the building of Robert Stephenson's and T. E.

Harrison's three-track High Level Bridge (1849—50) with a road deck below. It still stands and has been often illustrated. The four-track King Edward Bridge [587] was opened in 1906, giving access from the south to the west end of Newcastle Central Station and enabling East Coast expresses to pass through without reversal there.

Where the old, long branch of the Stockton and Darlington Railway climbed up the dales and over the Pennines to Westmorland, there were superb viaducts built in happier days by Thomas Bouch (who was to die, broken, after the fall of his Tay Bridge in 1879). Figure 588 shows that over the Tees near Barnard Castle. The iron traffic, for which the line was built, failed; passenger traffic was ever slight. The line is dead now and the bridges are gone.

588

NEW ENGLAND TRUSS BRIDGES

The completely covered timber truss bridge was a very common form in the early days of American railroads, though its lineage went back to ancient, long pre-railway practice in the Alpine countries, and fine old examples may still be seen spanning mountain rivers in the Tyrol. The bridge in Figure 589, at Contoocook, New Hampshire, was on the Concord and Clarence short line, formerly part of the Boston and Maine. The turnout on an ungated road crossing apparently worried nobody.

The steel truss in Figure 590 exemplifies

590

later practice in a similar situation, with incidental spring floods. This is at Bradford, Vermont. The photograph (1948) shows a Boston and Maine train from River Junction, Vermont, to Berlin, New Hampshire, headed by Canadian Pacific 4-6-2 locomotive No.2584 in between her regular night assignment between the B. and M. in the States and the C.P.R. in Canada. The train, rather than the bridge, is nearly as dated as the wooden truss at Contoocook. The slim Pacifics have since vanished.

410

BRUNEL IN THE WEST

I. K. Brunel's Royal Albert Bridge, Saltash, exemplified his unique tubular girders with the spans in suspension, which he first essayed at Chepstow. Figure 591 shows the Saltash bridge during construction, with the span on the Cornish side already in position. The Devon span, floated out and secured to the hulks of what once must have been rather beautiful ships, rests on its incipient piers, from which it is to be raised by hydraulic rams to its ultimate position. The structure was neither a true tubular bridge nor a true stiffened suspension bridge, but a compound of the two. It was completed in 1859, right at the end of Brunel's life.

Like several of the early Victorian engineers, he worked himself to death. This came following a stroke he suffered on hearing of an ac-

cident to the great ship, the *Great Eastern*, which he had schemed and which John Scott Russell had built. He lived just long enough to be lifted on to an arm-chair in a wagon, and then to be propelled slowly over his great bridge from Devon into Cornwall. After that there died a great artist as well as a giant engineer.

The bridge itself still stands. One of its top tubes neatly deflected a German bomb in the 1940s. But its splendid lines no longer can be appreciated from a distance. It was inevitable that ultimately it would be paralleled by a motor-road bridge (not shown here but which succeeded the rather charming ferry illustrated in Figure 592) but it was an appalling misfortune that the two bridges should stand closely side-by-side, each killing the other as a spectacle. The Philistine, however, does not care.

592

HAWKESBURY BRIDGE, N.S.W.

In New South Wales the first Hawkesbury River Bridge was opened on May 1, 1889. Figure 593 shows the inaugural train, headed by a B 205 class 2-6-0 engine, of which 70 were built between 1881 and 1885. The carriages, at that distance and angle, look neither British nor American but German, owing to the box-like clerestories stopping short of the roof ends.

The bridge was not a wholly fortunate one. As in the first Tay Bridge, in Scotland, the materials used in the piers were undoubtedly faulty, though there were to be no tragic results. It was 2,900 ft. long. In and after 1927 the piers were strengthened, yet this was but a makeshift.

In July, 1939, began the construction of a new Hawkesbury River Bridge, about 200 ft. upstream from the old one [594]. It is slightly

593

594

shorter — 2,764 ft. — while its deepest pier goes 183 ft. 7 in. into the riverbed. It was completed and then officially opened on July 1, 1946. Our view shows both bridges after the track had been lifted from the old bridge, but before its demolition.

ELECTRIC MAIN LINES

FIRST ELECTRIC LOCOMOTIVE

George Stephenson said, in old age, that while he had contributed to the advance of mechanical locomotion, a time was to come when electricity would be the great motive power of the world. After many attempts, in different countries, Werner von Siemens produced a practical electric locomotive, which hauled passengers round a line at the Trades Exhibition in Berlin, in 1879 [595]. The locomotive has survived the years — even the bombing of Munich — and Figure 596 shows it in the Deutsches Museum there. The early '80s saw the appearance of electric traction in Berlin (1881), Brighton, England (August 3, 1883) and Portrush, Giant's Causeway, Ireland (September 28, 1883).

595
596

PLATE XXXI Landwasser Viaduct, Switzerland.
PLATE XXXII Helensburgh-Bridgeton commuter train beside the Clyde.

SWEDISH TRAINS IN LAPLAND

Sweden today has a total State Railways network of 8,386 route miles, whereof 4,460 miles of route are electrified. Standard-gauge lines are worked on the single-phase system at 15,000 Volts, 16⅔ cycles, while 1,500 Volts d.c. is used on certain narrow-gauge lines, formerly in the hands of private companies.

An early conversion was on the Lapland iron-ore line, from Kiruna to the Norwegian frontier, with end-on connection to the Nor-

wegian Ofoten Railway down to the ice-free Atlantic port of Narvik. Eastern sections of the iron-ore line were electrified during 1920-23. From the middle 1920s electrification of the main lines went on continually, and for years, now, there has been unbroken electric traction from the extreme south at Trälleborg to the Lapland lines.

Figures 597 and 598 show iron-ore trains running on these lines. Figure 599 shows a standard inter-city express train in the southern part of the country.

599

PLATE XXXIII In the workshops of the
Berne-Lötschberg-Simplon Railway.

417

TRANS-EUROP EXPRESS

The late 1950s saw the rapid spread of Mr. den Hollander's Trans-Europ Express over the more important lines of Western Europe. They are relatively light trains of extremely comfortable day coaches, strictly limited and subject absolutely to reservation. The fares are high, but the object of the trains is competition with shorter-distance air-lines, and so far the experiment has proved a success. Traction is electric, or diesel-electric, or both, according to route.

Their advantage in European inter-city traffic is that, although much slower than aircraft in point-to-point speed, they show their patrons something of the country and, above all, cut out the tedious delays and frustrations of transport to and from airports.

Figure 600 shows a coach interior on the Paris-Brussels-Amsterdam route. The cars are fully air-conditioned, with meals and drinks continually available. Figure 601 shows a north-to-south T.E.E. on its way through Switzerland. The electric trains are adaptable for running under different systems in the countries they traverse. The hourly rating is 3,143 h.p. on 15,000 Volts $16\frac{2}{3}$ cycles (Germany and Switzerland) and 3,015 h.p. on 25,000 Volts 50 cycles (Northern France), 3,000 Volts d.c. (Italy and Belgium) and 1,500 Volts d.c. (Netherlands, Southern and Central France).

600

601

THE GOTTHARD LINE, SWITZERLAND

Throughout its history, the Gotthard line in Switzerland has demanded unusually powerful locomotives. The year 1939 saw the building of a double-unit electric locomotive which exerted 11,400 h.p. at rail and thus qualified at the time as the most powerful in the world. The '50s saw the development of a new design for express passenger haulage, class Ae 6/6, relatively light (120 metric tons) with the wheel arrangement Co-Co, but developing 5,820 h.p. at 46 m.p.h.

Figure 602 shows No. 11440, *Aargau*. As well as being a practical and economical engine it is a very stylish one, and its elegance is enhanced by a livery of light olive green and unpainted aluminium. All of the class are named after Swiss cantons and carry their cantonal insignia on shields each side, while the white cross of Helvetia is mounted on each end.

Figure 603 illustrates one of the class with an international express on the lowermost of three levels at Wassen, on the northern approach to the St. Gotthard Tunnel.

602
603

NO MEAN CITY

To most people except Glaswegians, the railway transport of Glasgow in the past meant terminal stations, and of these we show Glasgow Central in the great days of the Caledonian Railway [604] with the 2.00 p.m. 'Corridor' about to leave for London behind the legendary *Cardean* (1906). But from the late 1890s onwards the city was served by three underground railways, of which the Glasgow City and District, forming part of an oval with tangental connections to the eastern and western suburbs, was the oldest, being opened in the spring of 1886.

It was far from being a favourite in steam days, and several accidents did nothing to improve its reputation. The line east-to-west went over to electric traction on the 50 cycle system during 1960—61, with infantile pains at first. It then justified itself beyond even sanguine expectations, and certainly far beyond those of ordinary, critical citizens, and its success has resulted in an expansion of the electric system of British Railways in the Glasgow and Clyde coast area.

It is a trifle unusual to board what Americans would call a subway train and be borne out beside a great estuary to the roots of the mountains. Plate XXXII, facing page 416, shows such a train, eastbound beside the Clyde, on the route from Helensburgh to Bridgeton. In 1962 suburban lines south of the Clyde were added to the electrified network, and those to Gourock and Wemyss Bay have followed. Within the Clyde compass, the early '60s saw a railway renaissance.

604

EARLY ENGLISH MAIN-LINE ELECTRIFICATION

There is nothing new on British railways in the use of high or relatively high tensions at the contact line. In 1908 the Midland Railway experimentally electrified the Lancaster-Morecambe-Heysham lines on the single-phase system at 6,600 Volts 25 cycles [605]. In quite recent years, the line was used for primary experiments with 25 kV. traction before British Railways undertook electrification on this system in the London Midland, and Eastern Regions.

In 1909 the London Brighton and South Coast Railway began conversion of certain suburban lines in London, with a view to ultimate main-line electrification, on the 6,700 Volt single-phase system. Figure 606 shows an up Crystal Palace train near Clapham Junction. The system lasted for years until, in the interests of uniformity, the succeeding Southern Railway Company standardised on 660 Volt d.c. with third-rail contact.

605
606

422

ELECTRIC CITY TRAINS OF THE '30s

In Figure 607 is a Tyneside train near Whitley Bay in the 1930s. The cars were then recent, though this was the first electrification by a main-line British railway company (North Eastern Railway, 1903). Many of the original cars were destroyed in a tremendous depot fire. Both the old and the new cars were suburban rather than city transit vehicles, and had end vestibules only.

Of pure city type have always been the electric stock of the District Line in London, and Figure 608 shows a train of class P cars in Circle service at South Kensington. The design was carried out under W. S. Graff-Baker, a veteran of electric traction. The flared lower quarters had a psychological purpose, he told us. Waiting passengers were less inclined to stand close to the platform edge when the trains advanced with sweeping skirts. In the days of manually worked sliding doors there had been some shocking accidents, too, when people tried to jump trains at the last minute. Satisfactory automatic doors having been at last perfected, all new trains had them, and they were installed in many of the older cars dating from 1920. The 'P stock' dated from 1938.

423

609
610

BERNE-LÖTSCHBERG-SIMPLON RAILWAY

Electrification of the Berne-Lötschberg-Simplon Railway, during the years from 1910 onwards, was concurrent with its completion over and through the *massif* dividing the Aar and Rhône valleys. As an electric railway it was thus senior to the Swiss Federal Government's Gotthard line. Figure 609 shows one of its oldest heavy electric locomotives, built in 1913, with drive through jackshafts, yoke and side rods, with the wheel arrangement 2-10-2, or 1-E-1 by the German formula. In Figure 610 is one of the contemporary double-unit B.L.S. locomotives (Co-Co + Co-Co) which nowadays haul the international expresses between Berne and Brigue. In Plate XXXIII, facing page 417, a modern single-unit locomotive is lifted on to its bogies in the B.L.S. shops.

611
612

EARLY ALPINE ELECTRIC TRAINS

Electric trains advance on the Alps. Italy carried out experimental electrification as far back
as 1901—02, on the Milan-Varese and Valtel-
lina lines. The rather charming watercolours
[611 and 612] show a Pullmanesque motor
coach for working with trailers on the second-
named railway. One marks the gushing enthusiasm of the passengers, also the spare

candle-lamps at the sides of the carriage, against
a possible interruption of current supply.

The Swiss electrified the Simplon tunnel,
on the three-phase system (since replaced) immediately after its opening in 1906, but the
business of Alpine main-line electrification
began to be really spectacular with the opening of the Berne-Lötschberg-Simplon (1913);
then the conversion of the Swiss Federal Railways Gotthard line, on the 15,000 Volt single-

425

613
614

phase system, after the 1914—18 War.. Swiss conversion went on continuously thereafter. Figure 613 shows one of the original Gotthard passenger engines with drive through jackshafts and side rods, of class Be 4/6, built during the years 1920—23, and here shown in her old age at Brunnen in 1960. These were slow, but peculiarly sure.

The same qualification applies to the old Austrian Federal Railways 'Crocodile' [614], equipped like the Swiss locomotive by Brown, Boveri and Company, and put into service on the Arlberg line in 1923. This, too, is a recent photograph. The middle of the locomotive was articulated to the two six-coupled motor units. This flexibility, with the 'snout' ends, earned the nickname. Switzerland already had 'Crocodiles'.

GÖSCHENEN POWER STATION

We have seen many power stations, both steam- and water-powered: Lotts Road's great old power station between Chelsea and Fulham, primeval power-station of the London Underground lines, in its original form; Trollhättan in Sweden, Barberine in Switzerland, Walchensee in South Germany, to mention but a few of the impressive ones. But if *impressive* is the word, none has exceeded that at Göschenen, on the northern side of the St. Gotthard Pass, and the latest feeder to Swiss Federal Railways. The latter are electrified throughout, and their present traffic would astonish people who knew them only in the earlier days of the railway monopoly.

But the wonder of Göschenen is partly in its situation. Someone likened it to a cathedral, with an enormous crypt, inside a mountain. We saw it under construction, and its rough majesty at that stage more than justified the simile. Figure 615 shows the lower level, the crypt, in an unfinished state, with installation of the turbines lately begun. The alternators are above them, and Figure 616 shows the completed upper level.

One might imagine that Switzerland could not possibly lack power from falling water. The melting snows of great mountains are ever there, but according to climatic conditions there may be more water, or less. As yet, there

cannot be too many power stations in a land that has no indigenous fuel. In the past we have seen old steam locomotives helping out on fully electrified main lines, while during the war years there was even the incredible sight of steam engines electrically fired, with an element in the boiler and a pantograph collector on the cab roof. It was not an economic way of using electric power, but there was a shortage of new machinery.

THE ORANGE AND THE BLUE: SOUTH AFRICA

Today, the organisation of South African Railways and Harbours provides a supreme example of an integrated transport system. It works 13,650 miles of railway route; chiefly on 3ft. 6in. gauge, and 31,820 route miles of road motor services. Its air services began in 1934 (South African Airways) and in 1945 it started the Springbok service, jointly with B.O.A.C., between Johannesburg and London. Its railways provide by far the greatest proportion of revenue. Electrification began in the middle '20s, in Natal, and recent figures showed 1,668 route miles electrified in the

617

618

Union. The 3,000 Volt d.c. system is used throughout with overhead contact.

These two views are characteristic of mainline electric traction in the Union. In Figure 617, the Orange Express is climbing into the interior from the orchard country of Western Cape Province, headed by a single class 4 E electric locomotive. Visible are 14 coaches, of mixed vintage (the seventh is a rather old dining car). All of them exemplify the clerestoried body form, now extremely rare in other parts of the world, but found in South Africa and Rhodesia to have great virtues in relation to the climate. Half-domed ends to the roofs bespeak wooden bodies; the other vehicles are all-steel.

In Figure 618 the Blue Train from the Cape to Southern Rhodesia is in the Hex River Valley. Once again, motive power is furnished by a single 4 E locomotive, but the train is made up entirely of all-steel stock. It will be seen that in nearly all the carriages the air-conditioning ducts follow the clerestory shape, partly from convenience and partly through South African tradition. The official term is 'modified monitor roof'.

ELECTRIC STYLING

Styling the electric vehicle, or locomotive, is a more complex task than ever was the styling of steam. The steam locomotive started with the immense advantage of an entirely functional shape which was at the same time a bold, heroic form. There was no need to disguise it as something else. At best, its lines bespoke neatness of design and, above all, what a great locomotive engineer called mechanical balance.

In our pages devoted to steam there are examples of beautiful engines. Take such different examples, each expressing a more or less national idiom, as the American Pacific in South Manchuria (Figure 465, page 322), the Gresley Pacific of the London and North Eastern (Figure 505, page 353), and the Maffei Pacific in Bavaria (Figure 425, page 298), which are three engines of the same basic type and in the author's opinion singularly beautiful engines. Then compare them with the Hungarian hobbledehoys on pages 288 and 289 which, though good engines, look as if they had been chucked together. With electric 'faces' it is altogether a different matter. The machine itself makes only a small part of the outline. A box encases it. But it must look something more than a box-of-works.

Some of the most beautiful electric locomotives yet built have been the Alsthom Co-Co in France (see page 434). But the London Midland Bo-Bo, built for the 25 Kilovolt system between London and the North-West, is a remarkably handsome locomotive, if less consciously elegant than the French design. It has visible balance. With multiple-unit or motor-and-trailer trains the thing is complicated by the necessary equation of engine and coach. The Dutch 'Benelux' trains, which work such shorter international services as those between Brussels and Amsterdam, succeed rather well. The train is in fact a flexible motor-car, and as such a great deal better looking than some of the mechanical expressions of vulgarity on the roads of the mid-20th century.

AMERICAN DEARTH OF ELECTRIFIED LINES

A nation so dominated by its oil barons as the United States would be, in our own time, unlikely to encourage electric traction beyond a certain point. Yet the Americans had achieved the first main-line electrification as far back as 1895, on the short, steeply-graded tunnel section of the Baltimore and Ohio Railroad between Camden and Waverly stations, Baltimore.

The Great Northern Railway electrified its old Cascade Tunnel in 1909 on the three-phase system, which it replaced by 11,500 Volts single-phase at 25 cycles in 1927. The new, much longer Cascade Tunnel was opened in 1929, and Figure 619 shows one of the more recent locomotives (5,000 h.p.) near Leavenworth, Washington. On the Great Northern, however, the diesel has now conquered all. A more fortunate electrification has been that of the Chicago, Milwaukee, St. Paul and Pacific Railroad, carried out with 3,000—3,400 Volts d.c. on its mountain divisions, and dating from the years 1915—27.

PLATE XXXIV Double-unit diesel-electric locomotive in Melbourne.

Even so, the entire Class I (main line) railroad system of the U.S.A. contains but 1,810 miles of route electrified compared with 12,706 route miles in the Soviet Union, 6,119 in Italy and 5,891 in Japan. Even Great Britain, long backward in main-line electrification, approaches the United States closely with 1,682 miles, excluding tube lines in London and Glasgow.

The General Electric freight locomotive in Figure 620 has an odd history. Intended for Russia just after the war in 1950, she was bought instead by the Milwaukee company,

being converted to standard gauge and, unofficially, dubbed 'Little Joe'.

America's apparently poor showing in electrified mileage has been due to various factors. The importance, in American business, of oil, is of course one of them, but potent ones are the very small passenger-traffic density in the motor era, and the practice of running enormous freight trains at relatively infrequent intervals, over immense distances on single track. The Pennsylvania Railroad alone provides something fairly comparable to a European electric main-line railway.

620

PLATE XXXV *The Fish*, an inter-urban electric train, leaving Sydney.

PLATE XXXVI Electric traction in the
Low Countries.

MAIN-LINE ELECTRIFICATION
IN FRANCE

By the middle of 1964 France had 4,748 miles of electrified main-line railway, compared with 1,682 in the smaller area of Great Britain and 1,810 in the immensely larger United States. In the French South Eastern Region, as in many other places, 1,500 Volt direct current has long been used. On this system runs the famous Mistral express [622] each way between the capital and the Mediterranean, one of the fastest trains in the world. It is worth remarking that two of the electric locomotives employed, representing two different classes, attained the world's rail speed record for orthodox motive power and rolling-stock — 205 m.p.h. between Bordeaux and Dax — in the spring of 1955.

It was in the French Alps that early practical experiments were made in the use of 25 Kilovolt single-phase 50 cycles electrification during 1950—51, but it has been in Northern France that the first extensive application has been made. Figure 621 shows a Trans-Europ Express headed by a Co-Co locomotive

621

PLATE XXXVII London-Midlands-Lancashire: standard British Railways 50 cycle electric locomotive.

and bound for Brussels and Amsterdam, at Paris Nord. The system allows for much lighter ancillary equipment and a great reduction in the number of sub-stations needed.

By way of contrast, Figure 623 shows a metre-gauge line in the French Alps — third rail with 600 Volt d.c. — with a motor-and-trailer train between Chamonix and Argen-

tières. Electrification in these parts dates back to the years 1901—08.

Especially noteworthy in this picture are the elevation of the conductor rail (an important point in snowy country, if the thing is to be used at all) and the cased air-cooled resistances, looking from a distance like clerestories, on the two motor coaches.

622

623

ELECTRIFICATION IN GERMANY

Between the wars there was extensive electrification of German main lines, more especially in the southern and Alpine areas, using the single-phase system at 15,000 Volts $16\frac{2}{3}$ cycles. Following World War II, conversion was made a national policy under both republics, the system being the same. By 1962 there were 2,775 miles of route thus electrified on the Federal Railway, plus 37 miles of the 1,200 Volt d.c. Hamburg City Railway. In East Germany, the rump of the old Reichsbahn had 586 route miles electrified, including 256 miles in the Halle Division. Figure 624 shows a train on the Höllental line in the Black

625

Forest (converted in the '30s) while in Figure 625 a class E 10 locomotive pulls out of Cologne, heading over the river.

There have been experiments with very high voltage on contact line on the Höllental Railway before the more fruitful ones in France. Hungary, too, had essayed a 50-cycle system in the early 1930s.

ELECTRIC CONVERSION IN NORTHERN ENGLAND

For many years the main Manchester-Sheffield line, with its branch to Wath-upon-Dearne and the great marshalling yards there, had suffered increasingly from congestion, chiefly that of the heavy South Yorkshire coal traffic going westwards over and through the Pennines. Between Dunford Bridge and Woodhead were two parallel single-track tunnels,

each just over three miles long, the older dating back to 1845, and both very foul and in poor repair.

Electrification of the line was decided upon many years ago, but was held up by the war. It was at length carried out in stages during 1951—54, on the 1,500 Volt d.c. system, and simultaneously with its completion came the opening of the new double-track Woodhead Tunnel, through which, be it added, no locomotive has ever passed under steam. The old

tunnels were then sealed up. It was an expensive conversion, but it rendered unnecessary the quadrupling of track.

The first electric locomotive for this line was built during the war, and sent immediately after it for some time to the Netherlands Railways, which were very glad of it during an acute shortage of equipment, while its performance could be closely watched. The Dutch named the locomotive *Tommy*, which afterwards became the official name. All through traffic on the line is now worked by Bo-Bo locomotives and by a rather heavier Co-Co class. Figure 626 shows a laden coal train from Wath coming up to Penistone in 1955, and in Figure 627 one of the Co-Co type is heading an ordinary goods train across the strengthened viaduct at Broadbottom near Mottram.

627

SWEDISH IRON ORE TRAINS

The Grängesberg-Oxelösund Company in Sweden is as much a part of the country's iron-mining industry as a public transport undertaking. The initials T.G.O.J. on the side of the electric locomotive [628] stand for a title translatable as 'Grängesberg-Oxelösund Traffic Company's Railways'. The system has 178 miles of route, and was electrified in stages during the years 1947–56.

Figure 629 illustrates an older view showing one of the three non-condensing turbine locomotives which formerly took their turn on the ore trains down to the Baltic coast. The system of electrification is the same — 15,000 Volts single-phase, $16\frac{2}{3}$ cycles — as that of the Swedish State Railways.

628

629

630

ITALIAN EXTREMES

This extraordinary scene covers nearly 20 centuries: Out in the Roman Campagna [630] an electric multiple-unit train of the Italian State Railways threads a gap in the ruins of one of the aqueducts built by the Emperor Claudius (born 10 B.C.) a great patron of Roman engineering. One fancies that he would have approved of electric railways in Italy.

Later centuries saw the rise of the Venetian Republic, with its superb island city, and after several more centuries a railway viaduct was built to it across the lagoon. This was destroyed by the Austrians — one of the first major acts of war against a railway — who then replaced it themselves, Venice having become an Austrian city. Now the Italian electric trains roll to and fro above the waters where the family takes Mamma out for a quiet

440

631

cruise in the late afternoon sunshine [631].

Pride of the Italian State Railways' Passenger Department, in the '60s, are the luxurious and somewhat expensive Elettrotreni Rapidi [632], which link the greater cities, travelling at speeds calculated to keep in check any serious drift towards internal air services. The motormen sit aloft in a sort of lantern deck; passengers jockey for the favoured position in a small saloon in the nose of the train. The cars are articulated in two pairs and one three-body unit. The system is 3,000 Volts d.c.

632

633

634

635

ELECTRIC MOTOR COACHES

Haulage by electric motor coaches may be by two methods: single, very powerful coaches, which change ends at terminals, or alternatively haul and propel (pull-and-push) with a control trailer at the other end and control cables (not power cables) through the intervening carriages. Or several coaches may be distributed through a train, with a proportion of one or more trailers to each motor, driven from the front and with control cables linking them; this is the multiple-unit system employed throughout the world.

Haulage by motor coach is exemplified in Figure 633 by a close-up of an express on the Bodensee-Toggenburg Railway in Switzerland (see also page 468). This company and the

Swiss South Eastern run a joint service between northern and central Switzerland, and the latter company even names its motor coaches as if they were express engines.

In Figure 634 is an example of an Australian interurban multiple-unit train on the New South Wales Government Railways. It consists of two four-coach rakes, each with a motor coach at the end and two trailers between.

An Indian multiple-unit suburban train is shown in Figure 635, Italian-built in this case at Kurla on the Central (formerly Great Indian Peninsula) Railway's Bombay lines. Full permissible advantage, it will be seen, has been taken of the Indian broad gauge in body construction. The Swiss train works on the 15,000 Volt single-phase $16\frac{2}{3}$ cycles system; the others on 1,500 Volt d.c.

ELECTRIC LINES IN NEW ZEALAND

When it was opened on August 4, 1923, Otira Tunnel [636] through the Southern Alps of New Zealand was proudly proclaimed as *the longest tunnel in the British Empire*. With a length of 5 miles, 564 yards, it was worked from the first by electric locomotives, and for years the tunnel line formed the only electric section of a main line in New Zealand. Still New Zealand can claim the longest British mountain tunnel, for the recent Rimutaka Deviation involved a tunnel of 5 miles, 821 yards, opened on November 3, 1955.

Commonwealth runner-up is the Connaught Tunnel of the Canadian Pacific Railway, 5 miles, 39 yards long in the Rockies; until comparatively recently worked by steam locomotives, and enormous ones at that. Next comes England, with the 4 miles, 628 yards of the Severn Tunnel, under the great estuary between Gloucestershire and Monmouth, and dating back to 1886.

This, be it added, is as yet the world's longest under-water tunnel. Several times flooded during construction, it has had elaborate pumping machinery perpetually in operation to keep it more-or-less dry. Diesel traction serves it today.

New Zealand has still a comparatively small mileage. There are 68 miles of route altogether, chiefly in the Wellington area, North Island. Figure 637 shows an express from Wellington to Auckland near Plimmerton in 1961, headed by an articulated Bo-Bo-Bo locomotive of class Ew which would take the train as far as Paekakariki. Throughout New Zealand's electrified lines the 1,500 Volt d.c. system is employed.

637

CROWDED INDIA

By the summer of 1964 India had 1,128 route miles of railway electrified, the oldest conversions having been in the Bombay suburban area, where those of the former Great Indian Peninsula Railway dated back to the years 1925—29. The suburban lines of the Western Railway (ex-Bombay, Baroda and Central India Railway) were dealt with in stages from 1928 to 1955. All these lines based on Bombay use the 1,500 Volt d.c. system, and Figure 638 shows a commuters' arrival at Bombay Churchgate. Close quarters are endured in India, and a train unloading passengers between two platform faces instantly fills both platforms.

In Figure 639 is an Eastern Railway suburban train in the Calcutta area. The Sealdah Division was dealt with during 1963—64, and uses the 25 kiloVolt 50 cycle single-phase system. While the Indian passenger has always accepted crowding, he also likes fresh air. The doors remain open in transit, and legs may even be thrust out to enjoy a breeze up the trousers (observe second door of second car!). In Figure 640 is the Co-Co main-line locomotive *Bidhan*, also on the Eastern 25 kV. system which, by 1964, amounted to 438 miles of route.

638

639

640

641
642

448

PLATE XXXVIII Inter-urban electric train;
Lyons-St Etienne line, France.

PLATE XXXIX Metre-gauge in the Swiss Alps.

NEW TOKAIDO LINE, JAPAN

By the middle of the 20th century the common Western view of land transport seemed to be: 'We *must* have motorways!' Or, in the States: 'Our highway transportation is gummed up. Let us build more State Highways parallel to the old railroads.' So it was done, and no doubt General Motors and Standard Oil were very pleased. The Eastern attitude was this: 'We must have better transport between our cities. Congestion is appalling. It will be eased best by building a new railway beside the old one, on broader gauge, for through traffic. The existing rails can carry the local traffic. If we build super-highways instead, movement in our cities will grind to a stop. Look what has happened in America!'

Japan, like the much less thickly populated countries of South Africa and New Zealand, had inherited a 3 ft. 6 in. gauge railway system from the 19th century. The great arterial route of the country was the Tokaido Line of Japanese National Railways, linking Yokohama, Tokyo, Nagoya, Kyoto, Osaka and Kobe. This was completed in 1889. Its electrification was completed late in 1956. On April 20, 1959 the first turf was cut for the New Tokaido Line, to be on standard gauge with special rolling-stock, on the 20 kiloVolt single-phase system at 60 cycles, to support a frequent, very fast interval service by day and night. Trial runs on a test section began in June, 1962, and on March 30, 1963, a prototype train attained a speed of 159.08 m.p.h.

The die was cast for the shape of railways in the Age of Aircraft, a more practical die than the cumbersome one of internal air-lines, with their formidable terminal problems. Figure 641 shows the faces of the trains to come. In Figure 642, one of them skims on its way below Fujiyama.

MINING LOCOMOTIVES, ANSHAN AND UTAH

Electric traction was used in mines, both underground and in open-cast workings, from an early stage. In the former case, the engines could be built to very confined dimensions; in all cases, they emitted no fumes and were safe unless the mine was damp-ridden and thus liable to explosion by spark. These two views have this much in common; that they both show open lines, and work of very similar sort is being done. Geographically they are far distant, for one is in the United States and the other is in China. Figure 643 shows part of a

643

three-unit electric locomotive at Anshan. Each unit is an almost complete locomotive, but they are permanently articulated and the cab is in the middle, with a pair of pantographs mounted over the bonnets fore and aft. The third unit is out of the picture to the left.

The American scene [644] is taken from the open pits of the Kennecott Copper Corporation at Bingham Canyon, Utah. The locomotive is one of 64 85-ton double-bogie engines used for transfer movements between mine and main railroad. It has its pantograph down, and the clouds about the ore-cars are smoke from hot brake-shoes on the descent. (We have seen this phenomenon on the Arlberg line in Austria; so dense was the smoke that we imagined a steam train must have gone through the great tunnel just before us!)

644

645

THE MOSCOW-LENINGRAD EXPRESS

In a world which, as far as railway transport is concerned, has come to be dominated by oil engines in the West and electric motors in the East, the gas turbine raises its head for surface transport in both. The Russian example of a gas-turbine locomotive in Figure 645 was recently built at the Kolomensky diesel-engine works for working passenger trains on the cheapest low-grade fuel. It is rated at 3,500 h.p. and has a top speed of 90 m.p.h. on passenger trains. As in Western Continental Europe, even in parts of Great Britain, electric traction

is highly esteemed in Russian mechanical engineering circles. Though Russia is rich in oil those responsible for its production have not yet succeeded in cornering the national economy.

The October Railway from Leningrad to Moscow is the most patrician of Russian lines; it is about equal in length to the West Coast Route between London and Glasgow, and is electrified throughout. Figures 646 and 647 show its northern and southern extremities, both in modest, windswept-looking terminals. The Red Arrow makes a comfortable connection overnight, not too fast, and that last qual-

646
647

ification is a recommendation where night trains are concerned on an inter-city stretch of 404½ miles (compare London Euston to Glasgow Central, 401½ miles). The locomotive is shown at Leningrad's Moscow Station, and the sleeping cars, with a buxom train hostess, in the Leningrad Station, Moscow. The system is 3,000 Volts d.c., though since 1955 much Russian mileage has been electrified on the 25 kV. 50 cycles single-phase system.

MOUNTAIN
RAILWAYS

BERNE-LÖTSCHBERG-SIMPLON

With the Simplon Tunnel completed, there was need for access from Central and North-eastern Europe. A French company built the Berne-Lötschberg-Simplon Railway, crossing from the Rhine basin to that of the Rhône. It was opened, with its great summit tunnel, 9 miles 140 yards long, on July 15, 1913.

Figure 648 shows Moreau, Chief Engineer (South) greeting Rothpletz, Chief Engineer (North) when the bores met in the middle of the mountain on March, 31, 1911.

Figure 649 shows the officially-named Victoria Tunnel, high above the Rhône. When blasting achieved an astounding piece of un-intentional sculpture, the name was almost inevitable.

648

Surely the Lötschberg line is a favourite of ours! It has difference, always an endearing quality in railways, quite apart from the superb mountain country. In earlier days that difference was apparent not only in the locomotives and the agreeably elegant station houses, but even in the permanent way. Unlike all others in Switzerland, but like all British and several French main-line railways, the B.L.S. used the bull-head section of rail, keyed into chairs, instead of the flat-footed T-rail used nearly everywhere else. This is clearly visible in the 'Queen Victoria' view. The bridges are magnificent. It is stimulating to ride over the roof of Europe, in one bright morning, from the waters of Rhine to the youthful Rhône.

649

BERNE NEW STATION

In an entirely enclosed station, steam traction is a nuisance and the exhaust from oil engines is at once disgusting and a menace to health. Electric traction makes possible a completely underground terminal, as, 60 years ago, the New York Central found when required, under new City laws, to use only electric trains in Manhattan. In Switzerland, *par excellence* the land of electric trains, the Main Station at Berne had long been an anachronism for the Federal Capital. In 1860 it had begun as a terminus on a spur. During 1889—91 it was converted into a through station. The project of rebuilding it a second time dates from the early 1950s. Completion of the new, underground station, which should increase its capacity by 90 per cent., is expected in 1968. Figures 650 and 651 show the transformation in progress, without interruption to 650 train and 3,000 shunting movements daily.

650

651

ITALY: TUNNELLING AND REALIGNMENT

For years, Italian railways had been a byword for inefficiency that was sometimes, but not always, picturesque. Monumental reforms, for which the Fascist Government tended to take the credit, were planned and initiated by the great General Manager, Carlo Crova, and the recovery of the Italian State Railways from the calamities of war, many years later, was still in the Crova tradition.

Doubling of old tracks, involving either the construction of new tunnels round the old ones [652] or new, more or less concurrent tunnels [653], was carried out in many places. The coastal scene with the prickly pear is in Sicily, on the line from Palermo to Messina.

652

The Apennine Tunnel of the then new direct line from Florence to Bologna, 11 miles 892 yards long, was opened during the Mussolini years, on April 22, 1934. In the world, as a tunnel unbroken by intermediate access, it is the longest after the parallel Simplon Tunnels of 1906 and 1922. It is not unusual for a very long tunnel to have a block post in the middle of it; there is one in the Mont Cenis, oldest of the great Alpine tunnels. In the Appenine Tunnel [654] it is elevated to the status of an intermediate station, grandly named Precedenze, though there is no public passenger traffic for it to handle. Men coming on or off duty while working in the tunnel find the station useful, however, for in either direction they are over $5\frac{1}{2}$ miles from the outside world. The station contains a double crossover.

653

654

MOUNTAIN RACK LINES I

Oldest of the Alpine rack-and-pinion mountain railways, and one of the oldest in the world, is the Vitznau Rigi Railway in Switzerland. Its Schnurrtobel Bridge is shown in Figure 655 with one of the original locomotives, built by the Swiss Central Railway in 1870. On both this and the Mount Washington Railway in the United States, (Plate XVII, facing page 129) which just preceded it, a vertical boiler was at first adopted in the original locomotive design, owing to problems of keeping the firebox crown covered with water on very steep gradients. A forward-inclined horizontal boiler was later adopted.

Mark Twain, who was so busy *tramping abroad* that he forgot to mention the Mount Washington line, likened the descent of the Rigi to 'sliding down the balusters in a railroad train' and remarked that on crossing the Schnurrtobel Bridge he had good opportunity for remembering his sins, and repenting of them, though afterwards he found that this

had been quite unnecessary, for the line was perfectly safe. The Rigi line was unusual among such railways in having the standard 4 ft. 8½ in. gauge. Most of its successors were on narrower gauges.

The Abt rack, used on many other steep-grade mountain lines, consists of two closely parallel rails with staggered teeth. A solitary British example of an Abt line is the Snowdon Mountain Tramroad in North Wales [656]. It attains the highest British railway summit — 3,540 ft. — and began regular traffic in April, 1897. The present photograph appears to have been taken about 1923—25. All the equipment is Swiss-built and all the locomotives, except the first, which had a sad end at the very beginning, are still in service.

The same is to be seen on the Brienz-Rothorn Railway in Switzerland, which climbs to a summit of 7,378 ft., and after certain vicissitudes became the last steam mountain railway in Switzerland. Figure 657 shows one of its original locomotives, built in 1891, beside the main road at Brienz.

655

656
657

459

PILATUSBAHN

Since it was opened on June 4, 1886, the Pilatus Railway has held its place as the steepest railway in the world to be worked by locomotive traction. Its ruling gradient is 1 in 2, and working is on the Lochner system, with horizontal pinions engaging on lateral racks. Until 1936 it was worked by steam rail-motors, as shown in Figure 658. With a vehicle built rather on the lines of a locomotive staircase, the only possible position for the boiler was across the frame. Even the 'kneeling cow' engine was out of the question here. The first of the steam cars was built in 1866. It and others of an early delivery were used in construction of the line. Eleven were built down to 1909. In 1937 the railway was converted to electric traction, as shown in Figure 659. It is about three miles long from the lakeside station at Alpnachstad to a terrace just below the 7,116 ft. summit.

658

RHAETIAN RAILWAYS

Unique in Europe is the combined system of the Rhaetian, Furka-Oberalp and Visp-Zermatt Railway Companies, comprising a metre-gauge network that extends from the Engadine and Grisons right across the roof of Europe to beyond the Rhône, and also, in the east, over the Bernina Pass into Italy. Construction of the Furka-Oberalp line was held up by the 1914—18 War, with the odd result that for some time the town of Andermatt possessed a railway station, *and* a locomotive, but there was no line to connect with any other place.

The great ferro-concrete bridge at Langwies [660] is on the Rhaetian Railway as is the splendid Wiesener Viaduct [661]; the Chur-Arosa Railway was added in 1942, having been independently constructed and opened in 1914.

The Rhaetian Railway is the largest company-owned line in Switzerland, with 245 miles of route. Electrification began in 1913 between St. Moritz and Schuls, and was completed in 1922, on the 11,000 Volt single-phase, $16\frac{2}{3}$ cycles system.

660

LÖTSCHBERG, CONSTRUCTION

Timber trestles are little associated with railways in the Alps, or indeed with European railways generally, as they are with old-time North America. But in temporary use during construction, they have often been useful, and Figure 662 gives a rare view of a contractor's train making a rather dizzy loop on groaning timbers during the building of the Berne-Lötschberg-Simplon Railway. The original print is dated September 25, 1912. Construction was completed in the following year. In Figure 663 is the Bietschtal Viaduct, on the way down from the Lötschberg Tunnel to the valley of the Rhône.

662

PLATE XL The Pilatusbahn in Switzerland.

DOMINE · DIRIGE · NOS

VIRTUTE · ET · INDUSTRIA

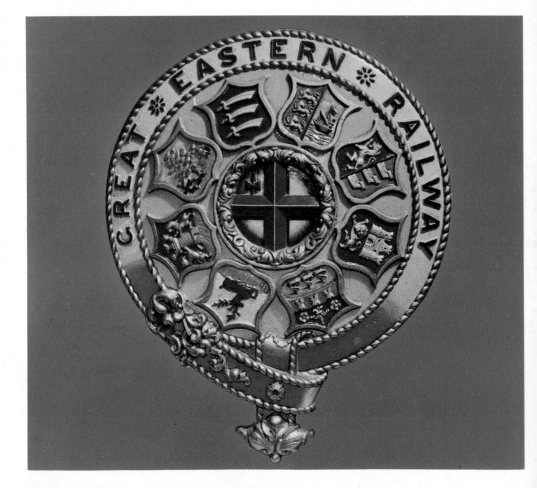

563

PLATE XLI The Great Western Railway's achievement, combining the arms, crests and devices of London and Bristol.

PLATE XLII Adamsware plate, showing an American locomotive taken from a Currier and Ives print.

PLATE XLIII Armorial bearings from a Great Eastern locomotive.

In 1871, the year of the Mont Cenis Tunnel's opening, the St. Gotthard Railway Company was formed at Lucerne, to build and run a central Alpine route from north to south. It involved the great tunnel from Göschenen to Airolo, with double track, 9 miles 562 yards from portal to portal. Work began on this, under Louis Favre, on June 4, 1872. Favre died in the workings in July, 1879. The two bores met on February 29, 1880, and at the end of 1881, a ballast train passed through on Christmas Eve. On May 27, 1882, the tunnel, then the longest in the world, was publicly opened. Its length, unbroken by external access, remained unexceeded until 1906, when the first Simplon tunnel, 12 miles 537 yards

long between Brigue in Switzerland and Iselle in Italy, was opened to traffic on June 1.

Unlike the Gotthard, this was single track, and the second Simplon Tunnel, 22 yards longer, came to supplement it on October 16, 1922. The Gotthard Tunnel was worked by steam traction until 1920, but the Simplon had electric haulage, at first on an archaic three-phase system, almost from the beginning. Figure 664 shows three levels on the Gotthard southern approach, at the Giornico spirals, with the Biaschina Gorge below. Figure 665 shows a train from Italy, with a Swiss locomotive, leaving the second Simplon Tunnel just south of Brigue. Figure 666 shows a southbound train leaving the southern portal of the Gotthard Tunnel at Airolo, headed by a Co-Co locomotive of the Swiss Federal Railways, named *Ticino* and built in 1952.

665

666

667

SWISS CROSS-COUNTRY LINES

Between them the Bodensee-Toggenburg Railway and the Swiss South Eastern Railway provide a cross-country route from St. Gallen, south of the Lake of Constance (Bodensee) and Arth-Goldau on the main Gotthard line, via Rapperswil, thus cutting a considerable mileage compared with that of the Swiss Federal Railways' route, and also avoiding the complexities of Winterthur and Zürich. Its traffic is relatively local, but of foreign visitors, Germans are aware of this short cut to the Goldau Valley and the Lake of Four Cantons.

Of a different sort is the Brunig line of the Swiss Federal Railways, on metre gauge with considerable rack sections, topping a summit of 3,396 ft. before dropping abruptly down to the Lake of Brienz and forming the most direct route between Lucerne and Interlaken. Figure 667 shows a Bodensee-Toggenburg train northbound, with the skyline of the Seven Princes beyond.

In Figure 668, a Brunig train is shown approaching the summit of the pass on its tremendous climb from Meiringen. Both routes were formerly worked by steam; the Bodensee-Toggenburg was electrified during 1931—32, the South Eastern in 1939, and the Brunig during 1941—42, all on the Swiss standard 15,000 Volts, 16⅔ cycles single-phase system.

MOUNTAIN RACK LINES II

One of the most interesting of the many mountain rack lines of Switzerland is the Gornergrat Railway. Like many others, it uses the Abt rack, and propulsion has always been electric for public service. During construction, however, a steam locomotive was used (built in 1892), and was kept for emergencies until 1920. In that year she was sold to the Monistrol-Montserrat Railway in Spain. Her more youthful duties were thus describable as a sinecure. The summit terminus of the Gornergrat Railway is 10,134 ft. above sea level, the second highest in the Alps. The gauge is one metre.

For a quaint contrast let us take the Achen-see Railway in the Tyrol [669]. It is unusual in that it leaves the main line station of Jenbach, on the main line eastwards from Innsbruck, on a violent gradient, straight up the mountainside. Its upper section, however, is more or less level, and on reaching this, the engine ceases to propel the train from below, runs round it, and hauls it for the rest of its short journey on ordinary track without rack assistance. Combined rack and adhesion lines are relatively common, and range from the Alps to the Andes, but such an arrangement on a short branch railway where, in Bryan Morgan's words, 'the kneeling-cow engine starts her train by walking abruptly upstairs', is pretty rare. On most lines the flat stretches, if any, are at the bottom.

669

ALPINE RAILWAYS, AUSTRIA

Austrian Alpine main lines, unlike those of Switzerland, generally follow courses from east to west, or east to south-west. North-to-south routes, such as the Mittenwald and Brenner lines, are comparatively short. The latter, incidentally, has no long tunnel, though reaching a summit of 4,496 ft. The Arlberg line, completed in 1884, passes through a tun-

nel 6 miles 650 yards long on its course from Innsbruck, Tyrol, to Feldkirch in the Vorarlberg.

Of more recent date is the Tauern line in Carinthia, which, with its 5 miles 551 yards tunnel, was completed in 1909. Figure 670 shows the Pfaffenberg-Zwenberg Bridge on the south side of the tunnel. The Arlberg line was electrified in 1923 and the Tauern line between 1933 and 1950.

GREAT NORTHERN RAILWAY:
NEW CASCADE TUNNEL, WASHINGTON

Longest tunnel outside Europe is that built through the Cascade Mountains and opened by the Great Northern Railway in 1929, 7.79 miles from portal to portal. On the left [671] is the western entrance, with the original *Empire Builder*, electrically hauled, just vanishing into the mountain. The train's tail-plaques bear the Great Northern insignium, a mountain goat.

Pictured on the right [672] is the eastern portal today. The great, calm, purring electric locomotives in their turn are gone. The eastbound freight train just emerging is headed by three gurgling and not very fragrant diesels. Neither are they very beautiful, against a harsh background of screes, but they are very useful, and two men control the three locomotives.

672

HIGHEST RAILWAY IN THE WORLD

One might expect the world's highest railway summit to be on some rack-rail line to a lonely summit. But it is on a main line, with standard gauge. This is the Central Railway of Peru, one of several lines owned and worked by the Peruvian Corporation, penetrating the high Andes and providing western links in South America's transcontinental rail network.

The abrupt rise of the Cordilleras from the Pacific coast is climbed by means of tremendous switchbacks, and on La Cima Pass an altitude of 15,848 ft. (4,830 metres) is topped on the new branch, 42 ft. higher than the La Cima old summit. Altogether, 10 summits above 14,000 ft. are crossed by railways in Peru. The scaling of these giant mountains

673

674

goes back into the previous century, and early railway construction was a mortal business for many. Engineering works are numerous and heavy. Figure 673 shows two levels on a characteristic part of the great ascent with, on the left, the grotesquely isolated form of a locomotive between two tunnel-mouths. Figure 674 shows a steel span sharing the Infernillo (Little Hell) gorge with the even more vertiginous mountain road.

In marked contrast to the mountain lines of North America, trains on the Central of Peru are modest things in relation to their immense surroundings. The cars are as light as is consistent with comfort and convenience. Oxygen is always carried to revive sufferers from *sorroche*, the sickness of high altitudes, and on that account, as well as that of formidable gradients, travel is leisurely from the coast to the great tops. Diesel traction took over during 1964—65, but for years previously traffic was handled by Beyer Peacock 2-8-0 engines, one of which is illustrated on the turntable in Figure 675.

PASSENGER AND FREIGHT HANDLING

SPECIAL TRAINS FOR CHICAGO WORLD FAIR, 1893

By the late 19th century the mighty Illinois Central Railroad, and many others, had made the Middle West. The Chicago World's Fair of 1893 was at once a demonstration of the expanding prosperity of the Middle-Western States and of the metropolitan importance of Chicago itself. Visitors descended on the exhibition in droves, not only from America but from nations all over the world. The principal countries exhibited, and the dominant theme was machinery, bigger and better, for every

purpose. At the same time the Fair was one of the first great international exhibitions to be laid out on landscaped lines; it had even an elevated intramural railway as if it were a town in its own right. Incidentally, the London and North Western Railway sent a locomotive (*Queen Empress*, sister to *Greater Britain*, see Plate XII), a sleeping car and a coach. Of course there were American exhibits galore, from locomotives and stationary engines to prairie windmills.

All this set a considerable traffic problem, to be shouldered entirely by the railways, for the motor was in extreme infancy, and Chicago's public transport consisted only of the horse-

676

cars and cabs. To deal with the rapid entrainment and detrainment of passengers in large numbers, the Illinois Central company improvised some special cars for transit between the city centre and the exhibition grounds on the South Shore. Unlike all other American cars they followed the European style, having cross seats and side-door access, though of doors proper there were none, simply waterproof curtains. It was rough, bu it was ready. High platforms, also very un-American, helped rapid ingress and egress.

Figure 676 shows passengers about to entrain. The cars filled in 15 seconds and emptied in 11 seconds. Old locomotives were used, with headlamps fore-and-aft, for the special World's Fair trains, non-stop between Van Buren Street and Jackson Park on special tracks; fare, 10 cents single and 20 cents 'round trip'. Many also used the regular suburban trains, and altogether about 19 million fares were booked during the six months down to October 31. Noteworthy in the photograph is the engine with its rear headlamp on the left, also, incidentally, the fine old patriarchal farmer and the little girl in a bustle.

Figure 677 is an Illinois Central scene by the way. The great plains of the Middle West were ever subject to disastrous floods. Then, as now, the train was the only thing likely to get through them. True, one hoped that the water would not reach up to the firebox, also that no hidden subsidence would be encountered.

COMMUTING TO CHICAGO

The American's love of the motor car has not destroyed the necessity for the commuters' train, indeed railroad passenger traffic has held its own more in the Middle-West than in the Eastern States where, over large areas, it has died of attrition. Figures 678 and 679 show how the Chicago, Burlington and Quincy Railroad deals with its suburban regulars, carrying them on two levels in what might be called gallery cars rather than double-deckers. The arrangement provides seats for a greater number of passengers, though access and egress are not too easy. For years the neighbouring Illinois Central Railroad used side-door coaches to overcome this problem, following its experience with the crowds at the Chicago World's Fair in 1893 (see the illustration on page 476).

678

680

CARLISLE MARSHALLING YARD

Sorting and marshalling of vehicles posed early problems which grew with the magnitude of freight and mineral traffic. About the turn of the century the London and North Western Railway, at Edge Hill, Liverpool, first expedited things by the use of gravity, with wagons being slowly propelled over a hump whence they ran down, singly or in groups, into a

gridiron of sidings, but the practice was not adopted on a grand scale until 1907, when the Great Central Railway inaugurated its 'concentration yard' at Wath-upon-Dearne.

The movement of coal from the South Yorkshire coalfield to many and diverse destinations needed expedition if it were not to become hopelessly congested. The modern, major marshalling yard is an immense installation covering many acres, and is divided into four

681

main areas; for reception and dispatch of trains in up and down — or in America, eastbound and westbound — directions respectively. The impetus of vehicles passing down the further end of the hump is checked, according to the loading and number of wagons, by electro-pneumatic retarders [680]. Operation is automatic.

The general view [681] taken just after completion, shows the yards at Carlisle, at the focal-point of traffic between the London Midland, and the Scottish Regions of British Railways. Carlisle Up Yard contains 48 classification sidings and 10 retarders. In Carlisle Down Yard there are 37 classification sidings and eight retarders. A primary retarder is installed on the downward slope of each hump towards the sidings which in turn are governed by group retarders. Control is central and, as shown, all the yards are floodlit.

AUTOMATIC MARSHALLING

It is a far cry from the ancient goods yard which in war, when bombed by the opposing side, was always called a marshalling yard. In our wartime monitoring experience it was surprising how many non-existent marshalling yards were bombed, according to official news-bulletins. But there are real ones a-plenty, ale round the world.

Figure 682 shows the control desk of the automatic marshalling yard at Millerhill, east of Edinburgh, in British Railways' Scottish Region. Figure 683 shows the Westinghouse 'Velac' automatic control panel for the electro-pneumatic retarders. Millerhill is smaller than Carlisle, but it contains 40 sorting sidings and eight reception sidings. There are 31 signals and seven point machines, one primary and seven group retarders.

682

BRITISH MARSHALLING YARDS

Freight concentration in British Railways, North Eastern Region: The aerial view in Figure 684 shows the up and down yards at Newport (County Durham) which together form the great Tees Yard, handling 7,500 wagons daily. The tall pylon in Figure 685, 376 ft. high, is at North Eastern Region's Tyne Yard, and supports a dish aerial. It is part of the micro-wave radio telephone link between Newcastle and York. The first such system to be used on British Railways, it was installed in 1964.

AMERICAN MARSHALLING YARDS

In Figure 686, at Conway Yard on the Pennsylvania Railroad, a single freight car is rolling down the plane and entering the primary retarder, one of a pair on the slope of the double-track hump. In the air view [687] is the Louisville and Nashville company's automatic marshalling yard at de Coursey, Kentucky, with the through lines bypassing it on the right. One of the trains appears to be about two miles long. The view is towards Cincinnati, Ohio.

686

488

FREIGHT HANDLING: COAL AND GRAIN

Markham Marshalling Yards, on the Illinois Central Railroad, seen from the control tower, with three lots of coal cars going down from the hump [688]. Markham became famous about 1930, a time of unprecedented trade depression, with the railroad companies fighting for their lives with their only weapon — heavy transport with expedition.

In Figure 689 is a 'Big John' grain car of the Southern Railway (U.S.A) coupled to a grain hopper of ordinary size. Both are, of course, covered; the big car is of 4,800 cu. ft. capacity, equivalent to 100 tons of grain. It has 12 hatches and eight discharge hoppers for rapid loading and unloading.

Insulated cars for perishable freight are everywhere important. That of the Burlington [690] is one of 575 built during 1965. Insulation is by polyurethane foam. They are the largest insulated freight cars in the United States.

689

690

489

THREE-DECK CAR HANDLING

Over 50 years ago, when the Chicago, Milwaukee and St. Paul company had electrified its Mountain Division, we were treated to a photograph of one of the new trains with the proud (and so American) caption: 'Handling Freight as Freight Never Before was Handled.' Certainly, the length of the train was prodigious. But the caption applies more than ever to several recent techniques developed in the United States.

The ordinary American freight car has not much changed its form, save that steel bodies have replaced wooden ones. But the transport of motor cars [691 and 692] is on a scale unequalled in the rest of the world. Mounting them on three levels still has its problems, even with the generous loading-gauge of American railroads, and there are places where they cannot go thus.

Both our illustrations are taken from the Santa Fe route to the West, and Figure 691, with the five-unit General Motors diesel in the foreground, shows the train winding through the dry, scrubby hills of Corva, Arizona.

693

694

FREIGHT HANDLING ON THE GREAT NORTHERN

Bulk movement and a minimum of transhipment make the essence of modern freight handling. These three views are all from the Great Northern Railway in the United States. The grain-hopper cars in Figure 693 each take approximately double the load of the old standard American freight-car. Figure 694 shows piggyback transport of road trailers conveying fruit. They have combined refrigeration and heating units for the conveyance of fresh apples at any time of the year. In Figure 695 centreflow hopper cars are being loaded with vermiculite near Libby, Montana. Each car has a capacity of 100 tons. On the middle car a sign vainly orders 'For Food Products Only'!

695

FREIGHT HANDLING OF HUGE LOADS

Mechanised methods of handling freight and minerals, on a large scale, form one of the railroads' principal weapons in a world of competitive transport. Figure 696 shows the loading of grain from elevator into a 100 ton covered hopper car of the Louisville and Nashville Railroad at Henderson, Kentucky. In Figure 697 a coal car of the same capacity is being tipped at a power station near Harrisburg. The entire operation, car-to-car, occupies three minutes.

Those were bulk loads; Figure 698 shows a single-item load, a million-pound (avoirdupois) pressure tank for an oil refinery, carried by the Louisville and Nashville Railroad in 1963. At the time of writing, this mammoth consignment still stood as a record load for land transport.

ENGLISH TRAIN FERRIES

Water breaks have bedevilled railway transport ever since railways first began to cover long distances. In a massive continent, such as North America, there has been less trouble, but Europe has always abounded in such gaps. Scotland saw the world's first real train ferries, though coal wagons had been barged in North Eastern England at least as far back as 1842. Thomas Bouch introduced them to the Firths of Forth and Tay in 1850 and 1851 respectively. How ironical that, years after, his bridge across the latter met with appalling disaster and, not so very indirectly, to his own unfortunate death.

From 1890, when the Forth Bridge was opened, Great Britain knew train ferries no more until the war of 1914—18, when they were much used for carrying loaded rolling-stock and locomotives for military purposes between England and France. The first public Anglo-Continental train ferry was inaugurated, for freight traffic only, between Harwich and Zeebrugge by Great Eastern Train Ferries and the allied Anglo-Belge company on April 24, 1924, using the old wartime vessels and equipment. Except for the Second World War, it has been functioning ever since. Figure 699 shows one of the present craft, the *Suffolk Ferry*, just off the dock at Harwich.

In Figure 700 is an exceptional out-of-gauge load — one of a series of trains conveying the equipment of a glass-works, very slowly but surely, from Central Belgium to South Yorkshire. Passenger train-ferrying between Dover and Dunkirk [701] began on October 14, 1936. Every night the Wagons-Lits company's cars pass decently, without fuss, between London, Paris and Brussels.

699

700

701

TRAIN FERRYING FROM LAPLAND TO SYRACUSE

In the years while British railways — having built the Forth and Tay Bridges — seemed to forget about train ferries, they came and flourished in the Baltic lands. The great Danish bridges were not yet built. Sweden and Norway were isolated from Continental land transport, as they still are, but for the ferries. The sub-continent of Scandinavia proper — no mean land-mass — was linked by them to Denmark and Germany quite early on.

There was a train ferry between Sassnitz on the Isle of Rügen, in North Germany, and Trälleborg, to the south of Malmö in Sweden, and one is glad to recall that the first vessels were built on the Tyne in the early 1900s. There was a train ferry between Copenhagen Docks and Malmö, and another between Elsinore and Hälsingborg. To this day, with the Little Belt Bridge long in use, the journey from Esbjerg to Stockholm involves two crossings by train ferry. Figure 702 shows a variety of vehicles — passenger, freight and oil-tankers — being driven on board a Swedish six-track train ferry.

Tidal variations in the Baltic are negligible by Channel standards, so the Scandinavian countries had far less difficulty in the equipment and provision of regular services than England at Harwich and Dover, especially Dover. The same tidal leniency belongs of course to the Mediterranean, and for many years the Italian State Railways have happily moved rolling-stock across the straits between Reggio di Calabria and Messina [703]. The vessel is on a more modest scale than the Swedish one, but the straits are narrow and the ships make repeated passages. It is thus possible to send a wagon from Wick in Caithness to either Lapland in the North or Syracuse in the South. Anyway, Italian wagons have long been familiar on British railways.

702

TRAIN FERRIES: ON AND OFF LOADING

To carry railway vehicles on a ship is a simple matter enough; but running them aboard and on to land again has always presented the major problem. Back in 1850, with the Forth and Tay train ferries, Thomas Bouch had used a long cradle running on rails down an inclined plane to overcome tidal differences, and today on the Channel ferry between Dover and Dunkirk special train-ferry docks are needed. Elsewhere, lift-cradles and hoists are generally sufficient.

In Baltic waters the difference in water-level is almost negligible, which is why train ferries were used in Denmark and across to Sweden from quite an early date. Figure 704 shows the original installation at Sassnitz, on the German-Swedish run via Trälleborg. The ends of two sleeping cars are just visible on the train deck of the Swedish ship *Drottning Victoria*.

Figure 705 is from a photograph taken at Harwich in 1948, showing the double-track cradle leading to the four-track steamer *Suffolk Ferry*, on the Harwich-Zeebrugge run.

705

PIGGYBACK FLAT-CARS

In a country so dominated by oil and motor interests, and crisscrossed by well subsidised State highways, American railroads maintain their existence and pay tremendous taxes simply through the virtues of the rail as a transport machine which is still the best for certain forms of conveyance, such as passengers in large conurbations or heavy freight over great distances. It is not favoured, as a public service, as it is in Communist countries; it is made to fight for its life. American railroads as they were in the 1920s for all their then virtues, would perish in a night. The rail had to come to what might be called mechanical terms with the motor, and so it has.

The idea of containers is ancient. It was known in the early days of French railways before the Second Empire, but it was with the appearance of the heavy motor that it came into its own. Figure 706 shows a 40-ton

straddle-lift crane lifting 24 ft. road-rail-sea containers on to a train of Southern Pacific flat-cars, from a 14-wheel articulated motor container carrier. Noteworthy is the fact that while the overhead crane inevitably runs on parallel rails, the straddle-frame is mobile to the extent of being mounted on, and achieving its locomotion through enormous balloon-tyred road wheels. It can freely range the freight yard.

Piggy-back haulage of motor trailers on flat-cars by railroad has become, in recent years, a nationwide feature of freight traffic. In Figure 707, 40-ton trailers are loaded, two to each flat-car, at the end of a ramp on which stands one of the tractor units for highway transport. The load appears to be somewhat dangerous.

These things exemplify the radical importance of transport *per se*. It is neither the train, nor the motor, which ultimately matters. Business is a spur, but not an end in itself.

707

708
709

STOCK AND AGRICULTURAL TRANSPORT

In both Australia and New Zealand the widely differing railways give indispensable service in the movement over long distances of the crops and the beasts which feed and clothe many other peoples. The immensely long Trans-Australian double-deck sheep car [708] (it is 85 ft. over headstocks) is on an American rather than an Anglo-Saxon scale. It is entirely of steel, to Commonwealth Railways' standards, with automatic couplers and continuous brakes, but its forerunners have been in Australia for a long time. In pre-motor days one might see the heads of several tramps or sun-downers sticking up among the warm, woolly bodies of the sheep on the upper deck (the lower deck, as may be imagined, had certain disadvantages quite apart from that of quick discovery and eviction).

On a much more modest scale, but still double-decked, is the New Zealand sheep truck in Figure 709, with the second contingent of Canterbury lambs following their leader to the upper level. Annual traffic is about 5,000,000 head. The scene quaintly suggests human beings boarding an air-liner, save that the sheep are probably better behaved.

From stock to arable: Figure 710 shows a wheat train, carrying 2,100 tons of grain, near Breeza, New South Wales Government Railways. It is hauled by three class 45 diesel-electric locomotives.

710

ALPINE MOTOR FERRIES

Driving over an Alpine pass is not a thing to be undertaken lightly, even in summer. The road is gruelling. In winter it is impassable. From the 1950s onwards increasing use has been made of ferry trains through the great tunnels. People drive on one end, over a ramp, and off the other as soon as the locomotive has been detached after passage through the tunnel.

The entire transit is extraordinarily rapid, and if an occasional driver has a touch of claustrophobia, it is better to have it while sitting on a train than when driving through a road tunnel such as that under the Great St. Bernard.

In Figure 711 railway officials are checking up on their motor-brigade at Mallnitz, outside the Tauern Tunnel in Austria. In Figure 712 a car train is entering the St. Gotthard Tunnel at Göschenen in Switzerland.

712

RAILWAYS AND INDUSTRY

As we have seen, the rail's origins at a remote time were with the movement of heavy minerals, from gold to coal, and it is still the ideal land conveyance for these things. Figure 713 shows a French coal train near Hénin-Liétard.

Compared with coal, oil is a newcomer, its importance having risen with the perfection of the motor engine, but this again is a commodity which has to be handled in enormous quantities as quickly as possible. Figure 714 shows the Spen oil depot of Charrington Hargreaves at Liversedge, in British Railways' North Eastern Region. In the foreground are electric rotary pumps passing oil from the railway tankers into the storage tanks.

Thirdly, there is the special vehicle for use in heavy industrial installations. All really large movable equipment moves on rails in great works. Figure 715 shows a molten iron carrier in Eastern France, unloading into a ladle.

713

714

715

FREIGHT LOADING AND UNLOADING

Palletising, in one form or another, with loading and unloading by vertical lift motor trucks, has become an essential accessory to certain classes of freight traffic in recent years. It is ideal for fragile or perishable consignments. Figure 716 shows an enormous freight car, 94 ft. long over the couplers, belonging to the Southern Pacific Railroad and used for vulnerable pressed-steel motor body components. The car has two sets of double doors each

716

717

side; its overall height is 17 ft. and its capacity is 10,000 cubic feet. In Figure 717, two vertical lift trucks are engaged in loading. Either loading or unloading takes 45 minutes.

Rapid loading and unloading of bulk loads, of quite another sort, is shown in Figure 718. This shows a composite steel/aluminium closed hopper car of the Canadian Pacific Railway under the mechanical loading equipment of a potash installation in Western Canada.

718

CAR-SLEEPER SERVICES

Although innumerable motor-cars are carried by North American trains, as freight, the car-carrier and car-sleeper services, whereby the private motorist is bedded down in a railway sleeping car, and his own car is carried in the same train, *and straight on till morning*, is essentially European. One is thus ferried from London to Perth, or from Glasgow to Eastbourne (drive on to Newhaven), or from Calais to Avignon. It is a highly civilised form of passenger transport, and now very widespread in Europe. Perth came first, in 1957.

Figure 719 shows a Continental car-sleeper, with one of the two-level open transporter wagons and the characteristic end of a Wagons-Lits car. The Wagon-Lits company's staff themselves seem to be a separate race. Possibly you will find in conversation that your conductor is a German-born French subject domiciled in Belgium, and he is probably trilingual.

British car-sleeper and car-carrier services are already long-established. Car-carriers, be it added, are daytime trains which shift the touring motorist far away from the metropolitan and certain provincial bottlenecks (e.g., Honiton and Exeter). Closed two-decker vans with power-lifts may be used, or ordinary type vans with large end-doors which present a long lighted tunnel as one drives on. When all vans are loaded the end-doors are closed and the car owners retire to their sleepers. The closed vans give the private cars more protection than do the Continental type. Figure 720 shows a car for Scotland being driven on at a London terminus.

719

720

SIDE DOORS FOR SPEEDY PASSENGER HANDLING

On another page we have shown the advantage of the British side-door train in the rapid entry and exit of passengers, which is of the highest value in heavy suburban passenger transport. Figure 721, taken in 1957 below the Ilford Flyover in British Railways' Eastern Region, shows both varieties of car. Above are the open-saloon vehicles with air-operated pneumatic sliding doors, similar to those on the underground lines, and below is compartment stock, with about 50 per cent lavatory-access, for regular travellers over longer distances from the city. Both trains are proceeding towards London.

Figure 722 shows a commuters' coach de-

721

722

signed by Oliver Bulleid and Lionel Lynes for the Southern Railway in the late 1940s which remains the prototype of this sort of stock. The plan and the door-arrangements are those of a compartment-type coach. The off-centre gangway, with seats three-by-two on each side of it, enables passengers to dispose themselves evenly. Every section has an outside door.

Very different is the American arrangement shown in Figure 723. Seating is on two levels, the upper set in galleries. In a severe climate the limited access allows the train to stay warm in winter where the British style of coach would be altogether superfluously air-cooled. But, as shown, with such limited access entry is slow and station stops are correspondingly longer. The American train is on the Burlington system in the Chicago area.

723

LONDON SUBURBAN SERVICES

These three views give quite separate aspects of the London suburban business traffic. Of Figure 724 we might write — for we often had that impression while looking on such a scene every morning from the detached position of an office window — that this is *the spawning of the electric eels*. The scene is Liverpool Street in London at 8.52 a.m. on June 14, 1961. The train at Platform 15 is withdrawing, while that on No. 14 has just let out its passengers. The same thing has just happened on Platforms 16 and 17. The lesson it rams home is the rapid egress (and ingress) of passengers on services run with the primeval European side-door carriage. Nothing can match it, even though its patrons may have no particular affection for it.

Figure 725 shows Harlow Town Station on this same Great Eastern Line. The place is peculiar. There is a new town at Harlow, a self-sufficient town; nevertheless the station handles commuters to and from London. The photograph was taken late on a midsummer evening. The breadwinners have gone home. A London-bound freight is quietly sliding through on the far side. In Figure 726 is a suburban train-washing plant, also in British Railways' Eastern Region.

724

725
726

727

INTERURBAN AND INTER-CITY

Inter-urban and certain inter-city trains have long been composed of block sets with motor and trailer cars, like suburban commuters' trains, but with more elaborate appointments. The South Coast services in England were indeed an extension of the Southern Railway's suburban network, which had been electrified from 1915 onwards (London and South Western Railway) on the 660 Volt d.c. system with third-rail contact. The coast was reached in 1933, and Figure 727 shows a London to Eastbourne and Hastings train on the Quarry Line near Merstham, about 1935. The train contained both a buffet car and a Pullman. A Russian multiple-unit inter-urban train is shown in Figure 728.

A British inter-city Pullman business train, a diesel in this case, is exemplified by the Bristol Pullman, in Western Region [729]. Though the days of the Pullman Car Company as such are no more, the name has been retained, as well as the fine feudal Pullman coat of arms, as long respected symbols of comfort and convenience.

728
729

CITY RAILWAYS

CITY AND SOUTH LONDON UNDERGROUND

The world's first underground electric city railway was the City and South London. It was opened between Stockwell and King William Street on December 18, 1890, at a deep level throughout, with access by lifts. At Stockwell a steep ramp led to the workshops and power-station on the surface, and Figure 730 shows one of the original trains — a small electric locomotive and three 'padded-cell' cars — in the Stockwell car sheds. It was considered that as there was no scenery, proper windows were unnecessary. Conductors bawled the station name down the cars at each stop.

Later cars, however, were of more civilised sort, for people liked to see where they were. Figure 731 shows a steel car built by Brush in 1907. The line was extended southwards to Clapham Common. Northwards, the King William Street line under the Thames was cut out and a new northern extension taken up via the Bank through Islington to Euston. In 1900 came what we might term the first modern tube, the Central London Railway. This too began with haulage by locomotives, of much heavier design. They set up such troublesome vibrations that motor coaches, with trailers between, were soon substituted. Figure 732 shows stock of 1904.

We know the railway today as London Transport's Central Line. Like nearly all the old tubes it has been much extended with the years, and now stretches from Ealing to Ongar in Essex. The older City and South London Railway was rebuilt to present tube line standards during the 1920s, and now forms the City Line.

730

731

732

733

GLASGOW SUBWAY

In the infancy of deep-level underground railways — tubes as we know them — electric traction was still regarded with suspicion by some engineers. To its ultimate great cost, the Glasgow District Subway, having inner and outer circle lines and twice passing under the Clyde, was equipped with cable traction, and opened for traffic thus on December 14, 1896. Figure 733 shows the cable drums and tension equipment in the old power station. Though uneconomic, the line was cable-operated until 1935, when electric traction with third-rail contact was substituted for it. With this the line, now belonging to Glasgow Corporation, at last began to show a profit, and it continues to do so.

In rebuilding the rolling stock, the old car bodies were kept, though considerably improved. They work in pairs only, at very frequent intervals. In Figure 734, two of the much-rebuilt cars stand in the shops at Govan, which are reached by an oblong well with the two lines at the bottom and a car-hoist above. Down below, the inner and outer lines are unconnected by points. It is a modest tube, compared with the ramifications of London and Paris, or the architectural grandiosities of Moscow, but within its limits, and with a worsening traffic problem above ground, it is very useful. Figure 735 shows a platform scene at St. Enoch station; inner circle on the left, outer circle on the right. Note the blandly chivalrous porter (or is he perhaps accepting a tip?).

736
737

MONORAILS

Apart from the unintentionally funny Lartigue lines in France, Ireland and elsewhere, the first commercial use of monorails, about which so many are still arguing, was in the twin towns of Barmen and Elberfeld, now known as Wuppertal, in the industrial area of north-west Germany broadly termed the Ruhr. Langen's suspended system was used, with electric traction, over a route 8¼ miles long between Oberbarmen and Vohwinkel. It had its first section opened as long ago as March 1, 1901, and although a true monorail, it has always been called *die Schwebebahn* (the hanging railway). It serves the purpose underground lines serve in other cities.

In some places the lines run concurrently above the streets, with the same ugly effect as was achieved by the old but orthodox elevated railways in New York City. But over considerable distances the space over the River Wupper was appropriated, with much less nuisance and expense, though not everybody thought it particularly beautiful. Still, people did not go to gaze on the Wupper with the same delighted admiration as they felt for the Rhine or the Moselle, or for that matter for the lovely green Isar through Munich.

During the war of 1939—45, the line suffered severe damage, but again it was more easily reparable than some more solid structures under really heavy air attack. Figure 736 shows an over-river station on the line in its earlier days, with one of the original two-car trains and a somewhat 'conservatory' style of building. Note also the one-horse omnibus and the pendulous arc lamp. Figure 737 is recent. Observe the splendid bow span, also the articulated bodies of monorail train, tram and bus.

738

UNDERGROUND ELECTRIFICATION

With the example of the tube lines, electrification of the older underground city railways in London could not be delayed much longer. From the beginning of the new century, the Metropolitan and District companies conducted joint experiments, but agreed badly, and the Mersey Railway in Liverpool achieved the first conversion (1903). General electrification of London's under-street lines followed in 1905, the two companies having at last agreed on 600 Volts d.c. with outer conductor rail and centre-rail return.

Figure 738 shows a seven-car District train of 1905. The cars, though not built in America, closely followed the design of some already at work in the States (Boston, Mass.). An early attempt to use pneumatic doors was, however, very unfortunate, and these did not re-

739

appear for years. Noteworthy, in the train shown, is the capacious luggage compartment behind the cab. Victorian ideas died hard, and passengers were still expected to bring heaps of luggage, even under the streets of London. The Metropolitan Railway had further, by then, a considerable outer suburban user.

On the Uxbridge line, it improvised motor- and trailer-car trains from stock built for the steam-worked Aylesbury line in 1898 [739].

Compartments and side-doors allowed rapid detraining. For working trains to and from the Aylesbury line within the electrified city area, double-bogie locomotives were employed. A Westinghouse 'Camel' (the nickname was inevitable) is shown in Figure 740, coupled to a train of the old underground semi-rigid eight-wheel coaches. Observe the early, and somewhat ostentatious, use of the destination blind.

740

LONDON TRANSPORT

Three phases and three aspects on the London Transport Board's railways are here shown. The oldest [741] shows an excursion train of ex-London Tilbury and Southend side-door compartment stock headed by two of the District Railway motor vans which were built in 1905 for hauling the older Outer Circle trains over the electrified lines between Mansion House and Earl's Court. The Outer Circle, forgotten by many and unknown to many more, was in fact U-shaped, between Mansion House and Broad Street, partly steam worked. The train shown is leaving Ealing Broadway for Southend via the District line. For many years the change-over to steam was made at Barking. The service ended in 1939.

Figure 742 shows a multiple-unit train of 1935, of District Railway type, but first put

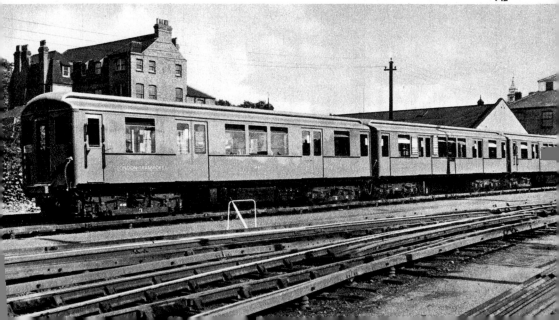

into service on the Hammersmith and City (Metropolitan) line. Air-operated doors had been in use on the deep-level (tube) lines since the early 1920s, but this was their first successful application to rolling stock of District type.

In Figure 743 we have the most familiar image of the London Underground system in this case furnished by an Elephant & Castle-Watford train on the Bakerloo Line at Piccadilly Circus. The squat 'tube' contour of the cars is peculiar to London, apart from the trains on the circular underground line in Glasgow.

743

NEW YORK SUBWAYS

In the New York City Transit Authority we have an organisation rather akin to the London Transport Board, having a virtual monopoly of internal passenger transport. New York's bus services are much less extensive than London's; the New York electric lines, subway and surface but excluding those of the main-line companies, amount to 237 route miles on standard gauge, compared with London's 244 route miles (216 owned by the Board).

Underground railways, or subways as they are called in the States, came relatively late owing to the difference in tunnelling through New York rock from boring London's clay.

N.Y.C.T.A. is the largest city transport undertaking in the Western Hemisphere. Figure 744 shows a Times Square shuttle train at one of the Interborough platforms under Grand Central Terminal, where the lines are on several levels. The Interborough system was acquired by the Authority in 1940.

Figure 745 shows one of the more recent subway cars on one of the surface sections, on a Coney Island express. In Figure 746 is a wintry night scene at an open subway-car yard on the city outskirts, with repair shops and power station in the right background. All the cars shown are of the older clerestoried type, somewhat akin to London's District Line cars of the middle 1930s.

744

745
746

THE BEAUTIFUL STOCKHOLM T-BANA

Stockholm is a city of surprises. Not the least occurs when one gets into an ordinary city underground train, at an ordinary though artistic city underground station, and finds the train mounting a startling ramp in the open air high above the gyrating motor cars with, for scenery, a skyscraper on one side and a charming timber-built windmill on the other [747].

Road congestion led to the building of the Stockholm underground system (the *T-bana*), the first section of which was opened in 1950, and extension has been going on from then. By the beginning of 1964 it comprised about 25 miles of route. Figure 748 shows passi-meters at Liljeholmen station, and Figure 749 a tunnel section.

The system was not absolutely the first of the Swedish capital's examples of underground construction; at Slussen on the south side of the river there had long been underground and semi-underground exits for suburban trams and for the Stockholm-Saltsjön Railway, the latter a combination of commuters' and holidaymakers' service, originally worked by steam. The *T-bana* is, however, a true 'underground', or in American parlance a 'subway' and carries over 600,000 passengers daily. At many of its stations it has become a gallery of modern decor and design.

747

748
749

THE UNDERGROUND AND THE TUBE

To this day there are two distinct forms of underground city railway transport in London; the deep-level tubes, and what are called the surface lines, though in the central area the latter also are underground. The surface lines have sprung from the old Metropolitan and District Railways, steam-worked before 1905, and built by cut-and-cover methods during the latter part of the 19th century. Both systems break surface on the perimeter of the city and extend into the suburbs; the Metropolitan line, indeed, gets as far as Aylesbury, far out in the green.

Figure 750 shows the burrowing junction at Wembley Park, with the stacks of Neasden Power Station in the distance. In the centre are two tube trains, mostly of 1938 cars but including (second in each) clerestoried cars of earlier design. The other trains are all of the largest Metropolitan Line stock, introduced from 1960 onwards. They are of orthodox underground type, with automatic air-operated doors, but the seating is on a fairly liberal scale in view of regular commuting use out to Amersham, nearly thirty miles from central London.

Deep in the heart of Suburbia [751] is the Piccadilly Line train at Rayner's Lane on the Uxbridge branch. This was originally a Metropolitan steam line. In 1903 it saw early experiments in electric traction. The station building above the tracks is characteristic of the architectural reforms carried out, particularly in the '30s, under the influence of Frank Pick.

751

752

CITY RAILWAYS: BERLIN AND TOKYO

London having given the world underground railways in cities, the world took them up. Paris and Berlin did so quite early, in 1900 and 1902 respectively. Figure 752, from a photograph taken between the wars, shows platforms of the three-level station at Alexanderplatz, Berlin, evidently caught during a very slack hour.

In Figure 753 is a standard multiple-unit train on the Ginza Line of the Teito Rapid Transit Authority, and Figure 754 shows a platform scene on the Hibiya Line, both in Tokyo. Noteworthy in the former are the conductor rails which, although affording top contact, have wooden guards over them. The supports of the collecting shoes project sideways from the bogies, under the superimposed boards.

753

754

CITY RAILWAYS: BAKERLOO AND CENTRAL LONDON

In Figure 755 is a Bakerloo car built in 1906, typical 'gate stock' of the London deep-level lines. The general design was similar to that of the Central London cars, but the finish and appointments were plainer. Getting from the middle of the car to one of the exits during the rush-hour was an ordeal, and sometimes an insoluble problem. The cars ran until the middle '20s.

Few people remember, or even know, that in its early days the Central London Railway ran a postal service like a main line railway. Figure 756 shows a train loading at Post Office station (now St. Paul's). In recent years the General Post Office has run its own tube system, with driverless trains carrying the mail containers.

MAIN LINE
DIESELS

THE NAPIER 'DELTIC' DIESEL

The Napier 'Deltic' engine, an 18-cylinder diesel, was applied in a pair to an English Electric locomotive in the middle 1950s. The original locomotive which, with its two engines, developed 3,300 h.p., was then the most powerful single-unit diesel-electric in the world. It is now in the Science Museum, South Kensington, London, having had long and critical road-tests in British Railways' London Midland Region. Among British diesel-electrics it made a new mark. But it was B.R. Eastern Region which produced the most valuable orders for 'Deltics'. They, truly, could be called the oil-engined successors of the London

and North Eastern's superb steam Pacifics on the East Coast expresses.

In 1961 the Deltics were on the Flying Scotsman, which, over the previous 99 years, had provided a daily, two-class passenger service in each direction between London and Edinburgh. In Figure 757 one of them passes along that agreeable riverside reach at Offord, going north. Figure 758 shows an up East Coast express near Grantham, also behind a Deltic. Two incidental features should be observed. In the foreground is an expansion joint in the long welded track. Beside it is the sign limiting speed to 100 m.p.h. on the curve going north. The two scenes were taken in August and October, 1964, respectively.

757

759

DIESELS IN SCOTLAND

It was in the 1950s that diesel traction began its great push against steam on British Railways, when in America the steam locomotive was already in full retreat. On the northern and eastern lines electric transmission was employed for all large locomotives, as in the United States. Figure 759 shows the East Coast express, the Heart of Midlothian, northbound from London to Edinburgh behind a Type 4 diesel electric locomotive, skirting the tranquil Ouse by Offord Church, Huntingdon. The time is August, 1958.

In Figure 760 is one of the standard inter-city diesel trains of British Railways Scottish Region about to leave Edinburgh Waverley for Glasgow Queen Street. The year is 1956; there are two steam locomotives just visible behind the leading diesel car. These inter-city diesel sets are very similar, as coaching equipment, to the fast inter-urban electric trains in the South of England. Internally they are to full main-line standards, and thirsty passengers will always find the bar open.

In the Scottish Highlands today, the diesels reign quite supreme. In Figure 761, two Sulzer-engined diesel locomotives in multiple head an Inverness to Perth express on the Highland line just south of Newtonmore, on the 16 mile climb out of Strath Spey to the 1,484 ft. summit of Druimuachdar Pass. The train consists of 10 carriages and two container wagons.

536

760

761

762
763

THE AUTORAIL

In France an *autorail* — a motor train — can be anything from a bus on rails to a quite considerable diesel multiple-unit. If, to an artist at any rate, it lacks either majesty or charm, it is extremely useful, and not least in fast service across country, where patronage is limited compared with that on the great main lines. In Figure 762 is *Le Catalan*, which runs from Geneva to the Spanish frontier town of Port Bou on the coast line to Barcelona. This shot was taken near Grenoble.

In Figure 763 a four-coach set from Ventimiglia to Nice passes above Menton-Garavan, just west of the Franco-Italian border (agaves, like prickly-pear, can make a formidable lineside hedge).

In Figure 764 is an *autorail-panoramique*, a French variant on the 'dome' theme. Propulsion is diesel-electric, tare weight 55 tons, top speed 80 m.p.h., and the car is essentially for touring in spectacular country. It is fully air-conditioned, with half its 88 passengers on the upper deck over the engineroom. Two trailers can be hauled.

764

765

DENMARK FIRST WITH DIESELS

Although there had been earlier experiments in other countries, Denmark has many claims to have been the nursery ground of the diesel engine in railway traction, and it was there, in 1929, that we first encountered diesel locomotives in the course of ordinary journeying. Both the locomotives on the left page were built and ran trials in Denmark during that year. Figure 765 shows one built by Burmeister and Wain.

It had two bogies, one on six wheels and the other on four. Quaint, to our eyes, is the body, comprising the engine-room and the two driver's cabs, designed to harmonise as far as possible with the clerestoried coaches then in vogue on the Danish State Railways.

The engine in Figure 766 was conceived on different lines. Built by Frichs of Aarhus, it outwardly resembled a small electric locomotive with the wheel arrangement 2-Bo-1 (four-wheel bogie, two uncoupled driving axles and

766

a trailing carrying axle). Difficulties in transmission were an early bugbear in diesel locomotive design; generally electrical transmission found most favour for large locomotives while mechanical transmissions were suitable for small ones and for light rail-cars or railbuses.

By the '60s the Danish State Railways, like most other national systems throughout the world, had become very largely 'dieselled'. Figures 767 and 768 show contemporary examples. The multiple unit train of eight cars including three motor vehicles is of a type used for fast internal passenger services and for the Esbjerg-Copenhagen boat train *Englaenderen*. It can be divided and transferred to train-ferry under its own power. The diesel-electric locomotive is for hauling ordinary vehicles, both freight and passenger. Its styling owes something to American influence, as in the high cab above a half-domed bonnet. The colour is dark red.

769

DIESELS SWEEP THE WORLD

In about a decade the diesel locomotive, in
one form or another, swept the world's railways wherever there was not high traffic
density with consequent electric traction. In
some places steam held out longer than in
others, but from the middle 1950s onwards
the change was rapid, sometimes abrupt. In
Figure 769, men of the Masai contemplate the
new face on a North British diesel shunter of
East African Railways and Harbours in the
station at Kajiado. The Bronze Age meets the
Oil Age.

Figure 770 is from Kingston, Jamaica, on
what was the senior member of British Colonial railways, and shows a modest 750 h.p.
English Electric Bo-Bo diesel-electric locomotive, one of the series numbered 81—92, first
introduced in 1955.

770
771

IRISH RESURGENCE

Between 1955 and 1965 the diesel engine more or less took over the world's railways. Whatever the objections against the diesel by many railway enthusiasts there is no gainsaying its cheapness in running and its round-the-clock availability. On the adverse side, breakdown liability is rather heavy. Its virtues, not uninfluenced by the power of oil in big business, soon overrode those less persuasive factors.

Even Russian government more or less decreed a diesel revolution on those railways which it was not busy electrifying. In Figure 771 is an express from Moscow to Kiev, headed by a double unit diesel-electric.

In Ireland the story was curious, almost tragi-comic. Ireland is not naturally a land of heavy railway traffic, and for a long time the railways had been in a bad way. There was no appreciable coal, and nothing like the Alpine sources of water power, but the rail was a lifeline. Differing, almost inevitably, the Northern Irish Government continued to let its railways rot, while the Republican Government aimed at a streamlined system of essential main lines. Oliver Bulleid, who had done so much on the Southern Railway in England to keep steam going, tried turf-burning in Ireland, then he too turned to diesels as his parting gift to Coras Iompair Eireann. In Figure 772 a diesel-hauled express is shown rounding Killiney Bay on its way from Waterford to Dublin.

772

THE AMERICAN STATE RAILWAY

Occurrence of a State-owned railway in the United States seems as improbable as that of a company-owned one in the Soviet Union. The Alaska Railroad did indeed begin under a company, but progress was slow, and bankruptcy came in 1908. But clearly a railroad was needed, though the country was not tempting to capitalists.

In 1914 President Wilson's Administration was authorised to acquire, construct and work railways in Alaska, and the Alaska Railroad's main line was completed between Seward and Fairbanks, 470 miles, in 1924. Additional lines included a branch to Whittier, which became a train-ferry terminal for traffic with what might be called the Metropolitan States of the Union, built under the urgency of war during 1941–43. Though few passengers are carried, freight traffic is valuable. Traffic is diesel-hauled, though the last available statistics showed the survival of a solitary steam locomotive.

Figure 773 illustrates Hurricane Gulch Bridge, a typical North American steel structure, with one of the rather scarce passenger trains crossing.

The Alaska Railroad is not the only line in the State, nor was it the first. The White Pass and Yukon Railway, a British undertaking dating from the first gold rush, dated back to 1898, was acquired by Canadian interests in 1951. Of 3 ft. gauge, it has 111 miles of route, all but 20 in Canadian territory. Also Canadian is the Pacific Great Eastern Railway, whose Budd-equipped Cariboo Dayliner is shown in Figure 774. Originally a purely local line, this is growing into a coastwise and inland system of great importance to British Columbia and the North-West generally. Headquarters are at Vancouver.

773
774

DIESEL RAILCARS OF THE 1930s

In the 1930s there was a renewed burst of enthusiasm for what had formerly been called a rail-motor; but this time the object was the provision of special high-speed diesel-engined cars, or pairs of cars, intended for rapid intercity passenger use with strictly limited accommodation of a superior sort.

The illustration in Figure 775 shows No. 3, one of the modest railcars of the Great West-ern Railway, built by A.E.C. at Southall. These were made in several varieties. There were cars for purely local services, intended to replace the old Churchward steam rail-motors which, though they had lasted longer than their kind on most other lines, were beginning to wear out. Provision of a lavatory, as in the example shown, made the car suitable for longer runs, and a small buffet also could be installed.

On the German State Railway, from 1933

775

onwards, handsome two-car units were built for the fastest inter-city services, beginning with the Flying Hamburger. It was a two-car train, with Maybach engines, and in the summer of that year it was running the fastest booked services in the world; 138 minutes westbound and 140 minutes eastbound over the 178.1 miles between the two cities. At that time the fastest regular steam train in the world was the Great Western's Cheltenham Flyer (71.4 m.p.h., Swindon to London, start to stop, over a distance of 77.2 miles).

This sort of limited diesel service paid off, as indeed it did in the American Middle West soon after, and other German cities were similarly linked. Electrical transmission was used. Figure 776 shows one of these German units and in Figure 777 is a very similar Belgian train. The maximum speed attained by one of the German trains was 133.5 m.p.h. This was achieved just before the war, on July 23, 1939, on a test run.

776

777

RAILBUSES

For years, passenger service on smaller English branch lines had been slowly dying, and in the 1950s attempts were being made to keep them going on a shoestring. Not only was the local bus a competitor, so was the cheap private motor car, aided by mass-production and hire-purchase. Indeed, as far back as 1933 someone high up in a southern English bus company, which ran through services to London, on being asked what he thought of the massive electrification of the Southern Railway, succinctly said this: 'No, we're not worried about improved railway services. We and the railways have different user. The ultimate menace is that of the private car.'

The hopes behind the railbus were for traffic off main railway lines, as between Audley End and Saffron Walden, or Gleneagles and Crieff. In such areas as those of South Germany and parts of Austria, and in the more remote parts of Scandinavia, the railbus has certainly achieved some success in maintaining a railway passenger link between otherwise rather isolated communities and their regional centres.

These three illustrations show a Scottish Region railbus on British Railways. The diesel-engined chassis is by Bristol and the body by Eastern Coachworks, the sponsors being the venerable Tilling Group. In Figure 778, the chassis is about to be run in below the lifted body. Figure 779 shows the completed railbus, and Figure 780 the control panel and motorman's seat.

778

781

NORTHERN IRELAND

The political division has scarcely favoured
railway prosperity in Northern Ireland, quite
apart from an admitted anti-railway bias
in some Government circles. Six counties
bounded by either the sea or a frontier do not
make an ideal railway terrain. Nearly all local
lines, and lines crossing and recrossing the
Border, have come under a ruthless axe. All of
the old Belfast and County Down Railway is
gone except what was once its suburban branch
to Bangor, which has important commuting
user from Belfast Queen's Quay Station.

A Bangor line suburban diesel is shown in

Figure 781, standing in Holywood station. Its
withdrawal would cause trouble. Along the
shores of Belfast Lough runs the line to Larne
Harbour, and from this diverges, at Green-
island, the old Northern Counties main line
to Derry.

In Figure 782 a multi-engined two-car diesel
unit heads a train of former steam stock at
Ballymena on its way from Belfast to Derry,
between a fine pair of *fin de siècle* station canopies. Figure 783 is from the main line of the
former Great Northern Railway (Ireland), and
shows the Enterprise express from Belfast to
Dublin running through Maze, with two-car
diesel units at front and in rear.

550

782
783

784

DIESEL'S VERSATILITY IN WESTERN REGION

None can deny the versatility of the large main-line diesel locomotive, which is well demonstrated by these three views from British Railways' Western Region. On what once was the Great Western Railway, much use has been made of the diesel-hydraulic locomotive, whereas other Regions have favoured electrical transmission for engines on heavy long-distance hauls. In Figure 784 the train is a down express passenger. (Note, incidentally, the elliptical arches of the overbridge, favoured so long ago by Brunel, and the Great Western lower-quadrant semaphores.)

In Figure 785 a large diesel-hydraulic locomotive pulls out with a train of standard Esso oil tankers, and in Figure 786 a smaller, Bo-Bo locomotive comes snarling down to the china-clay docks at Fowey in Cornwall. Part of the old passenger station is gone; the Fowey branch now exists on, and for, the fine Cornish clay which is shipped all over the world.

785

DIESEL SHEDS AND SERVICING

A change of motive power on a railway system involves a great deal more than the provision of new, different locomotives; or, if electric traction is adopted, the additional business of providing conductors, feeder lines and sub-stations. The old steam sheds were designed and laid out, many of them at a remote time, for the housing, servicing and running repairs of the railway engine as it was then known. At first diesels had to be dealt with, alongside the retiring steam, in the old sheds, which were in many ways unsuitable for a newer form of motive power.

The techniques of maintaining diesels and electric locomotives are in many ways different. There must therefore be different shed accommodation and different workshop equipment for effecting running repairs and working on serious breakdowns. The diesel, though its thermal efficiency and its availability are both superior to those of the orthodox steam engine, is also more delicate, in the sense that a minor

788

defect can incapacitate it. In short, it is not so tough as either the steam or the straight line-electric locomotive.

Both the illustrations are from the same modern diesel depot of Cardiff Canton on the South Wales line of British Railways' Western Region, replacing a well-known steam shed of many years standing. In Figure 787 is part of the shed proper, and the lofty repair shops. The eight locomotives in the foreground are of three different classes. External cleanliness is something differently considered in different countries.

Figure 788 illustrates a Western Region diesel-hydraulic locomotive passing through what might be called a needle-bath, with the addition of rotating 'flannels', an adaptation from well-established carriage cleaning practice, of which the Great Western was a pioneer.

DIESEL-HYDRAULIC

Hydraulic transmission for large diesel locomotives has flowered chiefly in British Railways' Western Region, once the Great Western Railway which could always be relied on to do something different. These three detail shots are of a 2,000 h.p. locomotive built in the early 1960s by the late North British Locomotive Company. Figure 789 shows the cab with seats for driver and co-driver. (The latter is still commonly called the fireman.) Figure 790 shows part of the brake equipment and Figure 791 the top of the engine casing, with the pressure gauges beyond.

789

791

790

RAILWAY MISCELLANY

WORKING MUSEUMS

With the rapid commercial decline of steam traction, this assumed a sporting interest, like sailing after the decline of the great clipper ships. In Great Britain, the United States, and Denmark, to name but three countries of very different dimensions, preservation societies have taken over some old steam lines and maintain them, for love, as working museums. In England and Wales there are several, and choice of an example is not easy, for they are fascinating and beautiful things, in pleasant places too.

The Bluebell Railway in Sussex takes its name from the 'Bluebell line' of the old London, Brighton and South Coast Railway, of which it is an isolated surviving part. On the left of Figure 792 in the yard of Sheffield

Park Station is one of the Great Western Railway's 'Earl' class engines, built for the lighter main lines of Central Wales. The passenger train, comprised of ancient Metropolitan coaches which had known both steam and electric traction, is headed by *Stepney*, one of the little 'Terrier' tank engines built by William Stroudley for the London, Brighton and South Coast company from 1870 onwards.

As far as possible, equipment is painted in correct period colours. The 'Earl' is green; *Stepney's* elaborate livery of yellow, with red, green and gold, has been faithfully restored; the carriages are oak brown with milk-white upper panels, heavily moulded. As well as giving delight to many who travel long distances to see them, the old trains are valuable for providing Victorian background in films and television plays.

792

OLD IRELAND

Even at the end of the 1940s under the impact of fuel shortage, political division and services reduced to minimum, the Irish railways were providing memorably good services under such adverse circumstances. The Great Northern Railway, indeed, was a model undertaking, especially as to trains and buses that connected. The equipment was old on most lines: Victorian on some, but nobody minded, especially as Southern Ireland at that time provided the best dining-car meals in the whole of Europe.

Figure 793 shows a Dublin-Belfast express of that time making a wintry start. Figure 794

793
794

shows an up train at Bundoran Junction on the G.N.R.; a scene that is no longer to be had. Between Bundoran and Castleblaney, a Dublin-bound train had to cross the border four times; at Belleek, west and east of Pettigo, and Clones.

Figure 795 is a now vanished scene too, in the deep South. It shows the modest branch train of Coras Iompair Eireann at Skibbereen in 1951, on a remote section of what had been the Great Southern Railway and, earlier still, the Cork, Bandon and South Coast Railway. The 2-4-2 tank engine and her single brake-third coach came from the Great Southern and Western company (incorporated in 1844, amalgamated into G.S.R. in 1925). The engine in this view was the work of J.A.F. (later Sir John) Aspinall, who later, in 1886, crossed over to work for, and make, the Lancashire and Yorkshire Railway.

795

ENGINES UNDER ATTACK

Compared with the motor, the aircraft and the ship, the railway has seen little use as a tactical weapon in war. But its strategic use was realised a century ago, and during the ensuing century's wars it has been both a decider of campaigns and a target for enemy air and ground attack.

Bridges, stations, marshalling yards, works and running sheds attracted everything that could be unloaded upon an enemy. During 1940 and 1941 the British railways had plenty of it, particularly the Southern and the London and North Eastern. A broken bridge could cause tremendous dislocation. Some people, however, were surprised at the toughness of the ordinary, and sometimes ancient, steam locomotive.

Figures 796 and 797 both show casualties on the Southern Railway during this time. In each case the victim was an old engine from the London and South Western company. Class T 14, No. 458 [796] had a direct hit in the running-shed at Nine Elms. The boiler was sprung and the frames broken, the latter usually a mortal injury. So it was in this case. The still older T 9 4-4-0 express engine [797] had a bomb through the boiler and firebox, exploding under the crank-axle. Main frames and cylinders were undamaged. This was a Fratton shed. She was repaired, and completed her half-century.

In cheerfuller vein is Figure 798. Women did most things short of driving heavy locomotives. This was Permanent Way Lookout-woman Shafto of the London and North Eastern. Let her represent thousands of others who toiled through the long war and were often under fire.

WARTIME MUNICH AND COLOGNE

Whether by aerial bombing, defensive wrecking or heroic sabotage by the Resistance in occupied countries, the ultimate destruction of railways from France to south-eastern Europe was on a fearsome scale. Bridges were down, stations were blasted, rolling stock blown to fragments, while railwaymen died like soldiers. German reprisals for a strategic

general strike of Dutch railwaymen went to the length of track lifting over considerable distances as well as confiscation of engines and vehicles.

British and American bombing reduced much of the old Deutsche Reichsbahn to a shambles. Figure 799 shows the famous Hohenzollern Bridge at Cologne in May, 1945, from the Deutz side of the river. With the familiar irony of war, Allied attempts not to

799

damage the Cathedral resulted in the survival of much of the structure in the Main Station (extreme right) and of the modest station of the Cologne-Bonn Railway down on the quay below it, while to the south of these the central area of the city was a waste of scorched and tottering walls.

In Munich [800] the ornate buildings of the old main station were pulverised (one wing, be it added, was burnt out by accident well be-fore the bombing). Its close neighbours on each side, the Starnberg and the Holzkirchen Stations, were likewise destroyed, and by 1945 only part of the parallel train halls stood gauntly above the ashes. Some of the trains, out in the country at the time, had dodged the bombs. So had one of the picturesque wooden platform trucks which we remember from be-fore the Hitler years. The station was later completely rebuilt.

800

ACCIDENTS

In the Victorian era Government Inspectors repeatedly blamed the railway companies for reluctance to instal mechanical safeguards against accident; while the railway companies (which, of course had to foot the bill) insisted that too much improvement led to decreased responsibility — and therefore reliability — in their staff. That attitude is fortunately extinct, but the fact has always remained that nearly every accident has been due to what is delicately called 'failure of the human element'. The derailment at Weedon in 1951 was due to a mechanical failure, and had spectacularly tragic results [801] but even in this case the failure was due to bad work by a fitter. Rail-way accidents are extremely rare, but when they happen, as in a shipwreck, there is usually a horrible grandeur about them. And the rail, unlike the sea, does not quickly hide the horrors.

The other two scenes are more describable as tragi-comic. The little London and South Western class O 2 tank engine went incontinently through a dead-end near Camberley at Christmas time, 1906 [802]. The Brighton D 1 tank engine [803] with her right side-tank unwrapped was in sidelong collision at a diamond crossing near Streatham Common on November 3, 1919. The accident might have been much worse. Again, it was due to human failure, though track-circuits, showing the position of the other, encroaching engine on the crossing, would have saved the situation.

802
803

MINOR RAILWAYS IN GERMANY

Visitors are often surprised to find how many relatively small, company-owned railways in the German States survived tremendous political upheavals as well as the destructive hand of war. The German minor steam railway of old Imperial days still could be seen here and there in the 1960s. Such a one is shown in Figure 804, a small tank engine of undoubted Prussian origin heading a local passenger train at Bodenwerder on the Vorwohle-Emmerthal Railway.

On an altogether grander scale has been the cross-country sort of line in the north-west, exemplified by the Westphalian Provincial Railway and the Bentheim Railway. The latter, close to the Dutch frontier, comprises two separate lines, and is now worked almost exclusively by diesel traction. It is a party to the *Verband Deutscher Nichtbundeseigener Eisenbahnen* (League of German Non-Federal-owned Railways) with headquarters at Cologne.

Figure 805 shows a Bentheim diesel passenger train passing two coupled rail-buses of the sort widely used on small German branch lines. The modern station building is noteworthy.

Of yet another sort is the inter-urban railway, of which the Cologne-Bonn Railway forms a fine example. It has 68 miles of route, mostly electrified, including two distinct lines between the cities it serves, the 'Foothills' and the 'Rhine Bank' lines. Its user is chiefly passenger, including an important commuting traffic, though there are also more than a thousand wagons serving the needs of local and through freight.

Figure 806 shows a recent electric motor coach, first- and second-class composite. Electric traction dates back to 1906, though the original equipment is long vanished. The d.c. system is used at 1,200 Volts.

804

805
806

RAILWAY TRIMMINGS

Railway heraldry was usually connected with the country the railway served. Thus the 'crest' (the term is not technically correct) of the Furness Railway [807] was thoroughly Catholic and Apostolic in deference to the fine ruins of Furness Abbey. In deference to Majesty, each of the two holy men supports a shield bearing the royal arms of England. The mythical creature at the Virgin's feet is suggestive of a long-tailed pterodactyl which, however, does not occur in the zoological index of the College of Heralds. The floridly rendered 'M S W J R' [809] adorned the sides of Midland and South Western Junction tenders down to 1923.

Since the opening of the Simplon Tunnel in 1906 was likely to divert traffic from the Mont Cenis, it was on the whole sporting of the Paris, Lyons and Mediterranean Railway to commemorate the event with a bronze and marble clock [808] at the Milan Exhibition of that year. The Spirit of Industrial Progress stands on the offside platform of a P.L.M. 2600 class locomotive while Mercury, God of Travellers, poses more cautiously on the near side, his attitude rather suggesting that he would put back the clock if he could.

The three colour plates facing page 465 show the armorial bearings of the Great Western and Great Eastern Railways [XLI, XLIII] and a modern piece of railway pottery [XLII] made by the English firm of Adams for the American market.

807

808

809

AMERICAN TRACK CLEARANCE

Snow clearance was a bugbear from earliest days, especially in North America, Northern Europe and most high-mountain country. The simplest clearing technique was to put three or more locomotives behind it and then charge deep drifts repeatedly. Either a way was battered through or the whole outfit was derailed [811]. This scene was near Ogden on the Central Pacific Railroad in 1872. Much later came the steam rotary snow-plough which screwed its way through big drifts. Figure 810 shows one on the Milwaukee Road near Hyak, Washington, in 1946. Figure 812 shows a modern American appliance which serves alike as spreader, ditcher, roadbed leveller and, when needed, as snow-plough.

810

811

812

SIGNALS
AND TELEGRAPHS

SIGNALBOXES: COUNTRY

As a piece of architecture the railway signal-box for more than a century has been unique, resembling no other building. Its forerunner was the telegraph tower, by which messages were signalled across country from hilltop to hilltop by semaphore in days before the electric telegraph, and in North America it has always been a 'tower', not a 'box'.

In the last century many signalboxes of the London, Brighton and South Coast Railway followed old telegraph tradition, for the box was mounted on legs and had the semaphores

on top of it, their tall masts passing right through the structure, which in windy weather groaned and even swayed like a sailing ship. A last survivor is shown in Hardham Junction Box [813] on the Mid-Sussex line. The photograph was taken in the 1960s and though the semaphores no longer sprang from the roof by then, the old box on its legs had not changed otherwise. The bases of the great supports which carried the weight of the manual frame and semaphores can be seen still, in this view.

More generally typical of the Victorian signalbox was the Summit Tunnel East Box of the Lancashire and Yorkshire main line

813

over the Pennines from Manchester and Leeds. Figure 814 shows this, with a fine lower-quadrant semaphore, with the home (stop) signal and the distant signal (which indicated the position of the next stop signal) below it, both at 'clear'.

Belford Box on the main East Coast line in B.R. North Eastern Region [815] shows a modern interpretation, with its predecessor, not yet demolished, just beyond it. The architecture and mechanism are of our own time, but the structure is basically familiar; glazed cabin above, mechanism below, and the primeval outside staircase. Wherever he is, the signalman has a clear view of the roads he controls.

814
815

816

817

SEMAPHORE SIGNALLING

For nearly a century British semaphores worked in the lower quadrant, that is to say the horizontal position of a stop signal showed *danger*, while a lowered position indicated *proceed*. In early days, a 45 degrees downward inclination indicated *caution* and a perpendicular position (inside the originally slotted post) meant *clear*. Slotted posts lasted longer than the three-aspect indications, the 45-degree drop then indicating *clear*. Distant signals, with fishtail notches cut in the ends, gave advance indications of stop signals to come. They could be passed, in the horizontal position, but drivers had to apply their brakes in readiness.

Figure 816 shows an old gantry of slotted-post semaphores near Norwood Junction on the London, Brighton and South Coast Railway in the 1890s. Then as now, the red side

of the arm faced the direction of movement. Slotted posts were vulnerable to packed snow, and this was a contributory cause of the Abbots Ripton accident on the Great Northern in 1876. The G.N.R. afterwards adopted French's balanced semaphores, in which the arm was centrally-pivoted on an iron bracket. Some last survivors are shown, near Finsbury Park, in Figure 817. (Observe the new colour-light signals mounted, but not yet in use, on the same gantry.)

The gantry in Figure 818 had a curious history. It belonged to the London and North Western Railway, and was at Rugby. When the new Great Central Railway came at the end of last century, its viaduct disturbed visibility of signals, so the G.C. company was required, at its own expense, to raise the London and North Eastern gantry so that its upper portion cleared the top of the girders on the viaduct.

818

SIGNALBOXES OLD AND NEW

A contrast, though not so much of a contrast as it might seem at first. The mechanical locking frame at Preston [819] has a singularly Victorian look about it, with the old block telegraph instruments above the levers and the raftered roof typical of the old type of signalbox found on the London and North Western Railway.

The same never could be said about the all-electric box at Rugby [820] though it is still on the old, classic, historic London and North Western main line from the Metropolis to the North, the oldest main line out of London. But in the old box at Preston, track circuits and the illuminated track diagram made of it a different installation from that which controlled train movements during the Race to Aberdeen in 1895.

819

821

SIGNALLING CONTROL DESKS

We have come a long way since a youthful signalman in Scotland first discovered that he could sit in a hut and control two fixed signals at once with a clothes line and a counter-weight. First mechanical and then electrical engineering improvements have brought us over that distance in time. Figure 821 shows the largest route relay interlocking control desk in the world, at Glasgow Central. Eleven route miles are involved, with 170 fixed signals and 157 point mechanisms, while the number of possible train routings involved exceeds a thousand.

The push-button control panel at Short-lands Junction, in the suburban area of British Railways' Southern Region [822] operates 36 signals and 20 point mechanisms over 15 miles of route, with 52 possible train movements. That at Pretoria, South African Railways [823] involves only 5¾ route miles, but there are 105 signals, 75 point machines, and the number of routes involved is 392.

822

823

824

SIGNALLING: MARSHALLING YARDS

In Figure 824 is the control tower of the Tyne Marshalling Yard in British Railways' North Eastern Region. Behind it to the left is one of the yard's 150 ft. lighting towers. Tyneside is an area of intense traffic movement; freight, mineral and passenger. Figure 825 shows the Newcastle Control Room. Left-centre is the traffic regulator's dais; centre and right is the switch console, and beyond it, left-centre to right, the illuminated track diagram. At the bottom of this are the east and west terminal lines with the through platform roads in the middle and the through passing roads at the top. Left (below) and right (above) are the main East Coast connections. Left (above) is the old High-Level Bridge route to Gateshead and South Shields, and right (below) the connections to the Carlisle line. On the extreme left is the sound-proof glass-panelled box of the station train-announcer. On the upper part of the main wall, above the track diagram, are the train-describer panels.

825

AUTOMATIC COLOUR-LIGHT SIGNALLING

Colour-light signalling, *per se*, is of course ancient, but the first British installation of track-circuited automatic colour-light signals in Great Britain, showing two aspects, was on the Liverpool Overhead Railway in 1920. Previously, on the same railway, the intermittent-contact system, employed on many city railways thereafter, had been used since 1893.

Modern colour-light signals are of two forms, *main* and *subsidiary*. The former generally show three aspects: red for absolute stop, yellow for caution and preparedness to stop at the next signal, and green for clear; but very often there is a fourth aspect, double-yellow, meaning that the next signal is to be passed at restricted speed. In congested areas, a red may be preceded by a yellow and by two, or more, at double-yellow. The arranged sequence is further affected by the use of very fast schedules.

Subsidiary signals for running lines are generally route indicators for sidings or calling-on signals, showing two white lights at 45 degrees, with the running line signal remaining at red. Ground signals for shunting show a red and a white light, horizontally, for *stop* and two white lights at 45 degrees for *proceed*.

Figure 826 shows signals at the east end of Sheffield Victoria, in British Railways' Eastern Region, with running and subsidiary signals on the same posts. Figure 827 shows a four-aspect signal with junction indicator on the Great Eastern Line of B.R. Eastern Region. The equipment is immunised for use with 25 kV. 50 cycle electric traction.

826

827

LEVEL CROSSING

It is easy to say that the road-rail level crossing is an anachronism of the Railway Era, and some motor people would gladly abolish the lot, provided somebody else foots the bill. As it is there are fewer in Great Britain, in proportion to the volume of railway traffic, than in most other countries.

Firstly and most primitively we have the occupation crossing, leading to private property and under the control of the road user. That shown was at Partridge Green in Sussex [828]. In many countries it is ungated. A cautionary note as to its use: Don't open one gate, drive on to the line, and then leave your car there while you open the second gate. If you do, you may (as the Chinese put it on their notice-boards) 'meet with a sad end'.

828

829

830

The controlled double-gate crossing is familiar to all in Great Britain and Ireland. It is expensive and cumbersome, and the lifting barrier is really a much better thing, as Germans, Scandinavians and others, discovered long ago. That shown in Figure 829 is at Spath, B.R. London Midland Region. It is a deterrent, with full road signals, but a dishonest motorist can dodge through it, imperilling both himself and the oncoming train.

The most nearly perfect form is shown in Figure 830. This is at Ware, in the British Railways' Eastern Region. The barriers are complete and fairly substantial. The crossing is fully signalled, with flashing lights and loud warning bells.

ACKNOWLEDGMENTS

Illustrations appear by courtesy of the following contributors:

Alaska Railroad
Dr Ian Cameron Allen
Peter Allen
Associated Equipment
Co. Ltd
Marcel Aubert
Austrian Federal Railways
The Author's Collection
W.G. Bagnall Ltd
Baldwin Locomotive
Works
Baltimore & Ohio
Railroad Co.
Andrew Barclay
Musius Beebe &
Charles Clegg
Benguela Railway Co.
Berliner Verkehrsbetriebe
Berne-Lötschberg-
Simplon Railway
J. Bettenhausen, Dresden
R.E. Bleasdale
Bodensee-Toggenburg-
bahn
W. Borelli
British Museum
British Railways Curator
of Historical Relics
British Railways, Eastern,
London Midland,
North Eastern, Scottish
and Western Regions
British Transport
Commission
British Transport Films
Y. Broncard
Dr T.F. Budden
Buenos Aires &
Pacific Railway
Camera Press Ltd
Canadian Pacific Railway
J. Allan Cash
Chicago, Burlington &

Quincy Railroad
Chicago, Milwaukee,
St Paul & Pacific
Railroad Co.
Chilean State Railways
R.N. Clements
Commonwealth Railways,
Melbourne
Coras Iompair Eireann
Council of
Industrial Design
Danish State Railways
J.E. Dayton
Deutsches Museum,
Munich
Deutsches Lokomotivbild-
Archiv
Walt Disney Productions
Maurice W. Earley
East African Railways &
Harbours Board
Charles Edmondson
'The Engineer'
Kenneth Field
Finnish State Railways
Major Sam Forbes
Hubert Foster
Fotokhronika Tass
Fox Photos Ltd
French Railways
G.E.R. Loco Publishing
Co.
German Federal Railway
Glasgow Corporation
Transport
Gloucester Railway
Carriage & Wagon Co.
Gornergratbahn
Great Northern Railway,
Minnesota
Edward Griffith
Gulf Oil Co.
R.B. Haddon

Dr Philip R. Hastings
Hellenic State Railways
T.G. Hepburn
Illinois Central Railroad
Independent Railway
Companies, Cologne
Indian Railways Bureau
Indian Tourist Office
Ipswich Corporation
Italian State Railways
Jamaica Railway
Corporation
Japanese National
Railways
Hans Kronawitter
J.B. Kronawitter
Locomotive & Allied
Manufacturers'
Association
Locomotive &
General Railway
The Locomotive
Publishing Co.
London Electrotype
Agency
London News Agency
London Transport Board
London Transport
Executive
Louisville & Nashville
Railroad Co.
Malaysia House
Information Dept.
L.G. Marshall
O.J. Morris
Mount Pilatus Railway Co.
Mozambique Railways &
Harbours
Museon di Rodo
Museum of British
Transport
Nederlands Spoorweg
Museum

579

New Delhi, Ministry
of Railways
New South Wales Railways
New York Central System
New York City Transit
Authority
New York, New Haven &
Hartford Railroad Co.
New Zealand Railways
Nordmark-Klarälven
Railway Co.
Norwegian State Railways
Norwegian Travel
Information Office
Nuremberg Transport
Museum
Österreichisches
Eisenbahnmuseum
Pacific Great Eastern
Railway Co.
Peckett & Sons
Pennsylvania Railroad Co.
Radio Times Hulton
Picture Library
'Railroad Gazette'
The Railroad &
Locomotive Historical
Society, Boston
Railway Transport,
Tasmania
H.R. Ramus
Reading Company,
Philadelphia
Rhaetian Railway Co.
Rhodesia Railways
D.S. Richter
R.C. Riley
Henry R. Salmon
Santa Fe Railway
Science Museum, London
South African Railways
South Australian
Government Archives

Southern Pacific Company,
San Francisco
Southern Railways System,
U.S.A.
A.F. Sozio
Robert Spark
P. Spilsbury
Stedef
Richard Steinheimer
R.D. Stephen
W.W. Stewart
Stockholms Sparvägar
Studio St Ives Ltd
H. Sullivan
Sulzer Bros (London) Ltd
P. Sunderland
Swedish Railway Museum
Swedish Tourist Traffic
Association
Swiss Federal Railways
Swiss State Railways
Anton Tauser
Teito Rapid Transit
Authority, Tokyo
Tiroler Kunstverlag
Trafikaktiebolaget
Grängesberg-
Oxelösunds Järnvägar
Bishop Treacy
Ulster Transport
Authority
Union Pacific Railroad
U.S. Department of
the Interior
U.S.S.R. State Committee
for Co-ordination of
Scientific Research
Victorian Government
Railways
'La Vie du Rail'
Verkehrshaus, Lucerne
The Vulcan Foundry Ltd
(English Electric)

Westinghouse Brake &
Signal Co.
H.D. Whebell
Patrick B. Whitehouse
Gavin L. Wilson
Wuppertal City Works
Dept.
Yorkshire Engine
Company

Colour Plates:

The Author
Berne-Lötschberg-
Simplon Railway
British Railways
Canadian Pacific Railway
Capitol Bologna
East African Railways &
Harbours Board
Giraudon/Musée
Marmottan, Paris
Michael Holford
Louisville & Nashville
Railroad Co.
Mansell Collection
Museum of British
Transport
National Gallery, London
Nederlands Spoorweg
Museum
Norwegian State Railways
Radio Times Hulton
Picture Library
Swiss National Tourist
Office
Union Pacific Railroad
Young & Company's
Brewery Ltd

INDEX

INDEX

Figures in italics refer to illustrations; these are numbered separately throughout the book.